Labor, Capital, and Finance: Inte

Traditional textbook analysis of international
typically ignores basic features of the welfare state, such as income maintenance programs, income distribution schemes, and pension programs.
Similarly, the theory of finance and firm-level capital structure very seldom
treats international capital flows and their implications for real sides of
the economy, which emphasize central macroeconomic variables, such as
saving and investment. Under such circumstances, barriers to capital flows
are always undesirables, very much in the spirit of the gains-from-trade
postulate. Despite the many volumes that have been written on the globalization of capital markets and the desirability (or costliness) of regulating
capital flows, there has been astonishingly little work on the magnitude
and composition when there are distortions in these flows.

This book fills a gap in the literature by combining elements from these
seemingly disjoint parts of economics and presents them in a consistent
analytical framework. It lays the groundwork for the integration of capital,
labor, and finance into a unified treatment of globalization. The book is
intended as a compact textbook for advanced undergraduate and graduate
courses in special topics in international economics and public economics.
It can also serve as a reference text for applied researchers and policy-
oriented professionals.

Assaf Razin is Mario Henrique Simonsen Professor of Public Economics
at Tel Aviv University, and the Friedman Professor of International Eco-
nomics at Cornell University. He is Research Associate at the National
Bureau of Economic Research, Cambridge, Research Fellow at the Centre
for Economic Policy Research, London, and Research Fellow at CESifo,
Munich. He is also a Fellow of the Econometric Society and a frequent
visiting scholar at the International Monetary Fund in Washington, D.C.
Professor Razin's major previous publications include *Fiscal Policies and
Growth in the World Economy,* (with Jacob Frenkel and Chi-Wa Yuen),
Population Economics (with Efraim Sadka), *The Economy of Modern Is-
rael: Malaise and Promise* (with Efraim Sadka), *International Taxation*
(with Jacob Frenkel and Efraim Sadka), *A Theory of International Trade
under Uncertainty* (with Elhanan Helpman), and *Current Account Sustainability* (with Gian-Maria Milesi-Ferretti).

Efraim Sadka is Henry Kaufman Professor of International Capital
Markets at Tel Aviv University and Research Fellow at CESifo, Munich.
From 1982 to 1985 he served as chairman of the Eitan Berglas School of

Economics, Tel Aviv University, and from 1987 to 1989 he served as the Director of the Sapir Center for Economic Development there. In addition to being the author or coauthor of six books, three of which are cited above, and editor or coeditor of four others, Professor Sadka has published articles in the *American Economic Review*, the *Quarterly Journal of Economics*, the *Review of Economic Studies*, *Econometrica*, the *Journal of Political Economy*, the *Journal of Public Economics*, and the *Journal of International Economics*. He has often been a visiting scholar at the IMF. He is an Associate Editor of the journals *International Tax and Public Finance* and *Finanz Archiv.*

Advance Praise for *Labor, Capital, and Finance*

"This book provides an excellent overview of recent work on the economic effects of international factor and financial mobility, written by two of the leading contributors to this literature. It should be required reading for any student hoping to work in this area."

Roger H. Gordon, *University of California, San Diego*

"During the past century, international economics was dominated by the Hechscher–Ohlin of the world: Goods and services may be traded, but factors of production – capital and labor – stay put. Razin and Sadka's new book, by contrast, puts international factor mobility – particularly the challenges and opportunities that migration presents for modern welfare states and the crucial role that capital mobility can play in currency crises and in international and domestic financial markerts – at center stage Researchers and students will find this book to be a valuable reference, providing systematic and integrated treatments of these pressing topics."

David E. Wildasin, *University of Kentucky*

Labor, Capital, and Finance
International Flows

ASSAF RAZIN

Simonsen Professor of Public Economics
Tel Aviv University
and
Friedman Professor of International Economics
Cornell University

EFRAIM SADKA

Henry Kaufman Professor
  of International Capital Markets
Tel Aviv University

PUBLISHED BY THE PRESS SYNDICATE OF THE UNIVERSITY OF CAMBRIDGE
The Pitt Building, Trumpington Street, Cambridge, United Kingdom

CAMBRIDGE UNIVERSITY PRESS
The Edinburgh Building, Cambridge CB2 2RU, UK
40 West 20th Street, New York, NY 10011-4211, USA
10 Stamford Road, Oakleigh, VIC 3166, Australia
Ruiz de Alarcón 13, 28014 Madrid, Spain
Dock House, The Waterfront, Cape Town 8001, South Africa

http://www.cambridge.org

First published 2001

Printed in the United States of America

Typeface Times New Roman 10/12 pt.   *System* LATEX 2$_\varepsilon$ [TB]

A catalog record for this book is available from the British Library.

Library of Congress Cataloging in Publication Data
Razin, Assaf.
    Labor, capital, and finance: international flows / by Assaf Razin and Efraim Sadka.
        p.   cm.
    Includes bibliographical references and index.
    ISBN 0-521-78074-8 – ISBN 0-521-78557-X (pb.)
    1. Capital movements.   2. Labor mobility.   3. Emigration and immigration – Economic
aspects.   4. International finance.   5. International trade.   I. Sadka, Efraim.   II. Title.
    HG3891 .R39   2001
    332′.042 – dc21   00-066716

ISBN 0 521 78074 8 hardback
ISBN 0 521 78557 X paperback

Contents

Preface

This book is about the implications of international factor mobility and, more generally, globalization, on the effectiveness of social and economic policy. As a policy issue, the role of economic integration on the working of the welfare state is at the top of the agenda for most national governments. As an intellectual issue, it is the subject of a great deal of interest and exciting work, both theoretical and empirical.

We analyze causes and consequences of international factor flows and the effects of public policies on these flows in a framework that allows for imperfections in the markets for labor and capital and for some of the basic features of the welfare state, such as tax and transfer programs and old-age security; and basic features of emerging markets, such as information asymmetry.

The traditional textbook analysis of international trade and labor movements typically ignores the basic features of the welfare state such as income maintenance programs, income distribution schemes, and pension programs. Similarly, capital movements are mostly analyzed in a frictionless and perfect-information world economy. Under such circumstances, barriers to capital flows are always undesirables, very much in the spirit of the gains-from-trade postulate. Despite the volumes that have been written on the globalization of capital markets and the desirability (or costliness) of regulating capital flows, there has been astonishingly little work on the magnitude and the composition of capital flows when there are distortions. By the same token, the traditional public economics analysis of the welfare state is typically conducted in a closed economy. Similarly, the theory of finance and firm-level capital structure very seldom treats international capital flows and their implications for the real side of the economy, which emphasizes central macrovariables such as the economy-wide saving and investment.

This book fills a gap in the literature by combining elements from these seemingly disjoint parts of economics and presents them in a consistent analytical framework.[1] By doing this, it could lay the ground for the beginning of an integration of the aforementioned disciplines into a unified treatment of globalization. The book is intended as a compact textbook for advanced undergraduate and graduate courses in special topics in international economics and public economics. It can also serve as a reference text for applied researchers and policy professionals.

In writing this book, we greatly benefited from collaboration with colleagues.

Chapter 12 is an edited version of a paper coauthored by Gian Maria Milesi-Ferretti and Assaf Razin, "Current Account Reversals: Empirical Regularities," which was published in the volume edited by Paul Krugman, *Currency Crises*, University of Chicago Press, Chicago (2000).

Two sections of Chap. 1 draw heavily on a paper coauthored by Helpman and Razin, "Increasing Returns, Monopolistic Competition, and Factor Movements: A Welfare Analysis," which was published in the *Journal of International Economics* (1983).

Chapter 10 is based on our joint work with Chi-Wa Yuen, "Excessive FDI Flows under Asymmetric Information," which was published in the volume edited by Reuven Glick, Ramon Moreno, and Mark Spiegel, *Financial Crises in Emerging Markets*, Cambridge University Press (2001).

Likewise, Chap. 11 is based on our joint work with Chi-Wa Yuen, "Social Benefits and Losses from FDI: Two Non-traditional Views," which was published in the volume edited by Takatoshi Ito and Anne Krueger, *Regional and Global Capital Flows: Macroeconomic Causes and Consequences*, University of Chicago Press, Chicago (2000).

Chapters 5 and 6 draw on our joint work with Philip Swagel, "Tax Burden and Migration: A Political Economy Theory and Evidence," *Journal of Public Economics* (2001).

Chapter 8 is based on our paper, "Country Risk and Capital Flow Reversals," *Economics Letters* (2001).

We thank wholeheartedly our long-time collaborators, Gian Maria Milesi-Ferretti, Elhanan Helpman, Chi-Wa Yuen, and Phillip Swagel, for letting us use some of our joint work in this book.

In writing this book we drew also on our previous work as follows:

"International Migration and International Trade," in Mark R. Rosenzweig and Oded Stark (editors), *Handbook of Population and Family Economics*, Vol. 1B, Elsevier Science B.V. (1997); "Migration and Pension with International Capital Mobility," *Journal of Public Economics* (1999a); "Unskilled Migration: A Burden or a Boon for the Welfare State?" *Scandinavian Journal of Economics* (2000).

---

[1] Related books include Bhagwati and Feenstra (1987) and Wong (1995) on the international trade side, Smith and Edmoston (1997) and Stark (1991) on the migration side, and Razin and Sadka (1999b) on the public economics side.

Parts of this book were written while the authors were visiting the Economic Policy Research Unit (EPRU), Institute of Economics, the University of Copenhagen, and the School of Economics and Finance, Hong Kong University. We thank these two institutions for providing us with an excellent research environment. Financial support from the Research Grant Council in Hong Kong[2] is gratefully acknowledged.

We benefited also from discussions with the following colleagues and from their comments and suggestions: Giovanni Facchini, Chaim Fershtman, Elhanan Helpman, Itay Goldstein, Lars Gottlieb, Philip Lane, Gian Maria Milesi-Ferretti, Soren Bo Nielsen, Maurice Obstfeld, Adi Pauzner, Ariel Rubinstein, Peter Birch Sorensen, Phillip Swagel, Gerald Willmann, and Chi-Wa Yuen.

Evgeny Agronin and Shir Raz provided competent research assistance. We also thank Stella Padeh for her skilled and painstaking typing. Our students in graduate courses and workshops at Tel-Aviv and Stanford Universities, respectively, were exposed to various preliminary versions of chapters of this book. This experience has enhanced the content of the book.

Special thanks are due to Scott Parris, economics editor of Cambridge University Press. Having come across our earlier book, *Population Economics*, MIT Press, Cambridge, MA (1995b), he approached us with a question: "Why not write a similar textbook on globalization?" We considered his suggestion thoroughly and came out with the idea of writing this compact textbook that focuses on major analytical and empirical aspects of cross-border flows of labor, capital, and finance.

[2] Research Grant Council earmarked competitive grant 10202893.

Introduction

The world economy nowadays is experiencing an unprecedented openness. The fading of borders between independent economic systems – local, state, national, and supernational – allows capital, firms, and labor to move more freely around the globe, so as to better exploit differences in opportunities (employment, savings, investments, etc.) arising from ever-changing technological and economic environments, as well as in fiscal and monetary stances.

Globalization is not an entirely new phenomenon. The world economy experienced such a process approximately a century ago, until it was disrupted by the eruption of the First and Second World Wars. Nevertheless, the **current** trend of economic integration is historically unprecedented. We support Bordo, Eichengreen, and Irwin (1999) who conclude that "our world is different: Commercial and financial integration before World War I was more limited." A century ago, trade in goods was impeded by transport costs and imperfect information. Also, services that were then considered largely nontradable are now a growing component of the volume of trade. Intraindustry trade, especially among multinationals, is flourishing. Financial integration is deeper and broader than before as financial flows spread into more and more activities and sectors.

An exception to the higher degree of international integration now compared with that of a century ago is, however, the flow of labor. Hatton and Williamson (1992) provide the following historical perspective[1]: "In the century following 1820, an estimated 60 million Europeans set sail for labor-scarce New World destinations." In fact, net migration contributed a significant share of the total growth of the population in the United States in the nineteenth and early twentieth centuries.[2]

---

[1] See also Hatton and Williamson (1998).

[2] For instance, net migration accounted for between 32% and 43% of the total increase in the white population during 1880–1910. The only comparable intercontinental migration was the black slaves from Africa to the Americas and the Caribbean.

The development of new national institutions (e.g., national insurance) and international bodies (the European Central Bank, the International Monetary Fund, the World Trade Organization, to name a few) raises new subtle issues that are intertwined with globalization. As put succinctly by Bordo, Eichengreen, and Irwin (1999) "Does the growth of global markets pose a threat to distinctive national social systems? Does a world characterized by high levels of trade and large international capital flows jeopardize social cohesion and economic and financial stability and therefore require the strengthening of national safety nets . . .? And failing this, will governments retreat toward financial autarchy and succumb to populist pressures for trade protectionism?" Furthermore, the "new economy" is a fertile ground for the international mobility of technology. Indeed, studying international "spillover" effects of research and development, Helpman (1999) concludes that ". . . there exist significant, cross-country links that are driven by foreign trade and investment."

This book attempts to address many of these issues analytically, while providing some empirical analysis of analytical issues as well.

In Part 1, we first develop the traditional arguments for free welfare-enhancing flows of goods, labor, and capital. It serves as a review of traditional trade literature on the substitutability and complementarity among trade in goods, labor mobility, and capital flows. We use this background as a departure point for succeeding analyses of nontraditional benefits and pitfalls of these flows in the presence of social and political institutions that impose a set of constraints on globalization, such as safety nets, representative democracies, credit-constrained financial intermediaries, and imperfect information, such as between foreign and domestic savers/investors, which impedes international interactions.

Part 2 deals with labor flows. The economic theory of international migration, and in particular the analysis of the implications of the welfare state for the causes and consequences of migration, is systematically developed in this part.

Part 3 considers international capital and financial flows and addresses a number of issues related to open capital markets. In addition to serving as a review of the globalization of capital markets and the desirability (or costliness, as the case may be) of regulating capital flows, this part also analyzes the magnitude and composition of capital flows when the capital market is plagued by imperfect-information distortions. The various chapters in this part deal systematically with financial intermediation, debt, equity, and FDI flows.

PART 1

A STANDARD ANALYSIS OF INTERNATIONAL FACTOR MOBILITY

1   Beneficial Versus Distortionary Mobility of Factors of Production

INTRODUCTION

Classical economic setups suggest that factors of production move, if not constrained, from locations where their marginal product is low to other locations where their marginal product is high. In these setups, perfect competition with complete information prevails and there are no distortions (created by taxation, externalities, etc.), so that the private returns to the factor owners coincide with the social returns. Accordingly, factor mobility induced by private factor return differentials is beneficial for both the owners of the factors that actually move from one location to another and for the population in the source and destination economies.

Factor mobility may wear two guises. First, there is the mobility of the factor of production itself, without the owner's changing his or her national residence. Second, one can look at the mobility of the owner with his or her factor of production. The first kind of mobility is typical for capital. The phenomenon of guest workers can also be viewed as a factor mobility of the first kind. Guest workers are typically not eligible for all the amenities (especially in the area of social insurance) of the host country. In our new age of information technology, many professionals can provide their services by means of the Internet, and other electronic means, without physically moving to the location where their services are received – the so-called "weightless trade."[1] The second type of mobility typically characterizes labor and is usually termed migration. It raises a host of issues and considerations associated with the welfare state that are not relevant for factor mobility of the first kind: unemployment insurance, pensions, health insurance and care, education, etc.

The possibility of separation between the mobility of the factor of production and the mobility of its owner underscores also the distinction between the Gross Domestic Product (GDP) of a country and its Gross National Product (GNP). The first term includes all the value added (or income) that is produced in the country in question. The second term subtracts from the GDP of a country

3

the value added produced in this country by factors of production owned by foreigners and adds to it the value added produced abroad by factors of production owned by residents of this country. Factor mobility of the first kind affects primarily the GDP of the host and the source countries, whereas factor mobility of the second type affects both their GDP and GNP. When the welfare consequences of factor mobility are analyzed, it is the GNP that is relevant as it can serve as a macroeconomic proxy for welfare. For instance, it may be argued that the heavy subsidization of Foreign Direct Investment (FDI) in Ireland in the past two decades resulted in impressive GDP growth rates but with a much less pronounced effect on the well-being of Irish residents, as proxied by the Irish GNP growth rates.[2]

In this part, we focus our attention on factor mobility without factor owner mobility, while successive parts of the book deal with factor mobility of the second kind.

ONE-GOOD CASE

Suppose first that there is only one final good. Therefore, in this case, there is no scope for trade in goods (i.e., of one good for another), as in standard trade models. However, a person residing in one country who provides the services of the factor of production that he or she owns in the other country can still retract the remuneration accruing to that factor in the other country to his or her own country.

The welfare impact of factor mobility can be neatly presented with the aid of the familiar "scissors diagram" (Fig. 1.1) in which the marginal product of a mobile factor (say, capital) for two countries (home and foreign) that comprise the world economy are shown as originating at opposite ends. Following MacDougall (1960), suppose that originally the world allocation of capital is at A, with the home country having a higher marginal product of capital than the foreign country. If capital flows from the foreign country to the home country up until the point at which the marginal product of capital is the same in the two countries, bringing the world allocation of capital to point E, then the world output is at a maximum.

In a laissez-faire competitive environment with complete information and no barriers to factor mobility, an amount of AE units of capital will indeed flow from the foreign country to the home country. This is because in the aforementioned classical setup the market return to capital is equal to its marginal product, so that it will pay the owners of capital in the foreign country to invest the amount of AE units of it in the home country. Furthermore, not only world output (namely, the sum of the home and the foreign GNPs) rises, but the GNP of each country also rises as well: The GNP of the home country rises from $O_H MKA$ to $O_H MRQA$ (Note 3) and the GNP of the foreign country rises from $O_F NSA$ to $O_F NRQA$ (Note 4), so that world output rises by KSR.

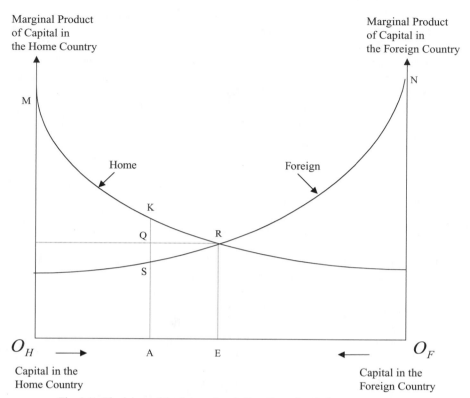

Fig. 1.1. The laissez-faire international allocation of capital.

TRADE IN GOODS

In this section, we extend the preceding analysis to the standard trade models in which some of the goods are traded for other goods; specifically, there are traded and nontraded goods. This setup guarantees that in the absence of factor mobility, primary inputs will be differently priced internationally not only in the absence of trade in goods, which is obvious, but also when trade in goods takes place [for the same reasons that are advanced in the standard trade models; see, for example, Jones (1967) and the next chapter].

Following Helpman and Razin (1983), we present in this section an analysis of welfare gains from factor movements for a small competitive economy with a constant returns-to-scale technology. For simplicity, we aggregate all traded goods into a single commodity Y and choose $p_Y = 1$ as its price. The aggregation is based on the assumption that relative prices of traded goods do not change as a result of factor movements (the small-country assumption in commodity markets), so that we can abstract from welfare changes that result from adjustments in the terms of trade of goods. We also assume that there is a single nontraded good X whose price in terms of Y is p.

Assuming the existence of a representative consumer or a social welfare function that is maximized with costless income redistribution, our country's welfare level can be represented by an indirect utility function $v(p, GNP)$, where GNP stands for the GNP (or income) measured in units of Y. Assuming that all foreign-source income stems from international mobility of capital, GNP equals GDP minus rental payments on domestically employed foreign capital. Hence,

$$GNP = GDP(p, L, K + \Delta) - \rho\Delta, \tag{1.1}$$

where $GDP(\cdot)$ stands for the GDP function, L and K stand for domestically owned labor and capital (assumed to be inelastically supplied), Δ stands for foreign capital used in the home country when $\Delta > 0$ and domestic capital used abroad when $\Delta < 0$. Finally, ρ represents the rental rate on Δ. Note that GDP depends on both the exogenously given stocks of primary factors (L and $K + \Delta$) and the relative price p of nontraded goods, which guides the intersectoral allocation of K and L. In fact, the function $GDP(\cdot)$ is a restricted revenue function in the sense that the total inputs of labor (L) and capital ($K + \Delta$) to the two industries are exogenously given.

By using the envelope theorem, we can derive the partial derivatives of the restricted profit function $GDP(\cdot)$:

$$\frac{\partial GDP(p, L, K + \Delta)}{\partial p} = X, \tag{1.2a}$$

$$\frac{\partial GDP(p, L, K + \Delta)}{\partial L} = w, \tag{1.2b}$$

$$\frac{\partial GDP(p, L, K + \Delta)}{\partial (K + \Delta)} = r, \tag{1.2c}$$

where w and r are the domestic wage rate and the domestic rental price of capital, respectively.

When foreign capital is used in the home country, then $\rho = r$; the assumption is that foreign-owned capital commands the same rental rate as domestic-owned capital. On the other hand, when domestic capital is used abroad, its rental rate in the foreign country is ρ, which may or may not be a function of the size of investment abroad.

Choosing a transformation of the utility function such that in equilibrium so the marginal utility of income (i.e., $\partial v/\partial GNP$) equals one, differentiation of $u = v(\cdot)$, by use of Eq. (1.1) and the properties of the indirect utility and GDP

functions, yields

$$dU = \frac{\partial v}{\partial p}dp + \frac{\partial v}{\partial(GNP)}\left[\frac{\partial(GDP)}{\partial p}dp + \frac{\partial(GDP)}{\partial(K+\Delta)}d\Delta - \rho d\Delta - \Delta d\rho\right].$$

$$(1.3)$$

Using Roy's identity, we find that

$$\frac{\partial v}{\partial p} = -\frac{\partial v}{\partial(GNP)}D_X,$$

$$(1.4)$$

where D_X is the consumption of good X. Substituting Eqs. (1.4), (1.2a), and (1.2c) into Eq. (1.3) yields

$$dU = (r - \rho)d\Delta + (X - D_x)dp - \Delta d\rho.$$

$$(1.5)$$

[Recall that $\partial v/\partial(GNP) = 1$.]

X is not traded, in equilibrium $X = D_X$, and Eq. (1.5) reduces to

$$dU = (r - \rho)d\Delta - \Delta d\rho.$$

$$(1.6)$$

Suppose that r is smaller than the rental rate that domestic capital can obtain abroad. Then owners of domestic capital will shift part of it into foreign operations, thereby increasing domestic welfare because of the first term on the right-hand side of Eq. (1.6) (because $r < \rho$ and $d\Delta < 0$). If the foreign rental rate is unaffected by the home country's investment abroad, the second term on the right-hand side of Eq. (1.6) equals zero (because $d\rho = 0$). In this case, domestic welfare unambiguously rises ($dU > 0$). If, on the other hand, the foreign rental rate on domestic capital invested abroad declines with the size of the investment and we start with a positive investment level ($\Delta < 0$), the second term generates a negative welfare effect, but this negative welfare effect is negligible for small investment levels. In the case under discussion, dU evaluated at $\Delta = 0$ is positive, so that it pays to invest abroad, at least a little. [The negative welfare effect (which does not exist at $\Delta = 0$) stems from possible market power in foreign investment.]

Now suppose that r exceeds the rental rate that foreign capital receives abroad. Then foreigners will invest in the home country, earning the domestic rental rate of r. Thus $r \equiv \rho$ in this case and Eq. (1.6) reduces to $dU = -\Delta dr$. However, because of the diminishing marginal product of capital, the rental rate on capital declines with capital inflows so that for positive investment levels ($\Delta > 0$) welfare increases.

This analysis illustrates again the two points made in the one-good case. First, capital mobility can raise welfare. Second, in a competitive distortion-free environment (absent terms-of-trade effects), private considerations about the location of capital guided by the differential between r and ρ coincide with social considerations in the sense that social welfare increases as a result of private decisions to shift capital from the low-return to the high-return location.

FACTOR MOBILITY IN THE PRESENCE OF DISTORTIONS

It should be emphasized that the social benefit generated by laissez-faire capital mobility that was demonstrated in the preceding two sections holds in a classical setup, in which perfect competition with complete information and no other distortions (such as taxes) prevail. As a matter of fact, with imperfectly competitive markets and/or tax distortions, factor mobility may be harmful. Such deviations from the classical setups are more likely to occur in the factor markets rather than in the goods markets. Labor markets are particularly notorious for their imperfections, which are due to unionism, state regulation (e.g., minimum-wage laws), incomplete information about job availability and workers' characteristics, and relatively heavy payroll taxes. Similarly, capital markets are also plagued by imperfect information phenomena manifested by severe moral hazards, adverse selection, debt and bank runs, herd behaviour, etc. On the other hand, goods are typically homogeneous and information about them is transparent; trade enhances competition in their markets and indirect taxes tend to be uniform [e.g., Value Added Tax (VAT)], thereby avoiding intercommodity distortions.[5]

It is quite straightforward to show that laissez-faire factor mobility can be harmful in distortive environments. We shall consider two deviations from the classical setup: taxes and noncompetitive markets.

Taxes

It is most convenient to use the one-good case depicted in Fig. 1.2 (which is drawn on Fig. 1.1) in order to analyze the effects of taxes.

Recall that in the aforementioned case, social welfare increases when a well-specified quantity of capital (i.e., AE) moves from the foreign to the domestic economy. However, in a distorted environment, social welfare can fall either when too much capital flows in or when the flow of capital is reversed. For instance, suppose that the home and the foreign countries levy source-based taxes at rates τ and τ^*, respectively, on the income from capital that accrues in their jurisdictions.[6]

For instance, suppose that the foreign country levies a source-based tax at the rate of τ^*, which is equal to VG/VF, and the home country levies no tax (i.e., $\tau = 0$). In this case the schedule of after-tax return to capital in the foreign country falls from NP to $N'P'$ and a quantity of AF units of capital flows from the foreign country to the home country. World output changes from $O_H MKSNO_F$ to $O_H MGVNO_F$, amounting to a decline of RVG, minus KSR in world output. [Of course, a similar allocation can be achieved with both countries levying a

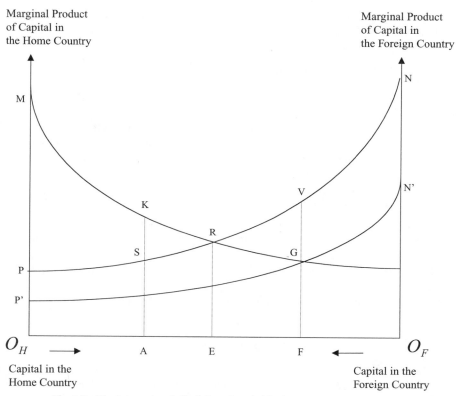

Fig. 1.2. The international allocation of capital in the presence of distortive taxation.

tax, but with the foreign country levying a higher rate (that is, $\tau^* > \tau > 0$).] Similarly, if the home country levies a much higher tax rate than the foreign country, then the direction of capital flows may be reversed, causing a decline in world output.

Increasing Returns

Another possibility of welfare-reducing factor mobility can occur when there are increasing returns, forcing prices to deviate from marginal costs. To illustrate this, we revert to the two-good model described earlier in this chapter while introducing to the model increasing returns to scale. We continue to assume that the traded good (Y) is produced with a constant-returns-to-scale technology. However, the nontraded good (X) is now a composite good of symmetric differential products, produced by N firms, each possessing increasing returns-to-scale technology. All of the N firms that produce X possess identical technologies. Thus they charge the same price, and, because of free entry that entails zero profits, they engage in average cost pricing. The free-entry assumption pins down analytically the number of firms (N) in the industry, as always. Good Y is produced with constant-returns-to-scale technology in which the unit (average) cost, denoted by $c_Y(w, r)$ is constant, unrelated to the scale of production. Therefore, at equilibrium in the market for Y,

$$1 = c_Y(w, r) \tag{1.7}$$

(recalling that Y is the numeraire whose price is set to unity). However, the average cost of production of X decreases with the scale of production. Denoting by x the scale of production of each firm in the X industry, we conclude that, at equilibrium in the market for X,

$$p = c_X(w, r; x), \tag{1.8}$$

where $c_X(w, r; x)$ is the average cost of producing x units of X.

Similarly, the unit capital and labor requirements in industry Y (a_{KY} and a_{LY}, respectively) are independent of the scale of production, whereas the unit capital and labor requirements in industry X (a_{KX} and a_{LX}, respectively) are assumed to be declining in the scale of production, x, because of increasing returns to scale. Thus equilibrium in the factor markets requires that

$$a_{LY}(w, r)Y + a_{LX}(w, r; x)X = L, \tag{1.9}$$

$$a_{KY}(w, r)Y + a_{KX}(w, r; x)X = K + \Delta, \tag{1.10}$$

where $X = Nx$.

Given x, the restricted revenue function that depends, as above, also on p, L, and $K + \Delta$, is essentially equal to $GDP(p, L, K + \Delta; x)$. The partial derivatives of this function can be found, as before, by the envelope theorem:

$$\partial GDP(p, L, K + \Delta; x)/\partial p = X = Nx, \tag{1.11a}$$

$$\partial GDP(p, L, K + \Delta; x)/\partial L = w, \tag{1.11b}$$

$$\partial GDP(p, L, K + \Delta; x)/\partial(K + \Delta) = r. \tag{1.11c}$$

As was already mentioned, the difference between this *GDP* function and that used earlier in this chapter is the dependence of the present one on x, the individual firm's output level (or, alternatively, its scale of production). We can observe from the set of equilibrium equations (1.7)–(1.10) that our nonconstant-returns-to-scale economy is formally similar to a constant-returns-to-scale economy with a technical progress coefficient. An increase in x reduces average costs $c_X(\cdot)$, because the elasticity of $c_X(\cdot)$ with respect to x is negative:

$$b'(w, r, x) \equiv \frac{\partial c_X}{\partial x} \frac{x}{c_X} = -1 + \varphi(w, r; x) < 0, \tag{1.12}$$

where $\varphi(w, r; x)$ is the elasticity of total cost (namely, xc_X) with the respect to the firm's output (namely, x).

Because of the increasing returns to scale, φ must be smaller than one, so that $b' < 0$. The absolute value of b', denoted by b, is

$$b(w, r; x) = -\varphi(w, r; x) + 1 > 0. \tag{1.13}$$

We can now adopt the familiar analysis of technical progress in the standard model of two factors, two-good and constant-returns-to-scale technologies developed by Jones (1965). He showed that

$$b = \theta_{LX} b_L + \theta_{KX} b_K, \tag{1.14}$$

where b_L is the absolute value of the elasticity of $a_{LX}(\cdot)$ with respect to x, b_K is the absolute value of the elasticity of $a_{KX}(\cdot)$ with respect to x, and θ_{jX} is the share of factor j in costs of production; $j = L, K$. As Jones (1965) shows, a one-percentage-point increase in x has the same effect on *output* levels as a b-percent increase in the price p, plus a $\lambda_{LX} b_L$-percent increase in the labor force, plus a $\lambda_{KX} b_K$-percent increase in the capital stock, where λ_{LX} is the share of labor used in the production of X and λ_{KX} is the share of the capital stock used in the production of X. This can be explained as follows. Suppose that x is increased by one percentage point and the number of firms N is reduced by one percentage point, so that the aggregate output in sector X (namely, Nx) does not change. As a result of the increase in x, each firm will increase its employment of labor by ε_{Lx} percent, where ε_{Lx} is its elasticity of labor demand with respect to output, so that the sector's demand for labor will increase by ε_{Lx} percent. On the other hand, because of the decline in the number of firms in the industry, the industry's labor demand will fall by 1%, so that $b_L \equiv 1 - \varepsilon_{Lx}$ is the proportion of the industry's labor force that is being released as a result of these changes. Because the industry employs the proportion λ_{LX} of the total labor force, $\lambda_{LX} b_L$ is the industry's saving of labor as a proportion of the total labor force. Similarly, $\lambda_{KX} b_K$ is the proportion of total capital saved by industry X as a result of a 1% increase in x, holding the aggregate output of good X constant (with the adjustment being made by means of a decline in the number of firms in the industry). In addition to these factor supply effects, a one-percentage-point increase in x reduces unit production costs by b percent.

By using the above-described elasticity relationship between the effects on output levels of a one-percentage-point increase in x and a b-percent increase in the price of p, plus $\lambda_{jX} b_j - (j = L, K)$ percent increases in the supply of factors of production, we can calculate the change in GDP as a result of a one-percentage-point increase in x as follows:

$$\frac{\partial GDP}{\partial x} x = \left(p \frac{\partial X}{\partial p} + \frac{\partial Y}{\partial p} \right) pb + \left(p \frac{\partial X}{\partial L} + \frac{\partial Y}{\partial L} \right) L \lambda_{LX} b_L$$

$$+ \left(p \frac{\partial X}{\partial K} + \frac{\partial Y}{\partial K} \right) K \lambda_{KX} b_K = w_L \lambda_{LX} b_L + r_K \lambda_{KX} b_X,$$

because of the envelope theorem (recall that $GDP = pX + Y$).[7] Hence, using the definition of λ_{jX} $(j = L, K)$, we obtain

$$\frac{\partial GDP}{\partial x}x = wa_{LX}Xb_L + ra_{KX}Xb_K = pX(\theta_{LX}b_L + \theta_{KX}b_K) = pXb,$$

$$\frac{\partial}{\partial x}GDP(p, L, K + \Delta; x) = pN(1 - \varphi), \tag{1.15}$$

where use has been made of the relationships $X = Nx$ and $b = (1 - \varphi)$.

Now define $\bar{r}$ as the increase in GDP that results from an increase in Δ, *holding p constant*. In the competitive case with constant-returns-to-scale technologies analyzed earlier in this chapter, this was shown to equal r – the market rental rate on capital. In the case considered, however, $\bar{r}$ is given by

$$\bar{r} = \frac{\partial}{\partial(K + \Delta)}GDP(\cdot) + \frac{\partial}{\partial x}GDP(\cdot)\frac{dx}{d\Delta}.$$

Using Eqs. (1.15) we can write this as

$$\bar{r} = r + pN(1 - \varphi)\frac{dx}{d\Delta}. \tag{1.16}$$

Because $\varphi < 1$ (because of the economies of scale at the firm level), Eq. (1.16) tells us that an inflow of one unit of capital will increase GDP by *more* than the market rental rate on capital if it brings about an expansion of every firm's output level in sector X. An inflow of the same amount of capital will increase GDP by *less* than the market rental rate on capital, or even reduce GDP, if it brings about a contraction of every firm's output level in sector X.

In more general terms, this means that the private sector may undervalue or overvalue the marginal productivity of capital (and that of labor) as far as GDP valuation is concerned, depending on the marginal effect of capital inflows on the size of operation of firms in the sector with economies of scale:

$$\bar{r} \gtreqless r \text{ as } \frac{dx}{d\Delta} \gtreqless 0; \tag{1.17}$$

that is, the private sector undervalues (respectively, overvalues) the effect of capital inflows on GDP when such inflows increase (respectively, decrease) the scale of production. Therefore, such a biased evaluation by the market of the effect of capital inflows on GNP and welfare can occur as well.[8]

For a complete welfare analysis of the effect of a capital inflow by the amount Δ, we must fill the above model with a formal specification of consumer preferences and the market organization of the increasing returns (nontraded) industry (e.g., imperfect competition with differentiated production). Such specification enables an explicit solution for the scale of production (x and consequently N) and the relative price p of the nontraded good, as described, for instance, in Helpman and Razin (1983).

CONCLUSION

We show that in a classical setup with perfect competition everywhere, no distortion and full information, the private return to a factor of production coincides with the social return. In such a setup, factor mobility induced by international differentials in factor returns is beneficial for both the factor owner and the source and destination countries, provided that distortion-free redistribution is made *within* each country.

We also show that once we deviate from the classical setup – for instance, through distortive taxes, market imperfections, etc. – private and social returns to factor of production may diverge and factor mobility may reduce welfare. Furthermore, when countries experience some market power, factor mobility may change the terms of trade. In this case, even when perfect competition and distortion-free environments prevail in each country, factor mobility can be detrimental to welfare. In the familiar Dornbusch–Fischer–Samuelson (1977) Ricardian model, a country receiving migrant workers may find its terms of trade deteriorating to such an extent so as to immiserise all the native-born workers. Naturally, these adverse terms-of-trade effects never occur in a small country.

2 Factor Mobility and Trade in Goods: Do They Substitute for Each Other?

INTRODUCTION

Autarky typically results in different countries having different commodity and factor prices. Think of protectionist pre-World War II Western Europe, vis-à-vis the American market or the former East-European bloc, vis-à-vis the industrialized countries. For instance, Table 2.1 highlights the wage gap betweem Eastern Europe (with hourly wages below 1 US$) and the industrialized countries (with hourly wages typically above 10 US$), just after the collapse of the Iron Curtain. If barriers to labor mobility were removed or eased up, labor could have been expected to move from low-wage countries (e.g., Eastern Europe) to high-wage countries (e.g., Western Europe). Similarly, capital would have been expected to move in the opposite direction.

A crucial question is whether trade in goods can narrow the wage and capital rental price gaps, thereby reducing the incentives for factor mobility. Put differently: Is trade in goods a substitute for factor mobility? In the preceding chapter, the existence of a nontraded good prevented trade in other goods from equalizing factor prices across countries. Hence, trade in goods could not serve as a perfect substitute for factor mobility. The rationale for this result is quite natural: Because trade is not all encompassing, it could not perfectly substitute for the mobility of the factors producing the nontraded goods as well. Thus, in order to sharpen the analysis of the role of trade in goods as a substitute for factor mobility, we assume in this chapter that all goods are traded.

Our starting point is a standard international trade model with two countries, two goods, homothetic and identical preferences, and constant returns to scale everywhere.

We first make an additional set of assumptions that together nullify all forces that can generate either commodity trade or factor mobility. By relaxing these assumptions, one at a time, we allow room for commodity trade and incentives for factor mobility. We can then also study their interaction and in particular whether trade in goods can substitute for factor mobility. Accordingly, we

Table 2.1. Wage Gaps and Population (1990)

Country	Wage Per Hour (US$)	Population (Millions)
Eastern Europe		
Poland	0.7	38
Hungary	0.7	11
Czechoslovakia	0.8	16
Bulgaria	0.2	9
Rumania	0.6	23
Yugoslavia	1.1	24
USSR (European)	0.9	222
Eastern Europe (total)	0.9	343
Industrialized Countries		
Germany (West)	11	61
France	8	56
Italy	11	57
U.K.	8	57
European Community (EC) (total)	9	340
European Free Trade Area (EFTA) (total)	13	25
Western Europe (total)	10	365
USA	13	250
Canada	13	27
Australia	14	17

Source: Layard et al. (1992).

initially assume the following:

(i) The two countries have the same relative endowments of capital and labor.
(ii) The two countries have the same technologies.
(iii) The number of goods and factors is the same. Specifically, we asume that there are two goods (X and Y) and two factors of production (labor (L) and (K)).

Under these assumptions, there will be no commodity trade between the two countries and no cross-country factor-price differentials that can lead to international factor mobility.

SUBSTITUTION

We relax assumption (i) and assume that the two countries differ in only their relative factor endowments. Suppose initially that labor and capital are internationally immobile. As we already mentioned, there are two goods, X and

Y, two factors, labor (L) and capital (K), and two countries, home (H) and foreign (F). This, of course, is the familar Heckscher–Ohlin–Samuelson model of international trade. Suppose, for concreteness, that good X is more labor intensive than good Y (in both countries, as they have identical technologies). By this we mean that when both industries are faced with the same factor prices, industry X will employ a higher labor/capital ratio than industry Y. Formally,

$$\frac{a_{LX}}{a_{KX}} > \frac{a_{LY}}{a_{KY}} \tag{2.1}$$

for all factor-price ratios, where a_{ij} is the unit input requirements of factor i in the production of good j and where $i = L, K$ and $j = X, Y$. By the factor-price ratio we mean the ratio of wage (w) to the rental price of capital (r).

We assume that country H is more abundant in labor (relative to capital) than country F, that is,

$$\frac{\bar{L}^H}{\bar{K}^H} > \frac{\bar{L}^F}{\bar{K}^F}, \tag{2.2}$$

where $\bar{L}^i$ and $\bar{K}^i$ are the endowments of labor and capital, respectively, in country i and $i = H, F$.

Suppose that good Y is the numeraire with its price set to unity in both countries, and denote by p^i, r^i, and w^i the price of good X, the rental price of capital and the wage rate in country i, respectively, where $i = H, F$.

First, observe the quite intuitive result that is due to Stolper and Samuelson (1941): An increase in the wage–rental ratio (w/r) raises the unit cost of the labor-intensive good (X) relative to the unit cost of the capital-intensive good (Y) and therefore must raise the relative price (p) of the labor-intensive good.

This result is demonstrated graphically in Fig. 2.1.[1] For a fixed p, the line XX represents the zero-profit locus for industry X, given by $p = ra_{KX} + wa_{LX}$. The absolute value of the slope of this line is a_{LX}/a_{KX}. The line YY is the analogous locus for industry Y, given by $1 = ra_{KY} + wa_{LY}$. The absolute value of its slope is a_{LY}/a_{KY}. The point of intersection between these two loci (point E) yields the equilibrium factor prices for the given price ratio p. Now, if p rises, the zero-profit locus for industry X shifts outward from XX to $X'X'$. The new factor-price equilibrium is at point E', in which the wage rate (w) is higher and the rental price of capital (r) is lower. Conversely, an increase in w/r raises p.

Second, the quite intuitive result that is due to Rybczynski (1955) (the dual to the Stolper–Samuelson result) asserts that at a given factor-price ratio, a higher labor–capital endowment ratio results in a higher X to Y output ratio (where good X is more labor intensive than good Y). To see this, refer to Fig. 2.2. The line LL describes the locus of output pairs (X, Y) that yield full employment of labor, given by $\bar{L} = Xa_{LX} + Ya_{LY}$. The absolute value of the slope of this

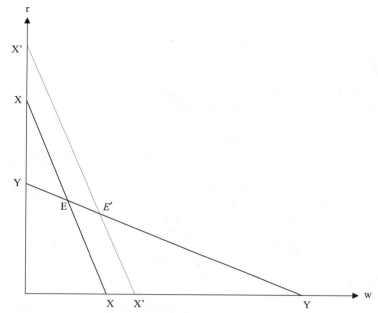

Fig. 2.1. The Stolper-Samuelson theorem.

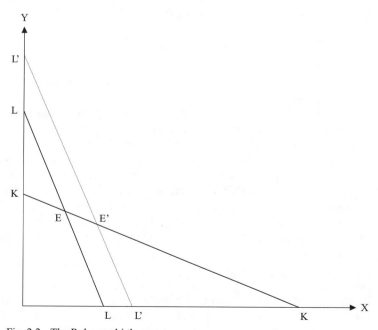

Fig. 2.2. The Rybczynski theorem.

line is a_{LX}/a_{LY}. Similarly, the line KK represents full employment of capital, given by $\bar{K} = Xa_{KX} + Ya_{KY}$. The absolute value of its slope is a_{KX}/a_{KY}. The equilibrium pair of outputs is at point E. Now, suppose that $\bar{L}$ rises. This shifts the labor full-employment line outward from LL to $L'L'$. The new pair of equilibrium outputs is point E', with a higher output of X and a lower output of Y.

Combining the above two theorems, we can draw in Fig. 2.3 the relative-supply curves RS^F and RS^H of the two countries. The relative supply of country $i = H, F$ is defined as X^i/Y^i. The Stolper–Samuelson theorem suggests that if the price of X (namely, p) is the same in the two countries, so is the wage–rental ratio (w/r). Hence, the Rybczynski theorem suggests that the relative supply curves are then affected only by the relative factor endowments. Then the relative-supply curve RS^H that describes the output ratio of the labor-intensive good (X) to the capital-intensive good (Y) in the labor-abundant country (H) is everywhere (that is, for each p) in a position to the right of the relative-supply curve RS^F in the capital-abundant country (H). Now, the assumption of the identical homothetic preferences implies that the two countries have the same relative-demand curve (RD in Fig. 2.3), which is also the world relative-demand curve $[(X^H + X^F)/(Y^H + Y^F)]$.

In autarky, equilibrium will be at point A for country F with a relative price ratio of $\bar{p}^F$, and at point B for country H with a relative price ratio of $\bar{p}^H$. Thus the Stolper–Samuelson theorem implies that

$$\frac{\bar{w}^H}{\bar{r}^H} < \frac{\bar{w}^F}{\bar{r}^F}, \tag{2.3}$$

where $\bar{w}^i$ and $\bar{r}^i$ are the autarky prices of labor and capital, respectively, in country i, and $i = H, F$.

Thus, when trade is allowed, good X will be exported from country H to country F until commodity prices are equalized across countries. Of course, at the same time good Y will be exported from country F to country H. With free trade the equilibrium price ratio is determined at the intersection of the world relative-supply curve with the world relative-demand curve. As was already pointed out, the curve RD is the relative-demand curve of each country and also that of the world. The world relative-supply curve is a weighted average of the relative supply curves of the two countries and must therefore lie somewhere between them. The world relative-supply curve is the curve RS in Fig. 2.3.

The free-trade relative price ratio is thus $\tilde{p}$, which lies between the two autarkic relative price ratios: $\bar{p}^H < \tilde{p} < \bar{p}^F$. By the Stolper–Samuelson theorem, the equalization of good prices (at $\tilde{p}$) implies also factor-price equalization. In this case, factor mobility is redundant: Trade in goods is a perfect substitute for factor mobility. We can say that although factors of production do not directly

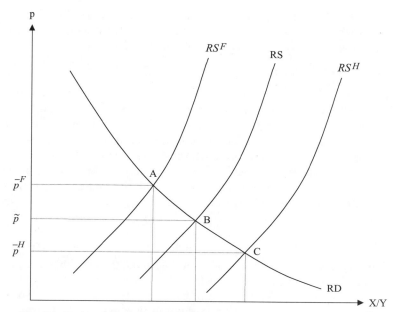

Fig. 2.3. Free-trade versus autarkic equilibria.

move from one country to another, they nevertheless move indirectly between them, because they are *embodied* in the goods that are traded.

To see this point, we can follow Vanek (1968) in calculating the *factor content* of the trade in goods. For this purpose, let us distinguish explicitly in our notation between output and consumption. Denote by Q_i^j and C_i^j, respectively, the output and the consumption of good $i = X, Y$ in country $j = H, F$. Denote also by M_L^H and M_K^H, respectively, the net labor and capital imported (indirectly, by means of trade in goods) by country H from country F. We can show (see Appendix 2.1) that

$$M_L^H = s^H(\bar{L}^H + \bar{L}^F) - \bar{L}^H, \tag{2.4}$$

$$M_K^H = s^H(\bar{K}^H + \bar{K}^F) - \bar{K}^H, \tag{2.5}$$

where s^H is the share of country H in worldwide income.

Equations (2.4) and (2.5) give a simple measure of the factor content of trade that depends on only initial factor endowments and the cross-country distribution of world income. Because country H exports good X, which is labor intensive, and imports good Y, which is capital intensive, the factor content of its net imports follows a similar pattern: The labor component is negative and the capital component is positive. That is, country H implicitly exports labor and implicitly imports capital by means of its trade in goods.

Thus, as Mundell (1957) first pointed out, trade in goods is a perfect substitute for an export of $-M_L^H$ units of labor from country H to country F in exchange for an import of M_L^H units of capital by country H from country F.

NONSUBSTITUTION

The result of the preceding subsection is rather special, even in our setup in which all goods are traded. In fact, if we relax either assumption (ii) or assumption (iii), trade in goods will no longer serve as a perfect substitute for factor mobility. When the number of goods exceeds the number of factors of production, trade in goods may still narrow down the autarkic factor price gap but not eliminate it altogether, leaving sufficient room for factor mobility. Furthermore, when technologies differ across countries, trade in goods may even exacerbate the factor-price gap, thereby generating more (not less) pressure for factor mobility.

More Goods than Factors

Suppose now that we relax assumption (iii) about the equal number of goods and factors of production. Specifically, suppose that we have a third traded good, Z. This case remains in the realm of the Heckscher–Ohlin–Samuelson model in which trade in goods (which serves to equalize goods prices) narrows down factor-price gaps, but does not eliminate them altogether. Suppose with no loss of generality that good Z is the least labor intensive of all three goods, that is,

$$\frac{a_{LX}}{a_{KX}} > \frac{a_{LY}}{a_{KY}} > \frac{a_{LZ}}{a_{KZ}}. \tag{2.1'}$$

First, observe that under free trade each country will produce only two goods. This can be seen in Fig. 2.4, which reproduces Fig. 2.1. For given goods prices (by international trade) the zero-profit loci for goods X, Y, and Z are given by the lines XX, YY, and ZZ, respectively. Note again that the slope of each line is given by the corresponding labor–capital intensity, and hence the line XX is steeper than the line YY, which, in turn, is steeper than the line ZZ. Unless, by sheer coincidence, all three lines intersect each other at the same point, only two goods can be produced. It also follows from Fig. (2.4) that the only possible combination of pairs of goods that are produced is either (X, Y) or (Y, Z). The combination (X, Z) that sets the factor prices at point E_{XZ} is impossible: At this set of factor prices, industry Y makes a strictly positive profit. Thus, the only feasible pairs of factor prices are (r_1, w_1) at point E_{XY} or (r_2, w_2) at point E_{YZ}. At the first point (E_{XY}), Z will not be produced because its price falls short of its unit cost. Similarly, at the second point (E_{YZ}), X will not be produced for the same reason.

Assuming that preferences are such that the demand for each good is always positive, it must be the case that all three goods are produced somewhere in the world. Which one of the two countries produces the pair (X, Y), and which one

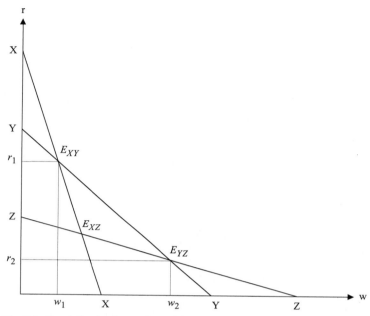

Fig. 2.4. Specialization in two (out of three) goods.

produces the other pair (Y, Z) depends on the relative endowments of capital and labor in the two countries.

We can observe from Fig. 2.5 (which reproduces Fig. 2.2) that the factor-price ratio (w_1/r_1) is compatible within only a certain range of the capital–labor endowment ratio. Note that at that factor-price ratio only X and Y are produced. Let the line LL represent the full employment of labor condition for the given factor price pair (w_1/r_1). Now, if the endowment of capital is K_*, then the full employment of capital condition is depicted by the line K_*K_*, in which only X is produced. Similarly, if the capital endowment is K^*, then only Y is produced. Thus, the factor-price ratio w_1/r_1 is compatible with a range $(K_*/L, K^*/L)$ of capital–labor endowment ratios. Similarly, the factor-price ratio w_2/r_2 is compatible with another range of capital–labor endowment ratios. The latter range must be to the right of the former range, as depicted in Fig. 2.6. This follows from two observations: (i) at the higher w/r ratio, which characterizes the production of the pair (Y, Z), only the capital–labor intensity rises in each of these two industries; and (ii) industry Z is more capital intensive than industry X, and hence the pair (Y, Z) requires more capital relative to labor than the pair (X, Y), even for the same w/r ratio.

At the free-trade equilibrium, we see from Fig. 2.6 that the factor-price ratio is (w_1/r_1) in country H and (w_2/r_2) in country F. The convergence of goods prices may narrow down the factor-price gaps, but does not fully eliminate them.

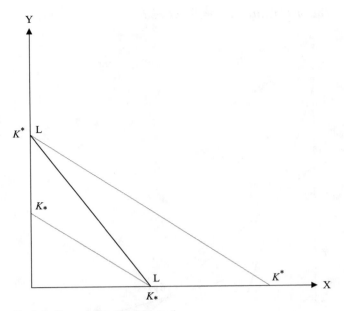

Fig. 2.5. Range of capital–labor ratios.

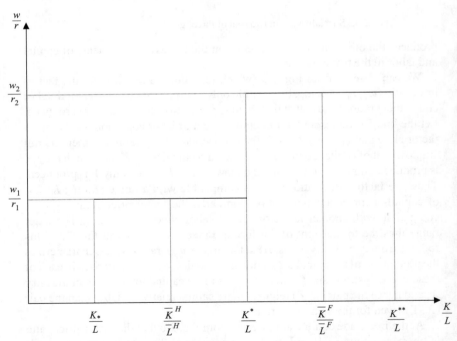

Fig. 2.6. Equilibrium relationship between factor price ratios and capital–labor ratios.

Complementarity between Trade in Goods and Factor Mobility

If we relax the assumption of identical technologies, trade in goods may even widen factor-price gaps. Hence, trade in goods may even increase the pressure for factor mobility. Furthermore, if such mobility is allowed, the volume of trade in goods may even increase. To focus attention on the differences in technologies, let us reinstate assumption (i) about identical relative factor endowments across countries and assumption (iii) about an equal number of goods and factors of production. In this subsection, we follow the analysis of Markusen (1983).

For simplicity and concreteness, suppose that country H has a more productive technology for producing good X than country F, in a Hicks-neutral sense, that is,

$$G_X^H(K_X, L_X) = aG_X^F(K_X, L_X), \ a > 1, \tag{2.6}$$

and that the technologies for producing Y are identical, that is,

$$G_Y^H(K_Y, L_Y) = G_Y^F(K_Y, L_Y), \tag{2.7}$$

where G_j^i is the production function of good j in country i, $j = X, Y$, and $i = H, F$.

In this case, we show that trade in goods does not suffice to equalize factor prices. Indeed, under free trade the wage in the home country, which is technologically superior in the labor-intensive good, is higher than in the foreign country, and the opposite holds true with respect to the rental price of capital,

$$w^H > w^F \quad \text{and} \quad r^H < r^F. \tag{2.8}$$

To see this, we plot the production possibility frontiers for the two countries in Fig. 2.7. Note that the frontier for H is achieved when the frontier for F is pulled to the right by the multiplicative factor α. Thus the slope at B, for instance, is $1\backslash \alpha$ times the slope at F_1. It is important to note that F_1 and B represent the same point (say, point F_2) on an identical contract curve in an identical Edgeworth Box of the two countries (Fig. 2.8). (The two countries have the same Edgeworth Box because they have the same factor endowments, and they have the same contract curve because their technologies differ by only a Hicks-neutral multiplicative coefficient). Thus, if both countries produce at the same point in the Edgeworth Box (say, point F_2 in Fig. 2.8, corresponding to F_1 and B in Fig. 2.7), then they cannot have the same commodity price ratio, which is required under free trade (recall that the commodity price ratio is equal to the slope of the production possibility frontier). Hence, with the equal commodity prices that are required under free trade, country H must produce less Y (and more X) than country F. Thus, suppose that country H is at H_1 and H_2 in Figs. 2.7 and 2.8, respectively, and country F is at F_1 and F_2 in Figs. 2.7 and 2.8, respectively.

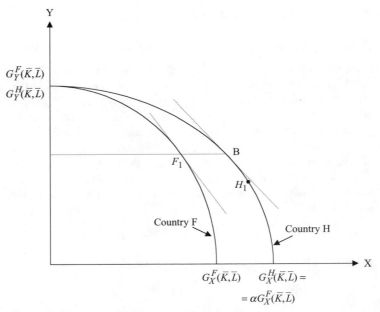

Fig. 2.7. Unequal factor prices: production possibility frontiers.

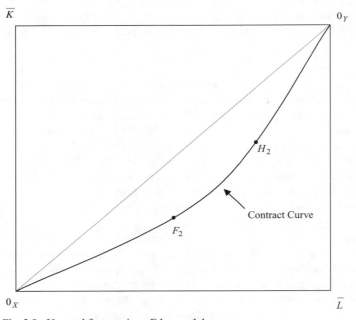

Fig. 2.8. Unequal factor prices: Edgeworth box.

Because the two countries have the same (homothetic) demand patterns, although country H produces a higher X-to-Y ratio than country F, it follows that country H exports good X (in which she enjoys a superior technology) and imports good Y. Given the convex shape of the contract curve, it follows that the factor-price ratio w/r is higher in country H than in country F. Because both countries produce good Y with the same technology and under the same price (namely, unity), it follows that inequalities (2.8) hold. Thus commodity trade does not equalize factor prices.[2] Furthermore, depending on demand patterns and the degree of factor substitution in production, it may well be the case that free commodity trade widens, rather than narrows, the factor-price differentials.

Now, suppose that factor mobility (labor and capital) is allowed alongside trade in commodities. Labor will move from country F to country H, and capital will move in the opposite direction. By the Rybczyinski theorem, at the initial commodity trade price, there will be an excess supply of good X in country H, and its imports of Y will further rise. Indeed, country H with its superior technology will specialize in the production of good X. Thus factor mobility reinforces trade in commodities. In this setup of international technological differences in certain industries, factor mobility and commodity trade complement each other.

Alternatively, complementarity between commodity trade and factor mobility can also be generated by external economies of scale. Being external to the individual firm, economies of scale still preserve perfect competition. Suppose for concreteness that there are external scale economies in the production of good X. If countries differ in absolute size, but have identical relative factor endowments, Markusen (1983) shows that the larger country will export good X. As this good is more labor intensive, the relative price of labor (w/r) in the free commodity trade equilibrium is higher in country H. Allowing labor to move from country F to country H will further increase the excess supply of good X in country H by means of both the Rybczyinski effect and the external-scale-economies effect, thereby generating an even higher volume of trade.

In a study on East–West migration that came out just after the breakdown of communism, Layard et al. (1992) emphasized the role of trade in goods as an alternative to labor migration:

> "Given the difficulties posed by the prospect of very large-scale migration from East to West, and the risk that such large-scale migration could actually leave worse-off the remaining population in the East, we need to ask what alternatives are available. Ideally, policy should try to bring good jobs to the East *rather than* Eastern workers to the West. International trade . . . *can* act as a substitute for migration. A free trade pact that ensures Eastern European countries access to the Western European market is the best single migration policy that could be put in place. In the amazing post-war reconstruction of Western Europe, the openness of the U.S. market was a crucial factor. Western Europe now has the opportunity of providing a similar service to the East."

The gains from trade in goods notwithstanding, we have pointed out that such trade can be a complement to labor (and capital) mobility. It does not necessarily equalize wages and may even widen the wage gap, thereby generating more incentives for labor mobility in the presence of technological advantage of one country over the other. Note also that the productivity advantage could merely reflect some superior infrastructure (roads, telecommunication systems, ports, energy, etc.), which is certainly the case in the East–West context. Thus, important policy elements should be investment in infrastructure (possibly funded by foreign aid) and direct foreign investment, which tends to also diffuse technology and raise productivity. Once productivity gaps are narrowed down, trade in goods can further alleviate the pressure for factor mobility.

In view of the empirical falsification of the factor price equalization theorems,[3] Davis (1992) introduced Hicks-neutral differences in technology across countries, uniform over all industries. He tested the hypothesis concerning convergence of relative industry wages across countries. The evidence found "strongly rejected the hypothesis of increasing uniformity across countries in the relative industry wage structure," despite the ongoing trend of trade liberalization.

APPENDIX 2.1 FACTOR CONTENT OF TRADE

In this appendix, we derive equations (2.4) and (2.5) that express the factor content of trade. Denoting by Q_i^j and C_i^j, respectively, the output and the consumption of good $i = X, Y$ in country $j = H, F$, we can calculate the net import vector of country H by

$$\mathbf{M}^H \equiv \left\{ \begin{array}{c} M_X^H \\ M_Y^H \end{array} \right\} = \left\{ \begin{array}{cc} C_X^H & -Q_X^H \\ C_Y^H & -Q_Y^H \end{array} \right\} \equiv \mathbf{C}^H - \mathbf{Q}^H.$$

Full employment in country $i = H, F$ requires that

$$\mathbf{AQ}^i = \left[\begin{array}{c} \bar{L}^i \\ \bar{K}^i \end{array} \right] \equiv \bar{\mathbf{V}}^i,$$

where

$$\mathbf{A} = \left[\begin{array}{cc} a_{LX} & a_{LY} \\ a_{KY} & a_{KY} \end{array} \right]$$

is the unit-input-requirement matrix. (Note that the matrix $\mathbf{A}$ is the same for the two countries because trade has equalized factor prices, the arguments of the a_{ij} coefficients.) From the assumption of identical homothetic preferences it follows that

$$\mathbf{C}^H = s^H(\mathbf{Q}^H + \mathbf{Q}^F) = s^H(\mathbf{A}^{-1}\bar{\mathbf{V}}^H + \mathbf{A}^{-1}\bar{\mathbf{V}}^F) \equiv s^H\mathbf{A}^{-1}\bar{\mathbf{V}},$$

where s^H is the share of country H in worldwide income and $\bar{\mathbf{V}} \equiv \bar{\mathbf{V}}^H + \bar{\mathbf{V}}^F$ is the world factor endowment vector.

Hence,

$$\mathbf{M}^H = \mathbf{C}^H - \mathbf{Q}^H = s^H \mathbf{A}^{-1}\bar{\mathbf{V}} - \mathbf{A}^{-1}\bar{\mathbf{V}}^H.$$

Therefore, the factor content of the net import flows that is $\mathbf{AM}^H$ can be expressed as

$$\mathbf{AM}^H = s^H\bar{\mathbf{V}} - \bar{\mathbf{V}}^H = s^H \begin{bmatrix} \bar{L}^H & +\bar{L}^F \\ \bar{K}^H & +\bar{K}^F \end{bmatrix} - \begin{bmatrix} \bar{L}^H \\ \bar{K}^H \end{bmatrix},$$

which is Eqs. (2.4) and (2.5) in matrix form.

PART 2

LABOR MIGRATION INTO THE WELFARE STATE

3   Intertemporal Social Insurance and Migration

INTRODUCTION

In Part 1, we dealt with factor mobility. We distinguished between the factor of production and its owner. By factor mobility we referred to the mobility of the factor itself, without the owner's changing her or his country of residence. This distinction might be applicable to capital or, in the case of labor, to guest workers. However, in the case of labor, the relevant mobility typically includes both the factors of production *and* the owner of the factor. This kind of mobility is referred to as migration.

Migration is intertwined with welfare issues. The incentives for migration are shaped by the various ingredients of the welfare state, beyond the economic return (i.e., the marginal product) of labor as a factor of production. Pension contributions and benefits, unemployment and disability benefits, public education to children, health care, etc., are all part and parcel of the incentives for migration. These elements may be equally important as the return to labor in the form of wages in generating the pull-and-push factors of migration. The size of the aforementioned payments and benefits, the scope and the composition of the income redistribution embodied in them, and the degree of eligibility of migrants to benefit from them determine not only the incentives to migrate, but also the effect of migration on the well-being of the native-born population and, consequently, the attitude of this population toward migration.

In this part, we analyze these issues. To this end, we find it useful to distinguish between long-term intertemporal aspects and short-term intratemporal aspects. We start in this chapter with the intertemporal welfare analysis of migration. As the intertemporal social insurance (old-age security) system is a central pillar (intertemporal and intergenerational) of the welfare state, we choose to focus on this system, analyzing its interaction with migration.

It is commonly agreed that the pension system is heavily burdened in most countries and is in need of reform.[1] For instance, Gruber and Wise (1999, p. 34), state that "the population in all industrialized countries is aging rapidly,

31

and individual life expectancies are increasing. Yet older workers are leaving the labor force at younger and younger ages . . . Together, these trends have put enormous pressure on the financial solvency of social security systems around the world." In many countries, the theoretical tax (contribution) rates, that is, the rates that would balance the system, are significantly higher than the statutory rates. For example, Brugiavini (1999) reports that this theoretical rate reached 44% for Italy in 1991.

Migration may have important implications for the financial soundness of the pension system. As put succinctly by the *Economist*: "Demography and economics together suggest that Europe might do better to open wider its doors. Europeans now live longer and have fewer babies than they used to. The burden of a growing host of elderly people is shifting on to a dwindling number of young shoulders" (February 15, 1992).

Naturally, a country is most likely to benefit from the migration of young, highly skilled individuals. This is because such migrants would typically be net contributors to the state pension system, that is, their contributions are expected to exceed their benefits (in present-value terms). For instance, a recent study, initiated by the U.S. National Research Council, estimates the *overall net fiscal* contribution of migrants with at least high school education who arrived in the U.S. at ages between 20 and 35 at approximately $150,000 over their own lifetime; see Smith and Edmonston (1997). Things are less obvious when the migrants are low skilled. For instance, the aforementioned study estimates that migrants with less than high school education, aged 20–40 years on arrival, impose an overall net fiscal burden of $60,000–$150,000 over their own lifetime. Therefore, our analysis is focused on the case of young, unskilled migrants.

The flow of unskilled, low-earnings migrants to developed states with a comprehensive social security system, including old-age security, has attracted both public and academic attention in recent years. Being relatively low earners, migrants may be net beneficiaries of the welfare state.[2] Therefore, there may arise an almost unanimous opposition to migration in the potential host countries. Although young migrants, even if low skilled, can help society pay the benefits to the current elderly population, it may nevertheless be still reasonable to argue that these migrants would adversely affect the current young population if the migrants are net consumers of the welfare state.

However, here comes into play the ingenuity of Paul Samuelson's concept of the economy as an everlasting machinery even though each one of its human components is finitely lived [Samuelson (1958)]. In this chapter, we use this concept in a dynamic model of a welfare state with immigration and show that even though the migrants may be low skilled and net beneficiaries of a pension system, nevertheless all the existing income (low and high) and age (young and old) groups living at the time of the migrants' arrival would be better off. Therefore, on these grounds, the political economy equilibrium will be overwhelmingly promigration. Furthermore, this migration need not put any burden on future generations.

This unambiguous result obtains whether or not the low-skilled migrants are net beneficiaries or net contributors to the old-age social security system. That is, the result obtains when the contributions of the migrants to the pension system both fall short of or exceed the present value of the pension benefits. Indeed, when the market rate of interest exceeds the biological rate of interest (i.e., the population growth rate), which is usually the case, and the percentage of skilled in the native-born population is relatively small, then the low-skilled migrants may even be net contributors to (rather than net consumers of) the pension system.[3]

The unequivocal Pareto-improving effect of migration in our welfare state is obtained in a fixed factor-price environment that is typical for a small open economy because of either capital mobility or factor-price-equalizing trade in goods. However, when migration affects factor prices,[4] particularly depressing wages of unskilled labor,[5] it may create some antimigration elements that may counterbalance the initial positive effect on the pension system. Indeed, with a sufficiently small substitution between capital and labor, the factor-price effect may well inflict losses on some income groups of the current generation and some future generations.

Before turning to the analytical study outlined above, we briefly review some new evidence from the U.S. on the fiscal burden of migration.

THE NEW AMERICANS

Recently, the U.S. National Research Council sponsored a comprehensive study on the overall fiscal impact of immigration into the U.S. The study looked carefully at all layers of government (federal, state, and local), all programs (benefits), and all types of taxes. For each cohort, defined by age of arrival to the U.S., the benefits (cash or in kind) received by migrants over their own lifetimes and the lifetimes of their first-generation descendents were projected. These benefits include Medicare, Medicaid, Supplementary Security Income (SSI), Aid for Families with Dependent Children (AFDC), food stamps, Old Age, and Survivors, and Disability Insurance (OASDI), etc. Similarly, taxes paid directly by migrants and the incidence on migrants of other taxes (such as corporate taxes) were also projected for the lifetimes of the migrants and their first-generation descendents. Accordingly, the net fiscal burden was projected and discounted to the present.

In this way, the net fiscal burden for each age cohort of migrants was calculated in present-value terms. Within each age cohort, these calculations were disaggregated according to three educational levels: less than high school education, high school education, and more than high school education.

The findings are summarized in Fig. 3.1, which is also Fig. 7.10 in Smith and Edmonston (1997). Chart A of Fig. 3.1 suggests that migrants with less than high school education are typically a net fiscal burden that can reach as high as approximately $200,000 in present value, when the migrants' age on

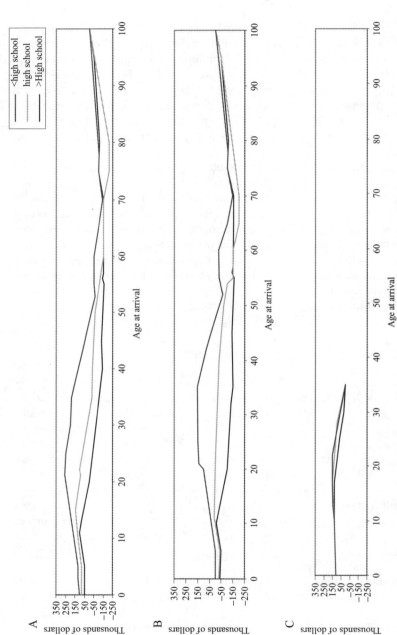

Fig. 3.1. Net present value of total fiscal impact: A, Generation 1 by age at arrival and education status, self, and descendants; B, generation 1 by age at arrival and education status, own lifetime; C, generation 1 by age at arrival and education status, and descendants. Monetary values are in 1996 U.S. dollars. This figure is reproduced from Fig. 7.10 in Smith and Edmonston (1997).

34

arrival is 50–55 years. On the other hand, a young migrant, aged approximately 20 years on arrival, with more than high school education, is expected to make a positive net fiscal contribution of approximately $300,000 in present value.

We now return to an analytical examination of the welfare implications of migration on the pension system, the central pillar of the intertemporal, intergenerational redistribution of the modern welfare state.

PENSION AND MIGRATION: FIXED FACTOR PRICES

Consider an overlapping-generations model, in which each generation lives for two periods. In each period a new generation with a continuum of individuals is born. Each individual possesses a time endowment of one unit in the first period (when young), but no labor endowment in the second period (when old). There is a pay-as-you-go, defined-benefit (PAYG-DB) state pension system. At each period, the benefits paid to the elderly population are fully financed by the contributions made by the current working young population, and there is no pension fund accumulated. The benefits that each individual receives at old age are predetermined by the government and are typically unequal on an actuarial basis to the contributions made by this individual at her or his working age.

Innate Ability and Schooling

There are two levels of work skill, denoted by low and high. A low-skill individual is also referred to as unskilled and a high-skill individual as skilled. Born unskilled, she or he can nevertheless acquire skills and become a skilled worker by investing e units of time in schooling. The remainder of her or his time is spent at work as a skilled worker. There is also a fixed pecuniary cost of education denoted by $\gamma \geq 0$.

The individual-specific parameter e reflects the innate ability of the individual to acquire a work skill. The lower e is, that is, the less time she or he needs for acquiring a work skill, the more able the individual is. The parameter e ranges between 0 and 1 and its cumulative distribution function (cdf) is denoted by $G(\cdot)$, that is $G(e)$ is the number of individuals with an innate ability parameter below or equal to e. For the sake of simplicity, we normalize the number of individuals born in period zero, when we begin our analysis of the economy, to be one, that is,

$$G(1) = 1. \tag{3.1}$$

For the sake of simplicity again, we model the difference between skilled and unskilled workers by assuming that a skilled worker provides an effective labor supply of one unit per each unit of her or his working time, whereas an unskilled worker provides only $q < 1$ units of effective labor per each unit of her or his working time.

In the first period of her or his life, the individual decides whether to acquire or not acquire skill; she or he also works, brings $1 + n$ children, consumes a composite, all-purpose good, and saves for retirement that takes place in the second period. In the latter period, she or he only consumes her or his retirement savings and her pension benefit.

Consider the schooling decision of the individual. If she or he acquires a skill by investing e units of her or his time, she or he will earn an after-tax income of $(1 - e)w(1 - \tau) - \gamma$, where w is the wage rate per unit of effective labor and $\tau > 0$ is a flat social security contribution (tax) rate. It is assumed that the fixed pecuniary cost of education (γ) is not tax deductible, as is usually the case in reality. If she or he does not acquire a skill, that is, spends all of her or his time endowment at work, she or he earns an after-tax income of $qw(1 - \tau)$. Thus there will be a cutoff level of e, denoted by e^* and given by

$$(1 - e^*)(1 - \tau)w - \gamma = (1 - \tau)qw, \tag{3.2''}$$

so that every individual with an innate ability parameter below e^* will acquire skill and become a skilled worker, whereas all individuals with innate ability parameters above e^* will not acquire skill and remain unskilled. Rewriting Eq. (3.2''), we explicitly define e^* by

$$e^* = 1 - q - \frac{\gamma}{(1 - \tau)w}. \tag{3.2'}$$

As we can see from Eq. (3.2') the tax has a distortionary effects: The higher the tax rate, the lower e^* is. That is, a higher tax rate leads to fewer people that acquire skill. It is clear from Eq. (3.2'') or Eq. (3.2') that if γ were replaced by $(1 - \tau)\gamma$, that is, the pecuniary cost of education were tax deductible, then the tax would have had no effect on e^*. Similarly, when $\gamma = 0$, the tax is neutral with respect to the decision of acquiring skill. In this chapter we focus on the distributional aspects of the old-age security system, abstracting from its distortionary effect. We therefore set γ equal to zero in this chapter so that

$$e^* = 1 - q. \tag{3.2}$$

We reinstate a positive γ in Chap. 4 in which the distortionary effects of the tax system play a major role in the determination of the overall tax burden.

Consumption and Saving

We denote first-period and second-period consumption by c_1 and c_2, respectively; an individual born at period zero and onward faces the following intertemporal budget constraint:

$$c_1 + \frac{c_2}{1+r} = W(e)(1-\tau) + \frac{b_1}{1+r}, \qquad (3.3)$$

where r is the interest rate,[6] $W(e)$ is the before-tax wage income for an individual with an innate ability parameter of e, and b_1 is the social security demogrant benefit paid to retirees at period one.[7] Note that

$$W(e) = \begin{cases} w(1-e) & \text{for} \quad e \le e^* \\ qw & \text{for} \quad e \ge e^*. \end{cases} \qquad (3.4)$$

We assume that preferences over first-period and second-period consumption are identical for all individuals and are given by a Cobb–Douglas log-linear utility function:

$$u(c_1, c_2) = \log c_1 + \delta \log c_2, \qquad (3.5)$$

where $\delta < 1$ is the subjective intertemporal discount factor. These preferences give rise to the following saving first-period-consumption and second-period-consumption functions for a young individual of type e:

$$S(e) = \frac{\delta}{1+\delta} W(e)(1-\tau) - \frac{b_1}{(1+\delta)(1+r)}, \qquad (3.6)$$

$$c_1(e) = \frac{1}{1+\delta}\left[W(e)(1-\tau) + \frac{b_1}{1+r} \right], \qquad (3.7a)$$

$$c_2(e) = \frac{\delta}{1+\delta}\left[W(e)(1-\tau) + \frac{b_1}{1+r} \right](1+r). \qquad (3.7b)$$

The Current Old Generation

In period zero, there are also $1/(1+n)$ old (retired) individuals who were born at period -1. The consumption of each one of them is equal to her or his savings from the first period, plus the social security benefit, denoted by b_0. In each period the aggregate savings of the old (retired) generation constitutes the aggregate stock of capital.

Migrants

Consider the following exercise: In period zero, m migrants are allowed in, but no more migrants are allowed later on.[8] It is assumed that these migrants are all young and unskilled workers and that they possess no capital. Once they enter the country, they adopt the domestic norms of the native-born population. Specifically, they grow up at the same rate (n), they have the same preferences [as given by Eq. (3.5)], and the ability index of their offspring is distributed similarly (according to the cdf G). The assumption of identical preferences is not essential for the conclusion and is made purely to simplify the exposition. However, the equal-ability-distribution assumption may be a subject of open debate in some rich countries. It may be argued that children of immigrants appear to have attributes such as relatively low birth weight and low school completion rates that weaken their earnings' potential later in life. However, to the extent that this slow integration process is not permanently extended forward to the next generations, our qualitative results are not significantly altered. Furthermore, a new empirical study by Card, DiNardo, and Estes (1998) challenged the claim that the children of unskilled migrants (from Mexico and Latin America) to the U.S. are likely to be assimilated slowly into the labor market. Using Current Population Surveys, this study found that these children tend to close approximately 50%–60% of the gap between average U.S. wages and the earnings of their fathers' ethnic immigrant group. Even more striking, immigrants' children do better than natives' children: Among American children with parents of the same socioeconomic class, those born to immigrants tend to attain more education and to enjoy higher earnings in their jobs.

Labor Supply

The aggregate supply of effective labor in period zero is given by

$$L_0 = \int_0^{e^*} (1 - e)dG + q[1 - G(e^*)] + qm. \qquad (3.8)$$

The first term on the right-hand side of Eq. (3.8) is the effective labor supply of the native-born skilled workers. The second term is the effective labor supply of the native-born unskilled workers [note that there are $1 - G(e^*)$ of them], and the last term is the effective labor supply of the unskilled migrants.

The aggregate supply of effective labor in period one is given by

$$L_1 = (1 + m)(1 + n)\left\{ \int_0^{e^*} (1 - e)dG + q[1 - G(e^*)] \right\}. \qquad (3.9)$$

Note that, because of migration and natural growth, there are altogether $(1 + m)(1 + n)$ young individuals born in period one.

The Stock of Capital

The aggregate stock of capital in period zero that is owned by the current old (born in period -1) is denoted by K_0. The aggregate stock of capital in period one consists of the savings of both the native-born young generation of period zero and the migrants. Thus, it is equal to

$$K_1 = \int_0^{e^*} \left[\frac{\delta}{1+\delta} w(1-e)(1-\tau) - \frac{b_1}{(1+\delta)(1+r)} \right] dG$$

$$+ \left[\frac{\delta}{1+\delta} q w(1-\tau) - \frac{b_1}{(1+\delta)(1+r)} \right] [1 - G(e^*) + m], \quad (3.10')$$

where use is made of the saving and earned-income equations (3.6) and (3.4). The term in the first square brackets is the saving of a skilled person with an ability parameter of e. The term in the second square brackets is the saving of an unskilled person. Note that because of migrations there are $1 - G^*(e) + m$ unskilled individuals in period zero. After some rewriting, Eq. (3.10') becomes

$$K_1 = \frac{\delta}{1+\delta} w(1-\tau) \left\{ \int_0^{e^*} (1-e) dG + q[1 - G(e^*) + m] \right\}$$

$$- \frac{b_1(1+m)}{(1+\delta)(1+r)}. \quad (3.10)$$

Output

In a small economy with free access to the world capital markets, the domestic return to capital will converge to the world rate of interest. Thus, migration has no effect on the domestic rate of interest. Furthermore, when the technology exhibits constant returns to scale, migration will have no effect on wages as well. Alternatively, we may view our single good as a composite of two traded goods. In a small Heckscher–Ohlin economy, the domestic good prices are nailed down by the world prices. Consequently, domestic factor prices are equated to the exogenously given world prices. Thus, in either case, gross national output [denoted by $F(K, L)$] is given by

$$F(K, L) = wL + (1+r)K. \quad (3.11)$$

We assume, with no loss of generality, that capital fully depreciates at the end of the production process. In this setup, w is the (fixed) marginal product of labor and r is the (fixed) net-of-depreciation marginal product of capital.

The Pension System

As was already mentioned, we consider a pay-as-you-go, defined benefit (PAYG-DB) pension system. The pensions to retirees are paid entirely from current contributions made by workers and the benefit takes the form of a demogrant. In period zero, total contributions amount to

$$T_0 = \tau w \left\{ \int_0^{e^*} (1-e) dG + q[1 - G(e^*) + m] \right\}, \quad (3.12)$$

as the term in the braces is the effective labor supply. Thus, the demogrant benefit b_0 is equal to

$$b_0 = (1+n)\tau w \left\{ \int_0^{e^*} (1-e)dG + q[1 - G(e^*) + m] \right\}, \qquad (3.13)$$

because there are $1/(1+n)$ retirees at period zero. Total contributions in period one are equal to

$$T_1 = \tau w \left\{ \int_0^{e^*} (1-e)dG + q[1 - G(e^*)] \right\} (1+m)(1+n), \qquad (3.14)$$

because there are $(1+m)(1+n)$ individuals in period one who are the indistinguishable offspring of the native-born in period zero and the migrants and because a proportion $1 - G(e^*)$ of these individuals are unskilled. The demogrant benefit in period one is equal to

$$b_1 = \tau w \left\{ \int_0^{e^*} (1-e)dG + q[1 - G(e^*)] \right\} (1+n), \qquad (3.15)$$

because there are $1 + m$ native-born and migrant retirees in period one.

Dynamics

The dynamics of this economy is quite simple. Because of the constancy of the factor prices, the economy converges to a steady state within two periods. The pension benefit in period two is going to be equal to b_1, the pension benefit in period one, because the common characteristics of the offspring of the migrants and of the offspring of the native-born population of period zero are stationary. Thus the pension benefits will equal b_1 from period one onward. The stock of capital will stabilize from period two onward because in period one it is still affected by the contribution to savings of the migrants who arrived in period zero.

In this stylized model, the welfare impact of migration on the economy is manifested through the pension benefit only. This is because factor prices are constant and schooling decisions are unaffected by migration.

The Benefits from Migration

On inspection of Eq. (3.13), we can observe that b_0, the pension benefit to retirees at period zero (in which the migrants arrive), increases with the number of migrants. Thus, as expected, the old generation at period zero is clearly better off with migration. This is because migration increases the number of workers and, consequently, the tax base. On inspection of Eq. (3.15), we can observe that b_1, the pension benefit paid to retirees in period one and onward, is unaffected by migration. In particular, and somewhat surprisingly, the young generation at the time at which the migrants arrive (both its skilled and unskilled members) is not adversely affected by migration. Thus, the existing population (both young and old) in period zero will welcome migration.

Furthermore, by creating some surplus in the pension system in period zero (that is, by lowering b_0 somewhat), the gain that accrues to only the old generation in our setup could be spread over to future generations as well. Thus, migration is a Pareto-improving change with respect to the existing and future generations of the native born. Evidently such a Pareto improvement will be experienced in each period in which a new wave of migrants comes in.

Somewhat surprisingly, this result obtains even though the unskilled migrants may well be *net beneficiaries* of the redistributive pension system, in the sense that the present value of their pension benefits exceeds their pension contributions. To see this, let us calculate the net benefit to an immigrant. The present value of her or his benefit is $b_1/(1 + r)$, and her or his contribution is $\tau q w$. Substituting for b_1 in $b_1/(1 + r)$ from Eq. (3.15), we can rewrite the net benefit (denoted by NB) as

$$ \text{NB} = \frac{1+n}{1+r} \tau w \left\{ \int_0^{e^*} (1 - e) dG + q[1 - G(e^*)] \right\} - \tau q w. \qquad (3.16) $$

By using Eq. (3.2) we can show (see Appendix 3.1) that $\text{NB} \gtrless 0$ if

$$ \frac{G(e^*)(e^* - e^-)}{1 - e^*} \underset{<}{\overset{>}{\gtrless}} \frac{r - n}{1 + n}, \qquad (3.17) $$

where e^- is the mean ability parameter of the skilled workers. Note that $e^* > e^-$, because e^* is the upper bound of the ability parameter of skilled individuals, whereas e^- is its mean. Thus, the left-hand-side of relation (3.17) must be positive. Hence, if $r < n$, then NB is certainly positive, that is, the migrants are the net beneficiaries of the pension system. However, it is typically assumed that $r > n$ (dynamic efficiency considerations).[9] In this case, if a large share of the population is skilled, then NB is still positive. To see this, observe that when the share of the skilled population (e^*) approaches one, then the left-hand side of relation (3.17) increases without bound. Hence, the left-hand side of relation (3.17) will exceed its right-hand side. In this case, migrants are net beneficiaries of the pension system.

However, when r is significantly larger than n, the share of skilled in the native-born population $[G(e^*)]$ is low, and the relative productivity of unskilled ($q = 1 - e^*$) is high, then NB will be negative. The intuition of how low-skill migrants can still be net contributors to a progressive pension system is grounded in the dynamic feature of the PAYG system. The benefits that the migrants are entitled to at old age grow in a PAYG system only at the rate of the population growth rate (n). However, to compare these benefits with the taxes paid by the migrants at their working age, we have to discount these benefits by the market rate of interest (r). Thus, ceteris paribus, the larger the gap $r - n$ is, the smaller the present value of the net benefit to the migrants is. Now, if migrant and the native-born workers are all similar [that is, $q = 1$, $e^* = 0$ and $G(e^*) = 0$], then no redistribution is performed by the social security system and the migrants, like all the native-born workers, are net contributors to the system. By continuity considerations, we can conclude that if the migrants are not substantially different from the native-born workers [that is, q is not significantly below one, e^* is not very high, and $G(e^*)$ is not very large], then they are net contributors to the pension system in the dynamically efficient case of $r > n$.

What we have established is that, regardless of whether or not the migrants are net consumers of the pension system, all existing and future generations may gain from migration. In our simple parable, migration was a one-time episode. Naturally, if this one-time immigration episode repeats itself in the future to generate a steady flow of migrants in each period, the gain that we showed to exist for the contemporaneous old generation would repeat itself too for all future old generations. Thus a steady flow of low-skill migrants would generate a steady flow of benefits to the native born.

Interpretation

An important lesson from this parable is that in a dynamic setup, which is both natural and essential for analyzing some important ingredients of the welfare state such as old-age security, certain seemingly costly shocks could turn out to be beneficial. The migrants could be net beneficiaries of the welfare state, so that, at first thought, they seem to impose a burden on the native-born population. However, in a dynamic context, this net burden could change to a net gain because the burden may be shifted forward indefinitely. If, hypothetically, the world would come to a full stop at a certain point in time, the young generation at that point would bear the cost of the present migration.

To illustrate this point, we construct the following example. Consider a finite-time (two-period) modified version of our model. Suppose the young generation of period zero and the migrants who arrive then bear no children and the world ceases after period one. Suppose further that the social security contribution (tax) rate remains τ in period zero. Hence, b_0 does not change [see Eq. (3.13)] and, as before, the old population living in period zero benefit from migration.

In period one, the last period, there will be no young people, no labor supply, and no social security benefits. National output is $(1 + r)K$. The young people born in period zero and the migrants live off their period-zero savings $[(1 + r)K]$. Obviously, the young people of period zero are not affected by migration. The migrants paid their social security taxes in period zero, receiving no benefits in return in period one. That is, the migrants are net contributors to the pension system (which ceased after period zero); they financed the increased benefit to the old population of period zero with no compensation to themselves.

In sum, the effect of migration is as follows: The old generation of period zero benefited, the native-born young generation was not affected, and the migrants financed in full the gain to the old population. In essence, it is a zero-sum game. If, in this zero-sum environment, the migrants are compensated in period one in some way or another for their social security contributions in period zero, it must be at the expense of the native-born old population of period one (the native-born young generation of period zero).

Summing Up

Even though the migrants may be net beneficiaries of the pension system in *total* in the two periods they live in, they nevertheless provide a net contribution to the public finances in the period during which they arrive (period zero). In this way, they exert a positive externality on the native population. In the next period (period one), the migrants draw pensions themselves but they also ensure the financing themselves by having reared enough children with sufficient human capital to take care of these additional pensions. Hence, the pensions of the migrants do not tax the children of the native population. Instead, the net cost that migrants impose when old (in period one) is deferred to the indefinite future. Thus, overall, the migrants yield positive externalities on the native population.

If rearing children were costless, migration of unskilled labor would have been equivalent to a once-off boost to the birthrate of unskilled labor, generating a positive externality on the rest of the population by helping to finance the PAYG pensions. Realistically, as rearing children may be quite costly, migration of unskilled labor is *more* beneficial to the native population than a once-off boost to the birthrate of unskilled labor, because with the migration of young working (already grown-up) people the child-rearing cost is avoided.

Furthermore, very often migrants do not all belong to the bottom end of the skill distribution, as posited in our parable. The phenomenon of the brain drain from the developing countries to the Organization for Economic Cooperation and Development (OECD) countries is a good example of skilled migration. Such migration is a net contribution to the public finances of the welfare state from the outset.

PENSION AND MIGRATION: VARIABLE FACTOR PRICES

We have shown in the preceding section that in an everlasting economy the migrants have a positive contribution on the existing old and possibly all other generations as well. In this simplified account of migration, the larger the number of migrants, the better off everyone is. This can be seen from Eq. (3.13), where the larger the m, the larger the b_0. Thus the native-born population would opt for having as many migrants as possible. However, when factor prices are variable, migration will generate a downward pressure on wages. This pressure can come about if capital mobility is not perfect or, alternatively, when the

Heckscher–Ohlin economy shifts across different industry structures as labor comes in; see Chap. 2. In this case of variable factor prices, the welfare calculus of the preceding section may be overturned.

Dynamics

Formally, national output is now given by a constant-returns-to-scale production function:

$$F(K_t, L_t) = L_t F(K_t/L_t, 1) \equiv L_t f(k_t), \tag{3.11a}$$

where $k_t = K_t/L_t$ is the capital–labor ratio.

This production function gives rise to the following factor-price equations:

$$1 + r_t = f'(k_t), \tag{3.18}$$

$$w_t = f(k_t) - (1 + r_t)k_t. \tag{3.19}$$

In period zero, the capital–labor ratio is given by

$$k_0 = K_0/L_0, \tag{3.20}$$

where L_0 is given by Eq. (3.8). At period one, the stock of capital (K_1) consists of period-zero savings (of the native-born young population and the migrants). This K_1 is given by Eq. (3.10), with w_0 replacing w. Thus, the capital–labor ratio is

$$k_1 = L_1^{-1} \frac{\delta}{1+\delta} w_0(1-\tau) \left\{ \int_0^{e^*} (1-e)dG + q[1 - G(e^*) + m] \right\}$$

$$- L_1^{-1} \frac{b_1(1+m)}{(1+\delta)(1+r)}. \tag{3.21}$$

The supply of labor is given by

$$L_t = (1+m)(1+n)^t \left\{ \int_0^{e^*} (1-e)dG + q[1 - G(e^*)] \right\}, \quad t \geq 1. \tag{3.22}$$

Hence, the capital–labor ratio is given by

$$k_t = \frac{1}{(1+n)(1+\delta)} \left[\delta(1-\tau)w_{t-1} - \frac{\tau w_t(1+n)}{1+r_t} \right], \quad t \geq 2. \tag{3.23}$$

Note that the dynamics of k_t from $t = 2$ and on is different from the earlier periods ($t = 0, 1$) because the composition of the skilled–unskilled population, which affects the savings of each period, does not depend on m for $t \geq 2$, as the offspring of the migrants are fully integrated in society.

The social security benefit in period zero, b_0, is given by Eq. (3.13), with w_0 replacing w, that is,

$$b_0 = (1+n)\tau w_0 \left\{ \int_0^{e^*} (1-e)dG + q[1 - G(e^*) + m] \right\}. \tag{3.13a}$$

Similarly, b_t for $t \geq 1$ is given by the right-hand side of Eq. (3.15), with w_t replacing w, that is,

$$b_t = \tau w_t \left\{ \int_0^{e^*} (1-e)dG + q[1 - G(e^*)] \right\} (1+n), \quad t \geq 1. \tag{3.15a}$$

Finally, the net benefit to a migrant from the redistributive pension system is given by

$$NB = \frac{b_1}{1 + r_1} - \tau q w_0. \tag{3.24}$$

Simulation Results

We resort to numerical simulations to illustrate the gains and losses from migration. The results are shown in Tables 3.1 and 3.2.

Suppose first that the economy is in a steady state with no migration, i.e., $m = 0$. This is described in the first row of the two tables as period -1. Then, in period zero, the economy is shocked by an influx of m low-skill migrants. We describe the path of the economy until it reaches a steady state again in

Table 3.1. The Effects of Migration with $\sigma = 1$

Period	Capital–Labor Ratio (k)		Social Security Benefit (b)		Welfare Losses of Highest Skilled (%)		Welfare Losses of Unskilled (%)	
	$m = 0.1$	$m = 0.2$	$m = 0.1$	$m = 0.2$	$m = 0.1$	$m = 0.2$	$m = 0.1$	$m = 02$
$-1(m=0)$	0.0096	0.0096	0.0444	0.0444	0	0	0	0
0	0.0088	0.0082	0.0468	0.0491	1.99	3.89	2.09	4.06
1	0.0091	0.0088	0.0438	0.0432	1.23	2.34	1.23	2.34
2	0.0094	0.0093	0.0442	0.0440	0.40	0.77	0.40	0.77
3	0.0095	0.0095	0.0443	0.0443	0.13	0.25	0.13	0.25
4	0.0095	0.0095	0.0444	0.0444	0.04	0.08	0.04	0.08
5	0.0095	0.0095	0.0444	0.0444	0.01	0.03	0.01	0.03
6	0.0096	0.0095	0.0444	0.0444	0	0.01	0	0.01
$\vdots$	$\vdots$	$\vdots$	$\vdots$	$\vdots$	$\vdots$	$\vdots$	$\vdots$	$\vdots$
∞	0.0096	0.0096	0.0444	0.0444	0	0	0	0

Note:

$$NB = \begin{cases} -0.0162 & \text{for } m = 0.1 \\ -0.0159 & \text{for } m = 0.2 \end{cases}.$$

Table 3.2. The Effects of Migration with $\sigma = 3.3$

Period	Capital–Labor Ratio(k)		Social Security Benefit (b)		Welfare Losses of Highest Skilled (%)		Welfare Losses of Unskilled (%)	
	$m = 0.1$	$m = 0.2$	$m = 0.1$	$m = 0.2$	$m = 0.1$	$m = 0.2$	$m = 0.1$	$m = 0.2$
$-1(m = 0)$	0.0032	0.0032	0.1595	0.1595	0	0	0	0
0	0.0030	0.0028	0.1721	0.1848	−0.09	−0.18	0.09	0.16
1	0.0031	0.0030	0.1594	0.1594	20.50	37.53	20.25	37.08
2	0.0032	0.0032	0.1595	0.1595	0.29	0.53	0.29	0.52
3	0.0032	0.0032	0.1595	0.1595	0	0.01	0	0.01
4	0.0032	0.0032	0.1595	0.1595	0	0	0	0
5	0.0032	0.0032	0.1595	0.1595	0	0	0	0
6	0.0032	0.0032	0.1595	0.1595	0	0	0	0
⋮	⋮	⋮	⋮	⋮	⋮	⋮	⋮	⋮
∞	0.0032	0.0032	0.1595	0.1595	0	0	0	0

Note:

$$NB = \begin{cases} -0.0173 & \text{for } m = 0.1 \\ -0.0173 & \text{for } m = 0.2 \end{cases}.$$

period ∞. Note that this new steady state is identical to the original one, as can be seen from the absence of m from Eq. (3.23), the dynamic equation of the model; compare the first and the last rows in each table. The path of the capital–labor ratio (k_t), the social security benefit (b_t), and the welfare loss to members of each generation are presented for $m = 0.1$ and $m = 0.2$. This loss is measured as the percentage increases in lifetime consumption that will restore utility to its premigration level.

The calculations were carried out for a constant elasticity of substitution (CES) production function. Table 3.1 presents the results for the Cobb–Douglas case (i.e., for $\sigma = 1$, where σ is the elasticity of substitution). The labor share is assumed to be 2/3. The distribution of e is assumed uniform over the intereval [0, 1]. Productivity of unskilled labor is one-half that of skilled labor, i.e., $q = 0.5$. The subjective discount rate is 5% annually; successive periods are 25 years apart from one another. The social security contribution rate is 30%. The annual population growth rate (n) is 2%.

As migrants come in, the capital–labor ratio (k_0) falls naturally. Also, the pension benefit to the old population (b_0) rises. The old people of period zero gain on two grounds: First, b_0 rises; and second, the rate of return to their capital $(1 + r_0)$ rises because k_0 falls. Thus, the old generation in period zero always gain from migration. Thereafter, the capital–labor ratio rises monotonically back to its steady-state level. The pension benefit in period one falls below the steady-state level but then rises monotonically to its steady-state level.

In contrast to the fixed factor-price case (i.e., $\sigma = \infty$), with variable factor prices and $\sigma = 1$, *all* income groups in every generation (except, of course, the retirees in period zero) lose from migration, as can be seen from the last four columns of Table 3.1. Furthermore, their loss is an increasing function of m. Note that the migrants are net contributors to the pension system, as NB < 0. Thus their contribution could not even enhance the welfare of the old generation at the time of the migrants' arrival without hurting every other generation.

For a higher value of σ than in the Cobb–Douglas case, some income groups in some generations may still gain. Table 3.2 presents simulation results for $\sigma = 3.33$. Here again the retirees in period zero naturally gain from migration. However, in this case the highest-skilled people in the generation born at period zero (i.e., when the migrants arrive) also gain. This group, which owns a larger share of the capital stock, is less affected than others by the downward pressure on wages exerted by migration. Unskilled people in all generations lose. Here again, the migrants are net contributors to the pension system as NB < 0. However, their net contribution does not suffice to support the gain to the retirees in period zero and to the highest-skilled people born at that time, so that all other people in all other generations are worse off.

CONCLUSION

Migration has important implications for the financial soundness of the pension system that is an important pillar of any welfare state. Although it is common sense to expect that young migrants, even if low skilled, can help society pay the benefits to the current elderly population, it may nevertheless be reasonable to argue that these migrants would adversely affect the current young population because the migrants are typically thought of as net beneficiaries of the welfare state that redistributes income from the rich to the poor.

In contrast to the adverse effects of migration in the static model, we used Samuelson's (1958) concept of the economy as an everlasting machinery, even though its human components are only finitely lived, and showed that low-skill migrants may be either net beneficiaries of, or net contributors to, an old-age social security system that is inherently progressive. However, regardless of whether the migrants are net contributors or net beneficiaries of this system, we show that migration is a Pareto-improving measure. That is, all the existing income (low and high) and age (young and old) groups living at the time of the migrants' arrival would be better off. This result obtains when the economy has good access to international goods and capital markets, so that migration exerts no major effect on factor prices. The effect of migration in this case is manifested entirely through the PAYG-DB pension system.

Therefore, in a dynamic model with capital mobility that freezes factor price, the political economy equilibrium will overwhelmingly support migration. Evidently this promigration feature can be weakened and possibly overturned when capital inflows are not sufficient to peg factor prices or when labor inflows change industry structure and factor prices. In these cases, even if migrants are net contributors to the pension system, their contribution does not suffice to support the increased benefit to the old at the time of the migrants' arrival; other people are made worse off.

APPENDIX 3.1

In this appendix, we prove that NB $\gtreqless 0$ when relation (3.17) holds. Substituting Eq. (3.2) into Eq. (3.16), we can see that

$$
\text{NB} = \frac{1+n}{1+r}\tau w \left\{ \int_0^{e^*} dG - \int_0^{e^*} e\,dG + (1-e^*)[1-G(e^*)] \right\}
$$
$$
- \tau w(1-e^*). \tag{A3.1}
$$

Because

$$
e^- = [G(e^*)]^{-1} \int_0^{e^*} e\,dG,
$$

$$
\int_0^{e^*} dG = G(e^*),
$$

it follows that NB $\gtreqless 0$ as

$$
\frac{1+n}{1+r}[G(e^*) - G(e^*)e^- + 1 - e^* - G(e^*) + e^*G(e^*)] \gtreqless 1 - e^*. \tag{A3.2}
$$

Hence, NB $\gtreqless 0$ as

$$
\frac{1+n}{1+r}[(e^* - e^-)G(e^*) + (1-e^*)] \gtreqless 1 - e^*. \tag{A3.3}
$$

Thus, NB $\gtreqless 0$ as

$$
(e^* - e^-)G(e^*) \gtreqless (1-e^*)\left(\frac{1+r}{1+n} - 1\right), \tag{A3.4}
$$

which yields condition (3.17).

4   Intratemporal Social Insurance: Attractiveness to Migrants and Attitude of Native-Born Population

INTRODUCTION

A key intratemporal feature of the welfare state is the emphasis placed on the tax system as an income redistribution mechanism. The welfare state uses progressive taxes and uses revenues to provide either cash or in-kind transfers to the poor population. Very often the transfers (health care, education, etc.) may be universal, accorded to all, but nevertheless they are quite progressive in the sense that they constitute a greater share of the income of the poor rather than that of the rich population. The old-age security insurance analyzed in the preceding chapter is a form of an intertemporal social insurance. In this chapter, we turn to an analysis of redistributive taxation that serves as a form of intratemporal social insurance.[1]

The intratemporal redistribution feature of the welfare state makes it an attractive destination for immigrants, particularly for low-skill immigrants. George Borjas (1994) reports that foreign-born households in the U.S. accounted for 10% of households receiving public assistance in 1990 and for 13% of total cash assistance distributed, even though they constituted only 8% of all households in the U.S. In this chapter, we explore the implications of various redistribution policies for the attitude of the native-born population toward migrants. In the next two chapters, we analyze the effect of migration on the shape and the magnitude of redistribution policies that are determined in a political economy equilibrium; at the same time, we address the question of whether the level of migration, when not restricted, is higher or lower in this welfare state than in the laissez-faire (no-redistribution) economy.

AN INTRATEMPORAL MODEL

Because we want to focus on intratemporal income redistribution, it is adequate to use a one-period static setup. To contrast the intratemporal feature of the analysis in this chapter with the intertemporal feature of the preceding chapter, it is useful to retain as much as possible the analytical framework of the preceding chapter. We therefore strip down the preceding model from its dynamic structure and consider a one-period static version of it.[2]

As before, there is a continuum of individuals. Each individual is characterized by the innate ability parameter e that is the time cost needed to acquire skill. The cdf of e is given by $G(\cdot)$, which is normalized as in Eq. (3.1). All individuals live for one period. They are born unskilled, each with a unit of labor time and K units of capital. By investing e units of labor time in education, an individual becomes skilled, which means that each unit of the individual's remaining labor time (that is, $1 - e$) is worth one unit of effective labor. If, however, she or he does not acquire skill (that is, she or he remains unskilled) her labor time is worth only $q(<1)$ units of effective labor.

The government can use an income tax only in order to redistribute income. Many studies [for instance, Mirrlees (1971)] suggest that the best egalitarian income tax may be approximated by a linear tax that consists of a flat rate (τ) and a lump-sum cash demogrant (b).[3] Because all families are of similar size and age structure, the uniform demogrant may capture also free provisions of public services such as health care, education, etc.

As in the preceding chapter, we continue to assume that the tax has no effect on the decision to acquire skill. Thus, the cutoff ability level (e^*) between acquiring and not acquiring skill is given by

$$e^* = 1 - q, \tag{4.1}$$

which is identical to Eq. (3.2).

We denote the consumption of an e individual by $c(e)$. It is equal to disposable income:

$$c(e) = \begin{cases} (1 - \tau)w(1 - e) + [1 + (1 - \tau)r]\,K + b & \text{for } e \leq e^* \\ (1 - \tau)qw + [1 + (1 - \tau)r]K + b & \text{for } e \geq e^* \end{cases}, \tag{4.2}$$

where $1 + r$ is the gross rental price of capital and, as before, it is assumed that capital fully depreciates at the end of the production process; the income tax (τ) applies to the net rental price of capital (r).

Note that the disposable income (consumption) distribution curve is piecewise linear in the ability parameter e. This refers to the native-born population. For individuals who do not acquire skill (i.e., those with an ability parameter e above the cutoff parameter e^*), the ability parameter is irrelevant and they have the same income. Naturally, within the group of individuals who do decide to become skilled (i.e., for $e \leq e^*$), the more able the individual is (i.e., the lower e is), then the higher her or his disposable income is. As can be seen from Eq. (4.2), this relationship is linear. The income distribution curve is depicted in Fig. 4.1. Note that the slope of the downward-sloping segment is $-(1 - \tau)w$. Also, note that e^* is unaffected by the income distribution policy (τ and b), as can be seen from Eq. (4.1). Finally, as we assume that the migrants

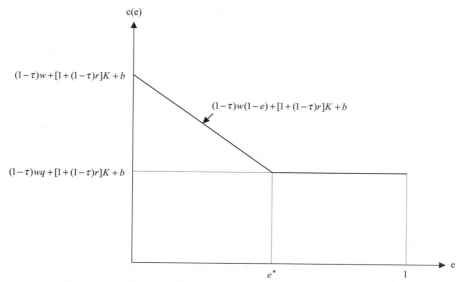

Fig. 4.1. The income distribution curve.

arrive with no capital, their disposable income is only $(1-\tau)qw + b$, which is below that of the unskilled native-born individuals.

We assume a standard (concave, constant-returns-to-scale) production function:

$$Y = F(K, L), \qquad (4.3)$$

where Y is gross output, K is the total stock of capital (recall that each individual possesses K units of capital and the number of individuals is normalized to one), and L is the supply of labor, which is given by

$$L = \int_0^{e^*} (1-e)dG + q[1 - G(e^*)] + qm, \qquad (4.4)$$

as in Eq. (3.8). We assume, as before, that the migrants (whose number is m) are all unskilled and possess no physical capital.

The wage rate and the gross rental price of capital are given in a competitive equilibrium by the marginal productivity conditions

$$w = F_L(K, L), \qquad (4.5)$$

$$1 + r = F_K(K, L). \qquad (4.6)$$

The income tax parameters τ and b are related to each other by the government budget constraint:

$$b(1 + m) = \tau(Y - K). \qquad (4.7)$$

Note that the base for the flat income tax rate is net domestic product $(Y - K)$, including labor income of migrants that is subject to the income tax.[4] Also, migrants qualify to the uniform demogrant b.

Finally, there are no barriers to migration so that m is determined endogenously by

$$(1 - \tau)qw + b = w^*, \tag{4.8}$$

where w^* is the opportunity income of the migrants in the source countries.

This model is used in the subsequent sections in order to investigate two issues: (i) How does the welfare state attract migration of various skill levels? (ii) More importantly, what are the effects of migration on the income distribution among the native-born population and, consequently, what is this population's attitude toward the migrants?

THE ATTRACTIVENESS OF THE WELFARE STATE TO MIGRANTS

Within this framework we address the first issue of whether the welfare state indeed attracts migrants. More generally, is it true that more taxes and more transfers attract more migrants in the context of our stylized model? Specifically, we study the sign of $dm/d\tau$.

To simplify the analysis we assume a uniform distribution of the ability parameter e over the interval $[0, 1]$. This assumption yields a simple labor supply function as follows:

$$L = \frac{1}{2}(1 - q)^2 + q(1 + m), \tag{4.4'}$$

where use is made of Eq. (4.1).[5]

Substituting Eqs. (4.3), (4.4'), (4.5), and (4.8) into Eq. (4.7) and rearranging terms yields

$$\left\{ w^* - (1 - \tau)q\, F_L \left[K, \frac{1}{2}(1 - q)^2 + q(1 + m) \right] \right\} (1 + m)$$

$$= \tau \left\{ F \left[K, \frac{1}{2}(1 - q)^2 + q(1 + m) \right] - K \right\}. \tag{4.9}$$

This equation describes the general equilibrium relationship between τ and m.

Total differentiation of the latter equation with respect to τ yields

$$[w^* - q\, F_L - (1 + m)(1 - \tau)q^2 F_{LL}] \frac{dm}{d\tau} = F - K - (1 + m)q\, F_L. \tag{4.10}$$

By substituting Eqs. (4.5), (4.8), $F = (1+r)K + wL$ (Euler's equation), and (4.4′) into Eq. (4.10), we conclude that

$$[b - q\tau w - (1+m)(1-\tau)q^2 F_{LL}]\frac{dm}{d\tau} = rK + \frac{1}{2}(1-q)^2 w.$$

$$(4.11)$$

It follows from the government budget constraint $[b(1+m) = \tau(rK + wL)]$ that the tax on labor income paid by an unskilled individual ($\tau q w$) must fall short of her or his demogrant (b), that is, $b > \tau q w$.[6] Because $F_{LL} < 0$, it follows from Eq. (4.11) that

$$\frac{dm}{d\tau} > 0.$$

$$(4.12)$$

Thus, more taxes and transfers attract more unskilled migrants.

This unambiguous conclusion that the more intensive the welfare state, the more attractive it becomes to migrants is restricted naturally to the main case that we discuss throughout of low-skill migration. If we allow for high-skill migrants as well, we can see in a natural extension of our stylized model that the welfare state attracts more low-skill migrants but fewer high-skill migrants, as long as "supply-side economics" does not prevail (that is, as long as raising taxes does not yield less revenues). This is shown in Appendix 4.1. Nevertheless, high-skill migrants from developing countries are still attracted to developed countries with an elaborate and extensive ("high" tax, "generous" benefits) welfare system, as the current debate in the U.S. over H-1B visa quotas for professional workers attests. These workers are mostly attracted to the high-tech new economy. Currently, almost one-third of the entrepreneurs and higher-level employees in Silicon Valley in California come from overseas. These migrants are typically net contributors to the welfare state. As put by Gary Becker: "Since skilled immigrants earn more than average workers, they pay more than their proportional share in taxes. They make few demands on the public purse for they have negligible unemployment rates, seldom go on welfare, make little use of medicare and medicaid, and commit few crimes. Being mainly in their twenties and thirties, they contribute much more to social security taxes than they will withdraw in retirement benefits" (*Business Week*, April 24th, 2000).

THE ATTITUDE OF THE NATIVE-BORN POPULATION TOWARD MIGRATION

Migration changes the income distribution among the native-born population and the attitude of the native-born people toward migrants is therefore shaped accordingly; for earlier analyses, see Wildasin (1994) and Razin and Sadka (1995a).

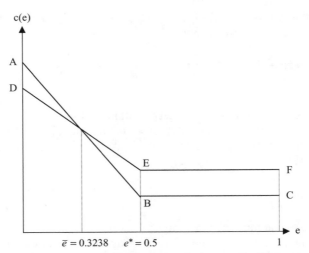

Fig. 4.2. The effect of migration on the income distribution among the native-born population (with no income redistribution policy). The parameter values are $q = 0.5$, $K = 1$, $w^* = 0.95qw$, where w is the wage rate in the no-tax-transfer, no-migration case; e is uniformly distributed over $[0, 1]$; the production function is a Cobb–Douglas function $F(K, L) = AK^\alpha L^{1-\alpha}$, with $\alpha = 0.33$ and $A = 4.5$.

A Benchmark Case: No-Redistribution Policies

Let us start with a benchmark case in which the government does not engage in redistributing income. This benchmark case highlights the gains from trade effect of labor mobility. In this case we set the tax-transfer parameters at zero (i.e., $\tau = b = 0$) and drop out the government budget constraint (4.7).

Suppose initially that there is no migration, so that m is set equal to zero and migration equilibrium condition (4.8) is dropped out. The resulting income distribution among the native-born is depicted by the curve ABC in Fig. 4.2, which is based on numerical simulations. Assuming that e is uniformly distributed, the area under the income distribution curve is equal to net output (i.e., $Y - K$), less payments to migrants (i.e., w^*m), which are initially zero.

Now we allow free migration. That is, we reinstate migration equilibrium condition (4.8) and reintroduce m as an endogenous variable. The ensuing income distribution among the native-born population is described by the curve DEF in Fig. 4.2. As expected, the gains from trade effect is impeccable in the absence of any costly redistribution: *Total* income of the native-born population (i.e., the area under the income distribution curve) rises as a result of the influx of migrants.[7]

The determination of the free migration number of immigrants is neatly described in Fig. 4.3. The aggregate labor supply of the native-born population

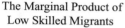

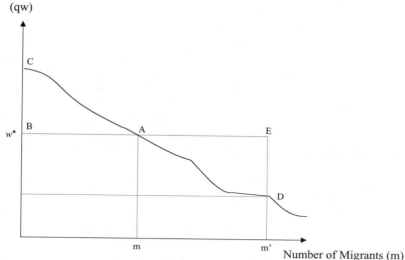

Fig. 4.3. Free migration: the income gain to the native-born population.

is perfectly inelastic. (Capital is also fixed.) Thus the labor supply of migrants changes the total domestic labor supply one to one. The downward-sloping curve describes the marginal product of low-skill migrants (qw) as a function of the number of migrants. The equilibrium level of m occurs at point A, where qw is equated to w^*. The standard gains from trade (to the native-born population) is measured by the trianglelike area ABC, which consists of the total output produced by the migrants ($OCAm$) less the amount of wages paid to them ($OBAm$).

However, the distributional effects of migration are in general not clear: Some *must always* gain, but others *may* lose. In our particular model, and for our specific parameter values, it so happens that some individuals (those with an ability parameter above $\bar{e}$; see Fig. 4.2) gain, but other individuals (those with $e < \bar{e}$) lose. Nevertheless, with an active redistribution policy *all* may lose, as we shall see below.

Redistribution Policy

Now consider a typical welfare state that redistributes income from the rich to the poor population. That is, it levies a positive flat tax ($\tau > 0$) on income (labor and capital) and uses the proceeds to finance a positive demogrant ($b > 0$). The immigrants are typically not only subject to the income tax, but are also eligible for the benefits of the welfare state, in contrast to guest workers.

We perform the following exercise. Suppose first that there is no migration. The closed-economy equations described above [Eqs. (4.1) and (4.3)–(4.7)] allow the government one degree of freedom in designing its redistribution policy (that is, the τ and b parameters). Thus, for each τ there is a corresponding equilibrium b. Consider a certain configuration of the equilibrium pair (τ, b). For this pair we find the income distribution curve given by Eq. (4.2). We then allow free migration, that is, we endogenize m and reinstate the free-migration equilibrium equation (4.8). We next redesign the tax-transfer pair (τ, b) in such a way so as to maintain the income of the native-born unskilled individuals at its premigration level and ask what happens to the income of the skilled individuals. The above exercise is carried out for various (premigration) tax-transfer configurations, starting from a very low level of redistribution up to a very high level.

Note that in the absence of migration, the redistribution is not distortionary: In the absence of a pecuniary cost of acquiring education, the redistribution policy affects neither the individual decision whether to become skilled or remain unskilled (that is, the determination of e^*) nor the supply of labor and capital. A dollar taxed away from some individuals ends up *entirely*, with no deadweight loss whatsoever, at the hands of some other or the same individuals. With migration, there is still no deadweight loss in the common use of this term: It is still the case that a dollar taxed away from some individuals ends up entirely in the hands of some other or the same individuals. However, there is a loss from the point of view of the native-born individuals because the low-skill migrants are typically net beneficiaries of the welfare state in the sense that their tax payments (namely, $\tau q w m$) fall short of their gross benefits (bm); thus a dollar of revenues collected from the native-born population does not end up entirely in the hands of the native-born population, as a portion of it leaks to the migrants.

Furthermore, note that, with a redistribution policy, the gains from trade (to the native-born population) may disappear altogether: Total income of the native-born population may actually decline as a result of migration. To see this, refer again to Fig. 4.3. The migrants who are low skilled and do not own any capital are net beneficiaries of the welfare state. That is, $\tau q w < b$, which means that their net income $[(1 - \tau)q w + b]$ is above their net marginal product $(q w)$. Because their net income is equal to their reservation income w^*, it follows that free migration occurs at a point such as D, where $q w < w^*$. In this case, the net gain to the native-born population is measured by the area ABC, less the triangularlike area AED. This "gain" from trade could well become negative when τ (and b) are sufficiently high. When this happens, it may also be the case that *all* (skilled and unskilled) native-born individuals lose from free migration.

Our simulations show (see Table 4.1) that when the flat tax rate (τ) in the absence of migration is between 35% and 55% (and the corresponding

Table 4.1. **Free Migration and Income Distribution Policy:**
Taxes, Transfers, and the Gains from Trade

Premigration[a]		Postmigration[b]			
τ	b/Y	τ	b/Y	m	Gains from Trade
0.35	0.2434	0.4024	0.1687	0.8748	(0.0646)
0.40	0.2782	0.3921	0.1648	0.8771	(0.0478)
0.45	0.3130	0.3902	0.1628	0.9009	(0.0341)
0.50	0.3478	0.3798	0.1587	0.9062	(0.0167)
0.55	0.3825	0.3737	0.1552	0.9261	(0.0011)
0.60	0.4173	0.3737	0.1539	0.9517	(0.0116)

Notes: τ, tax rate; b, demogrant; m, ratio of migrants to native-born individuals; Y, GDP.
[a] Exogenously given tax rate.
[b] Endogenous tax rate: The tax rate is determined so as to restore postmigration disposable income of low-skill individuals to its premigration level for each tax rate shown in the premigration cell. For example, $\tau = 0.4024$ is the endogenously determined tax rate corresponding to a postmigration disposable income of low skilled, which is equal to its premigration level at a premigration tax rate of 0.35.

demogrant b is between 24.3% and 38.3% of the GDP) indeed the skilled individuals all strictly lose from migration if the redistribution policy is adjusted to maintain the disposable income of low-skill native-born individuals at its premigration level. The aggregate gains (losses) to the skilled individuals are presented in the last column of Table 4.1. These gains (losses) to the skilled individuals are also the aggregate gains (losses) to the entire native-born population, as the redistribution policy is geared toward leaving the unskilled individuals intact. Thus migration cannot be a Pareto-improving shock for the native-born population when τ originally (before any migration takes place) exceeds 35%.

As was already mentioned, when the income distribution policy is geared to maintaining the income of the native-born unskilled individuals intact, then the net gain (or loss) to the native-born skilled individuals measures the standard gain (or loss) from trade to the native-born population. For instance, when premigration τ is between 35% and 55% (and the corresponding b is between 24.3% and 38.3% of the GDP), then the curves describing the disposable income distribution among the native-born population look like the curve ABC in Fig. 4.4. Now, if we allow free migration and adjust the tax-transfer parameters so as to maintain the disposable income of the native-born unskilled individuals intact, then the new disposable income distribution curves look like the curve DBC. (Note that among the native-born individuals the trianglelike area ADB in Fig. 4.4 measures the total net loss to the native-born population and is therefore equal to the area AED, less the area ABC in Fig. 4.3.)

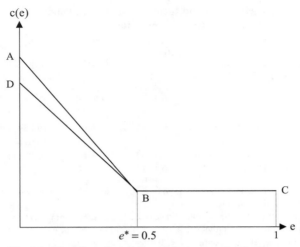

Fig. 4.4. The effect of migration on the income distribution among the native-born population (with an income distribution policy).

APPENDIX 4.1. THE WELFARE STATE AND THE SKILL MIX OF MIGRATION

Let us allow for high-skill migrants as well as low-skill migrants. Denote the number of low-skill migrants and high-skill migrants by m_ℓ and m_h, respectively. Suppose that their reservation wages in their home countries are w_ℓ^* and w_h^*, respectively. Then, Eq. (4.8) is replaced with two equations, one for each skill type:

$$(1 - \tau)qw + b = w_\ell^*, \tag{A4.8a}$$

$$(1 - \tau)w + b = w_h^*. \tag{A4.8b}$$

Labor supply equation (4.4′) becomes now

$$L = \frac{1}{2}(1 - q)^2 + q(1 + m_\ell) + m_h = \frac{1}{2}(1 - q)^2 + q + m_1, \tag{A4.4′}$$

where $m_1 \equiv qm_\ell + m_h$ is the labor supply of the migrants in efficiency units. The government's budget constraint [Eq. (4.7)] now becomes

$$b(1 + m_2) = \tau(Y - K), \tag{A4.7}$$

where $m_2 \equiv m_\ell + m_h$ is the total number of low- and high-skill migrants. Finally, the other equations of the model, (4.1), (4.3), (4.5), and (4.6), remain intact.

We can solve Eqs. (A4.8a) and (A4.8b) for b and w[8]:

$$b = \frac{w_\ell^* - q w_h^*}{1 - q},$$ (A4.1)

$$w = \frac{w_h^* - w_\ell^*}{(1 - \tau)(1 - q)}.$$ (A4.2)

Substituting Eqs. (A4.4′) and (A4.1) into Eq. (A4.7) we get

$$\left(\frac{w_\ell^* - q w_h^*}{1 - q} \right)(1 + m_2)$$ (A4.3)

$$= \tau \left\{ F \left[K, \frac{1}{2}(1 - q)^2 + q + m_1 \right] - K \right\} \equiv R(\tau, m_1),$$

where $R(\tau, m_1)$ are tax revenues. Substituting Eqs. (A4.2) and (A4.4′) into Eq. (4.5) yields

$$w_h^* - w_\ell^* = (1 - \tau)(1 - q)F_L \left[K, \frac{1}{2}(1 - q)^2 + q + m_1 \right].$$ (A4.5)

The latter two equations [(A4.3) and (A4.5)] can be solved for the labor supply (m_1) and the number (m_2) of the migrants as functions of the tax rate (τ). Total differentiation of Eq. (A4.5) with respect to τ yields

$$\frac{dm_1}{d\tau} = F_L \left[(1 - \tau)F_{LL} \right]^{-1} < 0,$$

because we assume that the marginal product of labor is diminishing (that is, F is concave). On inspection of Eq. (A4.3) we can see that

$$\text{sign} \left(\frac{dm_2}{d\tau} \right) = \text{sign} \left(\frac{dR}{d\tau} \right),$$

where $dR/d\tau = \partial R/\partial \tau + (\partial R/\partial m_1)(dm_1/d\tau)$. Suppose that supply-side economics does not prevail, that is, $dR/d\tau > 0$. (This is always true for small τ's.) Then, $dm_2/d\tau > 0$.

Thus, we have established that the labor supply of the migrants (m_1) falls while their number (m_2) rises when the tax rate (τ) is raised. That is,

$$\frac{dm_1}{d\tau} \equiv q \frac{dm_\ell}{d\tau} + \frac{dm_h}{d\tau} < 0,$$

while

$$\frac{dm_2}{d\tau} \equiv \frac{dm_\ell}{d\tau} + \frac{dm_h}{d\tau} > 0.$$

This can happen if and only if $dm_\ell/d\tau > 0$ and $dm_h/d\tau < 0$. Thus, more taxes and transfers attract more low-skill migrants but fewer high-skill migrants.

5   Intratemporal Social Insurance: The Interaction between Migration and the Size of the Welfare State

INTRODUCTION

In the preceding chapter, we analyzed the attitude of the native-born population toward migration. We examined the effects of migration on the aggregate income of the native-born people and its distribution among them. The scope of the welfare state itself was not the focus of analysis as the tax-transfer parameters were assumed exogenous (although, of course, constrained by the government budget constraint).

In this chapter, we examine how the redistribution policy is determined in a political-economy equilibrium. We then address in this setup the following issues: Does migration necessarily tilt the political-power balance in favor of heavier taxation and more intensive redistribution? Relatedly, how does migration affect income inequality among the native-born people? This chapter provides an analytical framework within which these issues are studied. The next chapter provides an empirical framework and evidence.

The extent of taxation and redistribution policy in our analytical framework is determined by direct democracy voting. The political-economy equilibrium is then determined by a balance between those who gain and those who lose from a more extensive tax-transfer policy. The model captures two conflicting effects of migration on taxation and redistribution. On the one hand, the low-skill low-income migrants who are net beneficiaries from the tax-transfer system will join forces with the native-born low-income voters in favor of higher taxes and transfers. On the other hand, redistribution becomes more costly to the native-born population as the migrants share some of the benefits at their expense. In this chapter we elaborate on how the aforementioned balance is shaped in the presence of migration.

REDISTRIBUTION POLICY IN A DIRECT DEMOCRACY

We continue to use the basic intratemporal model of an economy with migration and redistribution that is described in the preceding chapter with two modifications. As explained in the preceding chapter, the tax-transfer policy is not distortionary in the absence of migration. With no migration, there is also no "leakage" of tax revenues to migrants (through the demogrant) and, as a result, there need not be an interior solution for the equilibrium tax rate: It may go all the way either to zero or to 100%. We therefore reinstate a positive pecuniary cost of acquiring skill, which is not tax deductible; thus, e^* is now determined as in Eq. (3.2'):

$$e^* = 1 - q - \frac{\gamma}{(1-\tau)w}. \tag{5.1}$$

The second modification is done for the sake of simplicity: We consider the case in which migration is restricted by quotas. Formally, it means that m is exogenously given, so that Eq. (4.8), which specifies the equilibrium level of free migration, is dropped. It turns out that in this case of exogenous m, we can analytically derive the results when factor prices are not variable.[1] Thus, for analytical tractability in this chapter, we assume a linear production function:

$$Y = wL + (1+r)K, \tag{5.2}$$

where the marginal productivity conditions for setting up factor prices [Eqs. (4.5) and (4.6)] were already substituted into the production function. Also, we assume that e is distributed uniformly over $[0, 1]$, so that the labor supply Eq. (4.4) becomes

$$L = e^* - \frac{1}{2}(e^*)^2 + (1 - e^* + m)q. \tag{5.3}$$

Finally, the government budget constraint (4.7) implies that

$$b = \frac{\tau(wL + rK)}{1 + m}. \tag{5.4}$$

For any tax rate τ and exogenously given migration quota m, Eqs. (5.1), (5.3), and (5.4) determine e^*, L, and b as functions of τ and m: $e^* = e^*(\tau, m)$, $L = L(\tau, m)$, and $b = b(\tau, m)$. The number of migrants (m) is exogenous, but we nevertheless write e^*, L, and b as functions also of m because we wish to explore in this chapter the effect of m on these variables. Recall that consumption is a strictly decreasing function of the innate ability parameter (e) for the native-born skilled individuals, then constant for the native-born unskilled individuals. It is also constant for the migrants, but at a lower level than for the native-born unskilled individual because the migrants do not own any capital. This function is given by

$$c(e, \tau, m) = \begin{cases} (1-\tau)w(1-e) - \gamma + [1 + (1-\tau)r]K + b(\tau, m) & \text{for } 0 \le e \le e^*(\tau, m) \\ (1-\tau)wq + [1 + (1-\tau)r]K + b(\tau, m) & \text{for } e \ge e^*(\tau, m) \\ (1-\tau)wq + b(\tau, m) & \text{for } 1 \le e \le 1+m \end{cases},$$

$$\tag{5.5}$$

where for ease of exposition we artificially attribute a parameter e between 1 and $1 + m$ to the migrants simply in order to indicate that their consumption is below that of native-born unskilled individuals. For a given tax rate (τ_0), consumption as a function of e is depicted in Fig. 5.1. by the curve $ABCDEF$ (m is supressed).

The political economy τ is then determined by majority voting. By twice differentiating $c(e, \tau, m)$ with respect to e and to τ we find that

$$\frac{\partial^2 c(e, \tau, m)}{\partial e \partial \tau} = \begin{cases} w & \text{for} \quad 0 \leq e < e^*(\tau) \\ 0 & \text{for} \quad e^*(\tau) < e < 1. \\ 0 & \text{for} \quad 1 + m \geq e > 1 \end{cases} \tag{5.6}$$

Thus, $\partial^2 c / \partial e \partial \tau \geq 0$. Therefore, if $\partial c / \partial \tau > 0$ for some e_0, then $\partial c / \partial \tau > 0$ for all $e \geq e_0$. Similarly, if $\partial c / \partial \tau < 0$ for some e_0, then $\partial c / \partial \tau < 0$ for all $e \leq e_0$. This implies that if an increase in the income tax rate (τ) benefits a certain individual (because the higher tax rate can support a higher transfer b), then all individuals who are less able (that is, those who have a higher innate ability parameter e), including the migrants, must also gain from this tax increase. Similarly, if an income tax increase hurts a certain individual (because the increased transfer does not fully compensate her or him for the tax hike), then it must also hurt all individuals who are more able (that is, those who have a lower innate ability parameter e). These considerations imply that the median voter is a pivot in determining the outcome of majority voting. That is, the political-equilibrium tax rate maximizes the consumption of the median voter.

Denote the innate ability parameter of the median voter by e_M. Assuming that migrants are allowed to vote, then

$$e_M(m) = (1 + m)/2. \tag{5.7}$$

(Recall that the size of the native-born population was normalized to one and the ability parameter is uniformly distributed.) Diagramatically, suppose that τ_0 in Fig. 5.1 is a political-equilibrium tax rate. Suppose further for the sake of concreteness that the median voter is skilled, that is, $(1 + m)/2 < e^*(\tau_0)$. An increase of $\Delta \tau > 0$ in the tax rate must tilt the income distribution curve from $ABCDEF$ to $A'BC'D'E'F'$, so that all individuals who are more able than the median voter lose and all the rest gain. Similarly, if the tax rate is lowered to $\tau_0 - \Delta \tau$, then the income distribution curve tilts from $ABCDEF$ to $A''BC''D''E''F''$, so that all individuals who are more able than the median voter gain and all the rest lose.

As noted, the political equilibrium τ [denoted by $\tau_0(m)$] maximizes the consumption of the median voter, that is,

$$\tau_0(m) = \underset{\{\tau\}}{\arg \max} \ c[e_M(m), \tau, m]. \tag{5.8}$$

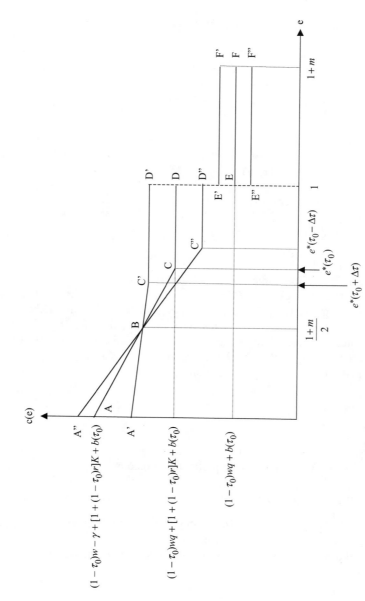

Fig. 5.1. Income distribution and a political-economy equilibrium.

63

Therefore, $\tau_0(m)$ is implicitly defined by

$$\frac{\partial c[e_M(m), \tau, m]}{\partial \tau} \equiv B(\tau, m) = 0, \tag{5.9}$$

where, by Eq. (5.5),[2]

$$B(\tau, m) = \begin{cases} -w(1-m)/2 - rK + b_\tau(\tau, m) & \text{if} \quad 0 < e_M(m) < e^*(\tau, m) \\ -wq - rK + b_\tau(\tau, m) & \text{if} \quad e^*(\tau, m) < e_M(m) < 1. \\ -wq + b_\tau(\tau, m) & \text{if} \quad e_M(m) > 1 \end{cases} \tag{5.10}$$

As a second-order condition for maximization we have

$$\frac{\partial^2 c[e_M(m), \tau_0(m), m]}{\partial \tau^2} = B_\tau[\tau_0(m), m] \leq 0, \tag{5.11}$$

where the subscripts stand for partial derivatives.

Note that the equation $B(m, \tau) = 0$ that determines the political-equilibrium tax rate $[\tau_0(m)]$ depends on, among other things, the median income versus the average income. For instance, consider the case in which the median voter is an unskilled native-born person, that is, $e^*(\tau, m) < e_M(m) < 1$. Because Eq. (5.4) implies that b is equal to $(wL + rK)/(1 + m)$, it follows that the equation $B(\tau, m) = 0$ implies that

$$I_M = \frac{\partial(\tau \bar{I})}{\partial \tau},$$

where $I_M = wq + rK$ is the pretax median income (net of depreciation) and $\bar{I} = (wL + rK)/(1 + m)$ is the pretax mean income.

THE EFFECTS OF MIGRATION ON REDISTRIBUTION

Having described the political-economy equilibrium, we now turn to the question of how this equilibrium is affected by migration.

Total differentiation of Eq. (5.9) with respect to m implies that

$$\frac{d\tau_0(m)}{dm} = \frac{B_m[\tau_0(m), m]}{B_\tau[\tau_0(m), m]}. \tag{5.12}$$

Because $B_\tau \leq 0$ [see Eq. (5.11)], it follows that the direction of the effect of migration (m) on the equilibrium tax rate (τ_0) is determined by the sign of $B_m[\tau_0(m), m]$.

By differentiating Eq. (5.10) with respect to m and evaluating it at $\tau = \tau_0(m)$, we conclude that

$$
B_m(\tau_0(m), m) = \begin{cases} \dfrac{w(q+m)}{1+m} - \dfrac{rK}{1+m} & \text{if} \quad e_M < e^* \\[3mm] -\dfrac{rK}{1+m} & \text{if} \quad e^* < e_M < 1. \\[3mm] 0 & \text{if} \quad e_M > 1 \end{cases}
\tag{5.13}
$$

See Appendix 5.1 for the derivation of the latter equation.

As noted, if the sign of $B_m[\tau_0(m), m]$ is negative, then an increase in the number of migrants lowers the political equilibrium tax rate (τ_0) and, consequently, the demogrant (b). Whether this is what actually happens depends on whether the median voter is skilled or unskilled. Consider first the case in which the median voter is skilled, that is, $e_M > e^*$. As can be seen from Eq. (5.13), the sign of B_m is not determined a priori. In this case, an increase in the number of migrants can either raise or lower the political-equilibrium tax rate and demogrant. Consider next the case in which the median voter is a native-born unskilled individual, that is, $e^* < e_M < 1$. In this case, an increase in the number of migrants unambiguously lowers the political-equilibrium tax rate and demogrant. In the extreme case in which the median voter is an (unskilled) migrant, an increase in the number of migrants has no effect on the tax rate and the demogrant.

The rationale for this result is as follows. It is most instructive to begin with the case in which the median voter is a native-born unskilled individual (that is, $e^* < e_M < 1$). In this case, the majority of the voters are unskilled and they are certainly protax. This majority has already pushed the tax rate upward to the limit (constrained by the efficiency loss of taxation). A further increase in the number of migrants who join the protax group does not change the political-power balance, which is already dominated by the protax group. However, the median voter who is a native-born member of this group (and, in fact, all the unskilled native-born individuals) would now lose from the "last" (marginal) percentage point of the tax rate because a larger share of the revenues generated by it would "leak" to the migrants whose number has increased. (Recall that, before more migrants arrived, this median voter was indifferent with respect to the marginal percentage point of the tax rate.) Therefore, the median voter and all unskilled native-born individuals now support a lower tax rate. Indeed, B_m, which is equal to $-rK/(1+m)$ in this case, reflects the marginal increase in tax revenues that are collected from the median voters (but not from the migrants who own no capital) and "leak" to the migrants. This is also why $B_m = 0$ in the case in which the median voter is an unskilled migrant (that is, $e_M > 1$) because the "leakage" element does not exist. In this case, an increase in the number of migrants does not change the political-equilibrium tax rate and demogrant.

Turn now to the case in which the median voter is a native-born skilled individual. The leakage elements, as in the case in which the median voter was a native-born unskilled individual, work for lowering the tax rate when m increases. However, now an increase in m tilts the political-power balance toward a median voter who is less able and has a lower income; she or he benefits more from a tax hike than the original median voter. Thus, an increase in m generates two conflicting effects on the political-equilibrium tax rate. Therefore, we cannot unambiguously determine the effect of m on τ and b.

A further insight into these conflicting effects can be gained when the second effect (that is, the shift in the political-power balance) is eliminated by assuming that migrants are not entitled (or choose not) to vote. In this case (see Appendix 5.2), we can show that

$$B_m[\tau_0(m), m] = \begin{cases} \dfrac{w}{1+m}\left(-\dfrac{1}{2}+q\right) - \dfrac{rK}{1+m} & \text{if } e_M < e^* \\[2ex] -\dfrac{rK}{1+m} & \text{if } e^* < e_M < 1. \\[2ex] 0 & \text{if } e_M > 1 \end{cases} \tag{5.13'}$$

As noted before, when the median voter is either a native-born unskilled individual or an unskilled migrant, then even if the migrants were to exercise their voting rights, they do not effectively tilt the political-power balance, and indeed Eqs. (5.13) and (5.13') are identical when $e_M > e^*$. However, when the median voter is a native-born skilled individual, it does matter whether the migrants do or do not vote. If they do not vote, then B_m is unambiguously negative (see Appendix 5.2 for the proof). When migrants do not vote, the tilting power-balance effect vanishes and only the leakage effect is at play and an increase in m lowers τ and b.

The effect of m on τ and b has an interesting implication for the income distribution among the native-born individuals. Recall that we showed that more migration leads, or can lead, to lower taxation and redistribution. For instance, this is always the case when migrants do not participate in the political process (namely, they do not vote) or when the median voter is an unskilled native-born individual. Then, more migration that leads the native-born individual to vote for a lower tax rate, and a lower demogrant has the unintended consequence of a greater inequality of the income distribution among the native-born population.

CONCLUSION

This chapter addressed the issue of how migration affects the power balance between the proredistribution and the antiredistribution coalitions. When low-skill migrants do not take part in the political process, then migration unambiguously lowers the extent of taxation and redistribution, thereby increasing the degree of inequality among the native-born population. For analogous reasons, if the nonvoting migrants were all skilled and brought with them the same amount of wealth as each native-born individual possesses, then the political-economy equilibrium degree of redistribution increases. This is because these migrants are net contributors to the welfare state. When migrants actively participate in the political process, migration still reduces the scope of redistribution if the median voter is a low-skill proredistribution individual. However, if the median voter is a high-skill antiredistribution individual, then migration may tilt the political-power balance in favor of more taxation and redistribution. The next chapter confronts these propositions with data from a set of typical European welfare states.

APPENDIX 5.1. MIGRANT VOTE

In this appendix, we prove Eq. (5.13).

Differentiating Eq. (5.10) with respect to m implies that

$$B_m(\tau, m) = \begin{cases} \dfrac{w}{2} + b_{\tau m}(\tau, m) & \text{if} \quad e_M < e^* \\ b_{\tau m}(\tau, m) & \text{if} \quad e^* < e_M < 1. \\ b_{\tau m}(\tau, m) & \text{if} \quad e_M > 1 \end{cases} \tag{A5.1}$$

Using Eq. (5.4), we conclude that

$$b_\tau(\tau, m) = \frac{wL + rK}{1 + m} + \frac{\tau w}{1 + m} \frac{\partial L}{\partial \tau}. \tag{A5.2}$$

Differentiating Eq. (5.3) with respect to τ implies that

$$\frac{\partial L}{\partial \tau} = (1 - e^* - q)\frac{\partial e^*}{\partial \tau}, \tag{A5.3}$$

where $\partial e^*/\partial \tau$ is derived from Eq. (5.1).

Substituting Eq. (A5.3) into Eq. (A5.2) yields

$$b_\tau(\tau, m) = \frac{wL + rK}{1 + m} - \frac{\gamma \tau(1 - e^* - q)}{(1 + m)(1 - \tau)^2}. \tag{A5.4}$$

We differentiate b_τ in Eq. (A5.4) with respect to m to obtain

$$b_{\tau m}(\tau, m) = -\frac{b_\tau(\tau, m)}{1 + m} + \frac{wq}{1 + m}, \tag{A5.5}$$

where use is made of Eq. (5.3) in order to obtain $\partial L/\partial m = q$.

Because $B[\tau_0(m), m] = 0$, we conclude from Eq. (5.10) that

$$b_\tau[\tau_0(m), m] = \begin{cases} \dfrac{w(1 - m)}{2} + rK & \text{if} \quad e_M < e^* \\ wq + rK & \text{if} \quad e^* < e_M < 1. \\ wq & \text{if} \quad e_M > 1 \end{cases} \tag{A5.6}$$

Substituting Eq. (A5.6) into Eq. (A5.5) yields

$$
b_{\tau m}[\tau_0(m), m] = \begin{cases} \dfrac{w}{1+m}\left(-\dfrac{1-m}{2}+q\right) - \dfrac{rK}{1+m} & \text{if } e_m < e^* \\[3mm] -\dfrac{rK}{1+m} & \text{if } e^* < e_M < 1. \\[3mm] 0 & \text{if } e_M > 1 \end{cases} \tag{A5.7}
$$

Finally, combining Eq. (A5.7) with Eq. (A5.1), we conclude that

$$
B_m[\tau_0(m), m] = \begin{cases} \dfrac{w(q+m)}{1+m} - \dfrac{rK}{1+m} & \text{if } e_M < e^* \\[3mm] -\dfrac{rK}{1+m} & \text{if } e^* < e_M < 1. \\[3mm] 0 & \text{if } e_M > 1 \end{cases} \tag{A5.8}
$$

This completes the derivation of Eq. (5.13).

APPENDIX 5.2. MIGRANTS DO NOT VOTE

Consider now the case in which migrants are not entitled (or choose not) to vote. Then, the ability index of the median voter is $e_M = \frac{1}{2}$, independently of m. In this case, a straightforward application of the same procedure yields

$$
B_m[\tau_0(m), m] = \begin{cases} \dfrac{w}{1+m}\left(-\dfrac{1}{2}+q\right) - \dfrac{rK}{1+m} & \text{if } e_M < e^* \\[3mm] -\dfrac{rK}{1+m} & \text{if } e^* < e_M < 1. \\[3mm] 0 & \text{if } e_M > 1. \end{cases} \tag{A5.9}
$$

This completes the derivation of Eq. (5.13').

Note also that when $e_M = \frac{1}{2} < e^*$, then $q < \frac{1}{2}$ [see Eq. (5.1)], which implies that $B_m < 0$ in this case.

6   The Effects of Migration on the Welfare State: Empirical Evidence

INTRODUCTION

The theoretical analysis of the preceding chapter complements the standard theory of the determinants of the size of the government in a representative democracy, in which the size of government or the scope of redistribution depends on pretax income inequality. Two economic interpretations are used to explain this result. Lovell (1975) emphasizes the size of the government as a provider of public goods, whereas our and other studies have considered the role of the government in redistributing income; Persson and Tabellini (1999) provide a recent survey. In both applications, the analysis shows that the size of government or the scope of redistribution depends on a particular measure of the skewedness of the income distribution: the ratio of the median income to the average income, which represents the price of collectively supplied goods in terms of private goods for the median voter. The more skewed the distribution of income, the more by which the mean income exceeds the median income and the lower this ratio; thus the higher the tax burden.

Empirical evidence of panel data on 11 European countries from 1974 to 1992 provides support for our theory as an additional explanation for the size of the redistributive system. A statistically significant role of immigration in affecting the tax rate is found after controlling for income inequality and for several social and demographic variables that would be expected to reflect the government's revenue needs and thus determine the tax rate. We find that the tax burden on labor income in these countries decreases with the share of immigrants out of the total population, as our theoretical investigation indeed implies in the case in which migrants do not participate in the political process. Most interesting, however, is that the educational composition of the immigrants matters in the way suggested by the theory, with an increasing share of immigrants with low levels of education leading to lower tax rates. The negative relationship between tax rates and the share of all immigrants thus reflects the predominant share of low-education individuals among immigrants and the larger share of low-education individuals in the immigrant population than among natives. In sum, we find that immigration matters for the tax burden, even after controlling for income inequality (predominantly among the native-born population), the generosity and the size of the welfare state, the dependency ratio, per-capita income, and the exposure of the domestic economy to international trade.

EMPIRICAL TEST OF THE HYPOTHESIS

We apply data on 11 European countries (listed in Table 6.1) over the period 1974 to 1992 to examine the empirical implications of the theory developed in the preceding chapter. In particular, we estimate regressions for the determinants of both the tax burden and the generosity of social transfers, considering both income skewedness as suggested by the standard theory and variables relating to immigration highlighted in our theory. We use data on European countries rather than across other advanced economies such as that of the U.S. because immigrants in Europe typically have access to a broader range of welfare benefits than those in the U.S. regardless of whether or not they are citizens. As a result, low-skilled immigrants in Europe are more likely to be net recipients of welfare benefits, whereas the opposite could be the case in the U.S. where immigrants (especially illegal immigrants) are not entitled to certain social welfare benefits. In addition, the definition of a migrant is relatively consistent across European statistical agencies but dissimilar from that of the U.S.

The empirical strategy is to estimate baseline specifications of the determinants of the labor tax rate and per-capita social transfers that include measures of inequality such as suggested by the standard theory along with other control variables and then to add data on the share of immigrants in the population. The empirical specification further examines whether the effect of immigrants on the tax equilibrium depends on the educational level of the migrants. The theory would suggest that additional low-skill immigrants could lead to lower taxes if the leakage effect dominates (and low skill immigrants tend not to vote). High-skill immigrants, though not considered explicitly in the model, could be thought of as having high incomes and thus would likely be net losers from any increase in the tax rate. They would not contribute to the anti-tax imperative of low skilled natives – in fact, more likely the opposite.

Additional control variables are used to account for expenditure-side pressures that would be expected to influence the amount of spending on transfers or revenue requirements of policymakers in setting the tax rate. These include government employment as a share of total employment to indicate the breadth of government involvement in the economy, a measure of openness to trade to capture exposure of external shocks, per capita GDP growth to control for business cycle effects, and the dependency ratio to control for demographic factors such as the aging of the population that might influence the tax burden.

Table 6.1. Summary Statistics on Migration and the Welfare State [Average for each Country (%)]

Country	Years	Labor Tax Rate	GDP Per Capita	Transfers/ GDP	Transfers Per Capita	Rich/ Middle	Rich/ Poor	Govt. Jobs Share	Dependency Ratio	Unemployment Rate	Trade Openness	Migrants/ Population
Overall		41.2	11,791	21.3	3,580	0.69	5.40	19.8	54.9	7.4	69.3	4.6
U.K.	1984–92	25.9	12,345	12.0	1.730	0.76	4.85	20.5	50.6	9.2	51.6	3.1
Finland	1983–92	33.3	12,659	20.3	4,132	0.60	4.66	20.5	48.5	5.8	52.7	0.5
Spain	1980–91	34.2	8,140	15.3	1,483	0.62	4.17	12.1	62.6	17.2	39.1	0.7
France	1974–82, 90	38.3	11,499	20.8	4,004	0.85	8.62	20.2	56.8	5.8	42.2	7.7
Germany	1974–92	39.8	12,339	16.8	2,646	0.73	6.79	15.0	53.8	5.7	53.1	7.2
Austria	1983–92	40.3	11,819	22.6	3,621	0.64	4.98	20.2	55.1	4.5	75.3	5.1
Italy	1983–91	40.3	11,499	22.2	3,327	0.71	4.65	16.9	59.9	9.3	38.6	1.0
Denmark	1982–92	43.0	13,174	19.5	4,055	0.66	6.74	29.9	45.1	9.4	68.8	2.7
Belgium	1974–91	44.4	11,243	26.5	3,878	0.63	4.41	18.9	59.2	9.2	126.2	8.9
Sweden	1974–92	48.0	13,060	21.0	5,297	0.70	5.45	30.7	48.2	2.4	61.3	5.1
Netherlands	1974–92	49.7	11,553	29.8	4,028	0.66	4.47	13.8	61.3	6.3	101.7	3.7
Correlations with labor tax rate												
COUNTRY AVERAGES (11 observations)			0.19	0.81	0.71	−0.09	−0.35	0.21	0.13	−0.40	0.56	0.36
ALL DATA (146 observations)			0.34	0.75	0.62	−0.12	0.06	0.25	0.06	−0.27	0.54	0.32

Notes: GDP per capita and transfers per capita are in real (1990) U.S. dollars; trade openness is defined as (exports + imports)/GDP; the dependency ratio includes unemployed individuals as dependent; the two measures of income inequality are the income share for the top quintile divided by the income share for the middle three quintiles (rich/middle), and the share of the top quintile divided by the share of the bottom quintile (rich/poor).

The baseline specification also includes two variables related to income distribution. The first is the ratio of the income share of the top quintile to the combined share of the middle three quintiles ("rich versus middle"). This is used in empirical tests of the standard theory because the disproportionate share of income accruing to those at the top of the income distribution determines the mean income, while the share of the middle is related to the median income (for which consistent cross-country data are not available). The standard theory predicts that the extent of redistribution depends on the preferences of the median voter – those in the middle rather than those at the bottom of the income distribution – which is why rich/middle is used in the baseline instead of other measures of inequality such as the income share of the top quartile relative to the bottom ("rich versus poor"). We also include the share of the bottom quintile relative to the middle three to control for other distributional influences.

Knowing whether or not immigrants exercise the right to vote would in principle be important, because if immigrants cannot or do not vote, then the prediction of the theory is straightforward in that the anti-tax coalition is un-ambiguously larger with low-skilled immigrants. As discussed below, however, little data exist on whether immigrants vote.[1] Our working hypothesis is that they do not; to the extent that this is correct, this sharpens the prediction of our model, since it means that the tax rate unambiguously declines with additional immigration.

Data Sources

Data on the stock of immigrants and educational composition of migrants are from the OECD Migration Statistics database, supplemented for years before 1980 by various issues of the OECD *Trends in International Migration* Annual Report. As shown in Table 6.1, the data encompass various periods for each of the 11 countries, so that an unbalanced panel is used in the regressions. Unfortunately, the migration data exist before 1980 for only five of the 11 countries and are the principal constraint in extending the sample to earlier years.

The Migration Statistics database also provides data on the educational attainment of immigrants and native-born individuals for three categories, with "low education" defined as completing less than the first stage of the second schooling level, "high education" as completing the third level of school, and "medium education" defined as the balance. Unfortunately, these data are available for only one year – 1995 – so we must assume that the educational composition of migrants and natives is constant over time. Some evidence on the validity of this assumption is discussed below. Data on the share of migrants who have become citizens are not available for most countries (and even then only for 1995), and of course these data do not provide insight as to the participation rate of nationalized immigrants in the political process. Because of this data constraint, we do not use information on the share of immigrants who are citizens in the empirical work.

Data on the labor tax rate from 1974 to 1992 are taken from Mendoza, Razin, and Tesar (1995) as extended by Milesi-Ferretti, Mendoza, and Asea (1997), and Daveri and Tabellini (2000); these are derived by use of revenue statistics to calculate an average tax rate on labor income. The measures of income skewedness are derived from the updated inequality database of Deininger and Squire (1996), which provides measures of income shares by quintile over time although data are not available for every year. Only the high quality measures in the database are used, and the missing observations are then obtained through linear interpolation (the shares do not vary all that much over time, although in most countries there is a general trend toward increased inequality).

Other data are taken from the OECD Analytical Database (ADB). These include per capita GDP, per capita transfers received by households, government employment as a share of total employment, and "openness to trade", defined as the sum of the imports plus exports as a share of GDP. The dependency ratio is calculated from the ADB as one minus the labor force as a share of the population. Per capita transfers include both social security and other transfers such as unemployment and disability compensation, although social security payments are by far the largest component of transfers in most countries. Transfers are deflated by each country's consumer price index (CPI) to provide real transfers in 1990 terms, translated into the common currency of U.S. dollars, and then divided by the population (also from the ADB) to provide per capita transfers. Finally, per capita GDP growth is calculated from the terms of trate adjusted measure in the Summers and Heston database.

Description of Data

Tables 6.1 and 6.2 summarize the variables used in the regression analysis. The 11 countries in Table 6.1 are listed in order of an increasing tax rate, so that it can easily be seen that high tax countries are generally those with more generous transfers, a feature that is also reflected in the strong (unconditional) correlations of 0.6 to 0.8 between the labor tax rate and transfers shown at the bottom of the table (per-capita transfers and transfers as a share of the GDP). The correlation between tax rates and the share of government employment is also positive but not nearly as strong as with transfers. Similarly, only modest or even negative correlations are found between the tax rate and the two measures of income distribution. In all countries, the bottom quintile receives approximately 5%–10% of income, the middle three quintiles approximately 50%–60%, and the top quintile 35%–40%.

Table 6.1. Summary Statistics on Education Levels in 1995 (Percent Shares of Native-Born Population and Immigrants)

Country	Natives			Immigrants		
	Low	Medium	High	Low	Medium	High
U.K.	46.5	34.9	18.6	57.9	21.8	20.4
Finland	37.0	44.8	18.2	39.9	50.4	9.8
Spain	67.8	18.1	14.1	47.0	27.4	25.6
France	40.3	43.0	16.7	53.3	30.7	16.0
Germany	19.1	62.0	18.9	46.3	42.9	10.7
Austria	31.7	61.9	6.4	47.4	43.7	8.9
Italy	64.2	29.5	6.3	53.3	30.7	16.0
Denmark	25.4	52.6	22.1	31.6	39.5	29.0
Belgium	45.3	34.1	20.6	52.8	27.7	19.5
Sweden	27.2	49.5	23.3	30.3	44.8	24.9
Netherlands	24.0	57.5	18.6	40.2	43.7	16.0

The dependency ratio varies widely across the 11 countries, with particularly high dependency rates (fewer workers per population) in Belgium, Italy, the Netherlands, and Spain, but little correlation with the tax rate. Somewhat surprisingly, countries with high unemployment rates have low labor tax rates, although this correlation of course does not say anything about causality or take into account other factors.

Openness to trade is included in the empirical work to address the hypothesis of Rodrik (1998) that a function of the welfare state is to provide social insurance against the adverse effects of external shocks, so that larger governments would be expected to be found in more open economies. Alternately, Alesina and Wacziarg (1998) suggest that the connection between openness and the size of government comes about indirectly through a size effect, in which small countries are both more open that large countries and have a larger government spending as a share of national income (and thus higher taxes). Finally, the last column of Table 6.1 shows that countries with a large stock of immigrants relative to their population tend to have higher tax rates, although the positive correlation is not as large as that between tax rates and transfers or openness, and this again does not imply causality or control for other determinants of tax rates.

Table 6.2 shows the breakdown of native individuals and immigrants by the three broad educational levels in 1995. As expected, the share of low education individuals is generally smaller for natives that for immigrants, although the opposite is the case in Spain and Italy, both of which have small immigrant populations relative to their populations. Conversely, the share of high education immigrants is larger than the share of high education natives in six of the 11 countries. Because the education data are available for only 1995, the shares of immigrants by education level used in the regression are created by assuming that these are constant over time and then by multiplying the share of immigrants in the population in each year by the share of immigrants by education level out of all immigrants, providing a measure of the shares of immigrants within each of the three educational levels out of the total population.[2] Medium- and high-education immigrants are combined for the estimation, so that the empirical work distinguishes between "low education" immigrants with less than the first stage of secondary school, and "high education" immigrants with more than this.

Some evidence that the shares of immigrants by education level might not have changed much over the course of the period in our data sample can be seen by using the February 2000 update to the Barro-Lee dataset on educational attainment (available on the World Bank website) to calculate the weighted average of the educational level of the population in the countries that are the sources of the immigrants. The stock of immigrants from each source country as a share of total immigrants in the destination countries is used as the weight. Several caveats are in order. First, the OECD migration dataset contains a breakdown of immigrants' source countries for only a limited number of years and countries (some destination countries report the region but not specific country of origin). Second, the education breakdowns in the Barro-Lee data do not precisely coincide with those in the OECD data. And third, the educational level of migrants might differ from the population in their country of origin, and could change over time by more or less than the education levels of the domestic population. Keeping these in mind, the average share of the "low" education population (defined as individuals with primary schooling or less) in the source countries falls from 65% in 1980 to 60% in 1985 and the 58% in 1990. The larger shifts in the educational composition of the source countries occurred in the period from 1960 to 1975 (for developing countries), or within the "low" and "high" categories rather than across the threshholds – from no schooling to primary school, or from secondary school to higher education. This latter phenomenon explains why it is preferable to combine the medium and high education levels in our empirical work rather than depend on too fine a breakdown to be fixed over time.

Results

Identical regressors are used in regressions for the determinants of the labor tax rate and the log of social transfers per capita in real dollars. The baseline specification includes the share of government jobs, the dependency ratio, openness, per capita GDP growth, the measure of income skewedness suggested by the standard theory (rich/middle), and the share of income for the poor relative to the middle. All regressions include country fixed effects.

Table 6.2. Determinants of Tax Rate on Labor Income (Dependent Variable: Labor Tax Rate, 146 Observations)

Determinant	1	2	3	4	5
Government jobs/total employment	0.879 (7.34)	0.877 (7.34)	0.620 (4.65)	0.901 (8.75)	0.699 (5.52)
Dependency ratio	−1.168 (−7.59)	−1.287 (−7.05)	−1.358 (−7.76)	−1.185 (−6.96)	−1.254 (−7.53)
Trade openness	−0.003 (−0.10)	−0.004 (−0.16)	−0.045 (−1.65)	0.008 (0.34)	−0.025 (−0.99)
per capita GDP growth	−0.015 (−0.25)	−0.035 (−0.55)	−0.006 (−0.10)	0.027 (0.45)	0.042 (0.72)
Rich/middle income share	−0.009 (0.18)	−0.033 (−0.62)	−0.019 (−0.37)	−0.033 (−0.68)	−0.022 (−0.47)
Poor/middle income share	−0.065 (−0.40)	−0.101 (−0.61)	−0.059 (−0.38)	−0.017 (−0.11)	0.006 (0.04)
Unemployment rate			0.327 (3.73)		0.259 (3.07)
Immigrants/population		−0.403 (−1.20)	−0.614 (−1.89)	−10.852 (−4.88)	−9.723 (−4.45)
Medium + high education immigrants/population				19.043 (4.75)	16.679 (8.73)
R^2	0.652	0.656	0.690	0.708	0.728

Note: All specifications include country fixed effects (coefficients not shown). The t-statistics are in parentheses.

Table 6.3 contains results for the determinants of the tax rate on labor income. Column 1 shows results without any variable for immigration. The tax rate on labor income is positively and significantly related to the involvement of the government in the economy as measured by the share of government jobs. In contrast, the measures of income distribution are both far from significant, and there is likewise little support for the hypothesis that the welfare state exists to provide social insurance against external shocks. The coefficient on the dependency ratio is negative and highly significant, even though the opposite might have been expected a priori, since a higher dependency ratio means that a smaller group of workers must support the non-active population and a higher tax rate might be needed to raise government revenue. In Razin, Sadka, and Swagel (2001), however, we show that this negative coefficient reflects an anti-tax effect spawned by the of the aging population. Just as low-skilled migrants represent a net drain on the welfare state and thus increase the anti-tax coalition by causing a shift in the the position of voters who are net losers, so too does the aging of the population represent a net cost to those who are still active. This leads to an increase in the size of the anti-tax coalition, and thus a negative relationship between tax rates and the dependency ratio.

The remaining columns of Table 6.3 add data on the stock of immigrants as a share of the population to the base specification, first for the share of all immigrants and then for immigrants by education level. In column 2, the share of immigrants out of the population have a negative sign, suggesting that the effect of immigrants in enlarging the anti-tax coalition dominates, though this coefficient is significant at only the 23% confidence level. A 1 percentage point increase in the share of immigrants in the population (a roughly 20% increase in the total stock of immigrants of all 11 countries) leads to a 0.4 percentage point decline in the labor tax rate. The other results are essentially unchanged with the immigrant share added to the regression.

The third column adds the unemployment rate. In contrast to the negative correlations in Table 6.1, there is a positive relationship between the unemployment rate and the labor tax rate once other factors are taken into account. As suggested by Daveri and Tabellini (2000), this possibly reflects the effect in the other direction of high labor taxes leading to high unemployment in Europe. With the unemployment rate added, the coefficient on the share of immigrants becomes more negative and significant at the 6% confidence level.

Column 4 shows the baseline specification with immigrants separated by education level. The results are consistent with our theory: low education immigrants have a statistically significant negative effect on the tax rate, whereas the combined category of medium and high education immigrants have a significant and positive effect. The results are unchanged in column 5 where the unemployment rate is again added. The composition of immigrants thus matters for the tax rate in the way predicted by the model: low education immigrants lead to lower taxes, while an increased share of medium and high education immigrants, who would likely not be net recipients of government benefits, leads to higher tax rates. Immigration might also increase income inequality and thus lead to higher taxes as predicted by the standard theory (although our empirical results are inconclusive on this point since the coefficient on the variable suggested by the standard theory, while negative, is not statistically significant), but our results show that immigration has an independent effect on tax rates, and this dependent effect works to reduce taxes, as is consistent with our theory.

Table 6.4 shows results for the determinants of social transfers per person (in the common currency of real dollars). As with the labor tax rate, the share of government jobs has a significant positive effect on social transfers, whereas the dependency ratio has a significant negative effect. In contrast to the results for the tax rate, the coefficients on both measures of income distribution are significant. However, the variable for income skewedness suggested by the standard theory has the wrong sign, with greater inequality leading to lower rather than higher redistribution. On the other hand, the negative coefficient on the poor/middle variable indicates that greater inequality leads to more generous

Table 6.3. Determinants of Per Capita Social Transfers (Dependent Variable: Social Transfers Per Capita in Real Dollars, 146 Observations)

Determinant	1	2	3	4	5
Government jobs/total	4.359	4.461	5.263	4.618	5.828
employment	(3.13)	(3.65)	(3.69)	(3.84)	(4.14)
Dependency ratio	−10.247	−3.908	−3.685	−3.346	−2.941
	(−5.72)	(−2.09)	(−1.96)	(−1.81)	(−1.59)
Trade openness	−2.028	−1.946	−1.819	−1.879	−1.682
	(−6.73)	(−7.35)	(−6.29)	(−7.19)	(−5.87)
per capita GDP growth	−1.388	−0.336	−0.425	0.009	−0.078
	(−1.95)	(−0.52)	(−0.65)	(0.01)	(−0.12)
Rich/middle income	−2.399	−1.115	−1.159	−1.117	−1.181
share	(−4.22)	(−2.07)	(−2.15)	(−2.11)	(−2.24)
Poor/middle income	−7.350	−5.424	(−5.554)	−4.959	−5.090
share	(−3.89)	(−3.21)	(−3.29)	(−2.97)	(−3.07)
Unemployment rate			−1.022		−1.514
			(−1.09)		(−1.62)
Immigrants/population		21.583	22.244	−36.328	−42.945
		(6.30)	(6.39)	(−1.51)	(−1.77)
Medium + high education				105.532	119.375
immigrants/population				(2.43)	(2.71)
R^2	0.497	0.616	0.620	0.633	0.641

Note: All specifications include country fixed effects (coefficients not shown). The t-statistics are in parentheses.

transfers. The coefficient on GDP growth is also significant in contrast to the results for the labor tax rate, suggesting a counter-cyclical role for social transfers (however, this coefficient is not statistically significant in the other specifications for transfers).

Adding the stock of immigrants out of the population in column 2 gives a strong positive effect of immigrants on transfers – the opposite as was found for the tax rate. To put this in perspective, average social transfers rose from $2300 in 1984 to $4500 in 1991 (in real 1990 dollars), a change of 0.8 in logs. Over this period, the share of immigrants in the population rose from just over 3.5% to not quite 4.4%. Multiplying this 0.8 percentage point change by the coefficient of 21.6 for the share of immigrants in column 2 indicates that the rising share of immigrants accounts for more than 20% of rising benefits (0.18 of the 0.8 log change in benefits). The results for the other variables are qualitatively unchanged, though the coefficient on GDP growth is no longer significant and the magnitudes of coefficients on the dependency ratio and the income distribution variables change somewhat. It is interesting as well that the fit of the transfers regression (the within-country R^2) improves markedly with the addition of the stock of immigrants, from 0.5 to better than 0.6, in contrast to the tax rate regression, where this hardly mattered. The results are essentially unchanged with the inclusion of the unemployment rate in column 3.

Separating immigrants by education in columns 4 and 5 of Table 6.4 provide results more in line with those for the labor tax rate in Table 6.3. As before, rising social transfers are related to medium- and high-education immigrants for the which the coefficients in both columns are statistically significant, while there are negative but not as strongly significant coefficients on the overal share of immigrants in the population (thus on the low-skilled immigrants).

Finally, there is a potential problem of reverse causality from the tax rate and benefits to the immigrant share. First, if taxes affect migration this would likely *strengthen* out results. This is because higher taxes or benefits would be expected to lead to more immigration of low-skilled workers (with higher-education immigrants moving for reasons other than benefits). But this means that in our regressions, this positive effect of taxes or benefits on immigration is partially offsetting the negative effect we find of migration on taxes (or covering up a negative effect of migration on benefits). However, it is also possible that countries with more elaborate welfare systems will choose to tighten their migration quotas, especially with respect to unskilled migrants. This can offer an alternative explanation for the negative correlation between the tax rate and migration share that we find in the data.[3] A useful extension of the empirical work of this chapter would be to develop and test a theory that jointly explains migration and taxes/benefits.

Conclusion

Earlier studies have examined the burden imposed on the modern welfare state by migration. For instance, Wildasin (1994) and Razin and Sadka (1995) show how all income groups of the native-born population may lose from migration with income redistribution schemes.[4] In the preceding chapter, we examined how these schemes are shaped in the context of a political-economy equilibrium. The theory suggests that migration does not necessarily tilt the political power balance in favor of heavier taxation and more intensive redistribution. The reason for this is that more native-born individuals from the middle of the income distribution (that is, the skill/ability distribution) may lose from the extra tax burden brought about by the need to finance the transfer to the migrants, and as a result shift to the side of the high-income anti-tax coalition. This shift may be larger than the increase to the pro-tax coalition brought about by the migrants who join this coalition. Our model thus complements the standard theory of the determination of the size of government in a representative democracy, which focuses on the role of income inequality in determining the extent of redistribution and thus the tax burden.

Our empirical results using data on 11 European countries from 1974 to 1992 are reasonably consistent with the implications of the theory. After controlling for variables suggested by the standard theory of the size of government in a representative democracy, and for a number of additional variables that would be expected to drive expenditures and thus determine the tax burden required to fund the welfare state, we find that a larger share of immigrants in the population leads to a smaller tax burden but larger per capita social transfers. When we examine the effect of immigration by education level, however, we find as predicted by our theory that a larger share of low education immigrants leads to a smaller tax burden and lower transfers, while a larger share of middle and high education immigrants has leads to higher taxes and more generous transfers.

PART 3

INTERNATIONAL CAPITAL FLOWS
INTO EMERGING MARKETS

7   Bank Runs and Capital-Flow Reversals

INTRODUCTION

Many emerging economies that had liberalized their capital markets generated massive capital inflows. Not much later, these inflows sharply reversed themselves during the financial crises that started in East and Southeast Asia in 1997, and then spread to Russia in 1998 and Brazil in 1999. In all cases, the liberalization of the capital markets was not accompanied by an appropriate reform of the banking sector that is preeminent in the financial system of these economies (although other financial intermediaries are growing in importance). Banks remained vulnerable to bank runs. Indeed, bank failures were intertwined with capital-flow reversals, generating balance-of-payment crises.[1]

In this chapter, we lay out the seminal model of bank runs that was developed by Diamond and Dybvig (1983). They were the first to formalize the maturity mismatch between a bank's assets and liabilities, which is at the root of the vulnerability of a bank. This vulnerability may lend itself to a bank run. We then show how international capital flows interact with bank failures.

THE DIAMOND–DYBVIG MODEL OF BANK RUNS

Suppose that there is a single all-purpose commodity that serves as both a capital good and a consumption good. There are three periods: The present, the short run, and the long run. In period one (the present), there are two types of investment opportunities. One is a short-run opportunity that matures in the second period, yielding a return of r_S. This short-run investment technology is available also in period two. Thus, a unit of the good invested in period one in a short-run opportunity can be reinvested in the same type of opportunity in the second period, accumulating to $(1 + r_S)^2$ units of the good in period three. The second type of investment technology that is available in period one is of a long-run nature, that is, it has an incubation process lasting two periods. Thus a unit of the good invested with this technology matures in period three, yielding an accumulated quantity of $(1 + r_L)^2$ units of the good. If this investment is terminated after one period only, that is, in period two, it accumulates to $1 + r_B$ units of the good. Naturally it is assumed that such an abrupt termination of a project that was a priori designed as a long-run project is costly in the sense that it yields on such termination a return (r_B) that is significantly lower than the return (r_S) of a project that was originally designed for the short run. Otherwise, noone will choose to invest in a short-term technology. On the other hand, a long-term investment that is held until its planned maturity date, that is, period three, yields a higher return than a short-term investment that is reinvested for an additional period. Thus, $r_L > r_S$. Summarizing,

$$r_L > r_S > r_B. \tag{7.1}$$

Consumers are ex-ante identical. Each consumer possesses an initial endowment in period one of one unit of the good; this consumer possesses no endowment in any other subsequent period. There is a continuum of individuals whose number is normalized to one. Therefore, the aggregate initial endowment in the first period is one unit of the good. To simplify the analysis, we assume that the individual derives no utility from consuming in period one, so that she or he invests all of her or his first-period endowment. We further assume that the individual consumes in either period two or three (but not in both periods), depending on whether a "need" arises in either period two or in period three.

In period one, no individual knows in which subsequent period (two or three) such a consumption (liquidity) need will arise. For a proportion λ of the consumers, the need will arise in period two; these consumers, will be referred to as early consumers. For the other $1 - \lambda$ consumers, the need will arise in period three; these consumers will be referred to as late consumers. In period one, all consumers are identical; each one of them faces a probability λ of turning out to be an early consumer and a probability $1 - \lambda$ of turning out to be a late consumer. There is no aggregate (macro) uncertainty in this economy: Exactly λ consumers will be early consumers and exactly $1 - \lambda$ consumers will be late consumers; also, the returns on the two types of assets (the short-term asset and the long-term asset) are safe. However, no one in period one knows which type of consumer she or he is going to be, so that there is a risk at the individual level but not at the aggregate level.

The expected utility of an individual in period one is

$$U(c_2, c_3) = \lambda u(c_2) + (1 - \lambda)u(c_3), \tag{7.2}$$

where c_i is consumption in period $i = 2, 3$ and u exhibits risk aversion (that is, u is concave).[2]

A crucial assumption in the model is that in the second period only the individual knows whether she or he became a late consumer or an early consumer. That is, the late-consumption or the early-consumption state of the world is private information and no contract contingent on these states of the world can be enforced.

No Financial Intermediation

Suppose first that there are no banks or any other financial intermediaries. In Fig. 7.1 the line AB describes the consumption-possibility frontier of a representative individual. If she or he invests all of her or his unit endowment in a short-term investment technology, then she or he will be able to consume $1 + r_S$ units in period two if she or he turns out to be an early consumer; she or he will consume $(1 + r_S)^2$ units in period three if she or he turns out to be a late consumer. This consumption bundle is described by point B. At the other extreme, if she or he invests all of her or his unit endowment in a long-term investment technology, then if she or he turns out to be an early consumer in period two, she or he will be forced to prematurely terminate her investment in period two, in which case she or he will get $1 + r_B$ units of consumption; if she or he turns out to be a late consumer, then she or he will hold her investment until its planned maturity, in which case she or he will be able to consume $(1 + r_L)^2$ units in period three. This consumption bundle is described by point A. Dividing her or his unit endowment between the two types of investment opportunities, she or he can attain any consumption bundle along the line AB. Given this consumption-possibility frontier, she or he chooses the consumption bundle D, in which her indifference curve $U(c_2, c_3) = U_A$ is tangent to this frontier.

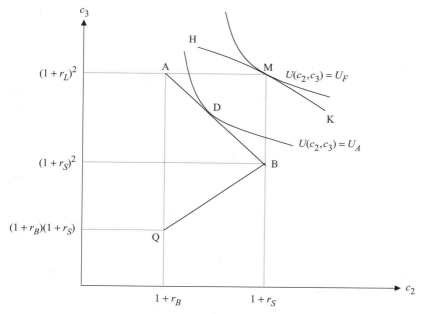

Fig. 7.1. The Diamond-Dybvig model.

Financial Intermediation

One of the roles of a financial intermediary is the so-called maturity transformation, that is, the matching between savers' needs of different maturities and investments of different maturities. Consider a perfectly competitive bank in which all consumers deposit their unit endowment. Because it is certain that exactly λ consumers will turn out to be early consumers and $1 - \lambda$ consumers will turn out to be late consumers, then if the bank invests λ units in short-term investment technologies and $1 - \lambda$ units in long-term investment technologies, it will have $\lambda(1 + r_S)$ units of consumption in period two and $(1 - \lambda)(1 + r_L)^3$ units of consumption in period three, without having to terminate any long-term investment. Being competitive, the bank will offer all consumers a deposit contract in period one that promises a return of r_S if the deposit is withdrawn in period two and a return of r_L per period if the deposit is withdrawn in period three. Note that the bank will not be able to distinguish between the two types of consumers in period two (because the type of a consumer is private information), and therefore it allows *all* (both late and early) consumers to withdraw their deposits in period two. However, it does not pay a late consumer to withdraw her or his deposit in period two if she or he expects that only early consumers will withdraw their deposits in period two. Therefore, the deposit contract is incentive compatible. Indeed, when only early consumers withdraw their deposits in period two, total withdrawals in this period are $\lambda(1 + r_S)$, which exactly matches the amount of short-term assets that mature and are at the bank's disposal in period two. This deposit contract offers the consumer the consumption bundle N in Fig. 7.1.

The bank can also follow different investment strategies other than investing λ units in short-term technologies and $1 - \lambda$ units in long-term technologies. Accordingly, it can offer different deposit contracts other than a return of r_S for withdrawals in period two and a return of r_L per period for withdrawals in period three. For instance, the bank can invest β units in short-term technologies and $1 - \beta$ units in long-term technologies. Accordingly, the bank can choose any $0 \leq \beta \leq 1$ and offer any pair (d_S, d_L) of short- and long-term per-period returns, respectively, that satisfy the following three constraints:

$$\lambda(1 + d_S) = \beta(1 + r_S) + \alpha(1 - \beta)(1 + r_B), \tag{7.3}$$

$$(1 - \lambda)(1 + d_L)^2 = (1 - \alpha)(1 - \beta)(1 + r_L)^2, \tag{7.4}$$

$$\alpha \geqq 0, \tag{7.5}$$

where α is the fraction of long-term projects that the bank has to terminate in period two in order to meet its short-term liabilities. Because there are λ early consumers in period two who will all withdraw their deposits in that period, the bank will have to pay them an amount equaling $\lambda(1 + d_S)$. The bank has a total of β units invested in short-term technologies. These investments will hand to the bank an amount of $\beta(1 + r_S)$ units of consumption in period two. If total withdrawals at period two $[\lambda(1 + d_S)]$ exceed total available liquid funds $[\beta(1 + r_S)]$, the bank has to call in a fraction α of long-term investments with a penalty of earning a return of only r_B. The fraction α has to satisfy Eq. (7.3). In period three, the remaining fraction $(1 - \alpha)$ of the long-term investments of the bank matures and provides an amount of $(1 - \alpha)(1 - \beta)(1 + r_L)^2$ units of consumption. This amount must suffice to pay total withdrawals that amount to $(1 - \lambda)(1 + d_L)^2$. This explains Eq. (7.4). Constraints (7.3)–(7.5) can be consolidated into two constraints as follows:

$$(1 - \lambda)(1 + d_L)^2(1 + r_B) + \lambda(1 + d_S)(1 + r_L)^2$$

$$= [\beta(1 + r_S) + (1 - \beta)(1 + r_B)](1 + r_L)^2, \tag{7.6}$$

$$\lambda(1 + d_S) \geq \beta(1 + r_S). \tag{7.7}$$

Thus, for each investment strategy, that is, for each pair $(\beta, 1 - \beta)$, there exists a continuum of deposit contracts, that is, pairs (d_S, d_L) that the bank can offer; these pairs must, of course, satisfy constraints (7.6) and (7.7). Put differently, for each pair $(\beta, 1 - \beta)$, there is a corresponding consumption possibility frontier in (c_2, c_3) space. The upper envelope of all of these frontiers, obtained when β is allowed to vary from zero to one, is termed the grand consumption-possibility frontier and is depicted by the curve *HNK* in Fig. 7.1. Note that point N is indeed feasible: First, N is characterized by an investment strategy $(\beta, 1 - \beta) = (\lambda, 1 - \lambda)$ and a deposit contract $(d_S, d_L) = (r_S, r_L)$. It is straightforward to see that these values of $(\beta, 1 - \beta)$ and (d_S, d_L) satisfy constraints (7.6) and (7.7). Next, note that N lies *on* the grand consumption-possibility frontier: If we maximize c_3 subject to $c_2 = 1 + r_S$ and constraints (7.6) and (7.7), then the only solution is $(\beta, 1 - \beta) = (\lambda, 1 - \lambda)$ and $(d_S, d_L) = (r_S, r_L)$.[3]

Point M is a competitive equilibrium in which each consumer withdraws her or his deposit in period two if and only if she or he turns out to be an early consumer. This is a "good" financial equilibrium that clearly dominates the autarkic (with no financial intermediaries) equilibrium D.

However, there is another "bad" financial equilibrium of a bank run. As put by the *Economist* (1999, p.107):

> "Most of a Bank's liabilities have a shorter maturity than its assets. There is, therefore, a mismatch between the two. This leads to problems, if depositors become very worried about the quality of a bank's lending book that they demand their savings back. Although some overdrafts or credit lines can easily be called in, longer-term loans are much less liquid. This can cause a bank to fail."

As long as the bank does not invest all of its assets in short-term technologies, then everyone knows that the bank will not be able to pay a return d_S in period two if *all* consumers run on the bank. This is because the competitive bank offered a short-term return d_S on the premise that only λ consumers (that is, the early consumers) would withdraw their deposits in period two; see Eq. (7.3). Thus even a late consumer will find it optimal to join a run on the bank, because in such a case the bank will be forced to terminate abruptly all of its long-term projects ("liquidate all of its assets") in period two and divide whatever resources are available among panicked depositors on a first-come, first-served basis. If a late consumer does not join the run, she or he will be left with nothing in period three. Thus, a bank run is another financial equilibrium.

This bad bank-run equilibrium is located somewhere on the curve QB in Fig. 7.1. To see this, consider the resources available to the bank to divide among its panicked depositors in period two. If it were to invest all deposits in short-term technologies, then it would be able to pay $1 + r_S$ to all of its depositors in period two. Thus, an early consumer would then be able to consume $1 + r_S$ units in period two. If the consumer turns out to be a late consumer, then she or he will reinvest her withdrawn amount of $1 + r_S$ in period two in a short-term technology to obtain $(1 + r_S)^2$ units of consumption in period three. This consumption bundle is described by point B in Fig. 7.1. At the other extreme, if the bank were to invest all of its deposits in long-term technologies, it would have to liquidate all its assets in period two in the event of a bank run and get $1 + r_B$ units of consumption. Hence, a consumer that turned out to be an early consumer in period two can consume $1 + r_B$ units of consumption in this period. A late consumer will receive $1 + r_B$ units in period two and invest it in a short-term technology and will be able to consume $(1 + r_B)(1 + r_S)$ units of consumption in period three. This consumption bundle is described by point Q in Fig. 7.1. Other intermediate investment strategies, including the strategy that underlies the good equilibrium M, are located somewhere along the line QB.

Summing Up

Financial intermediation can support a good equilibrium (point M) that unequivocally dominates the consumption-possibility frontier in the absence of financial intermediation (the curve AB). However, financial intermediation could also turn into a bank run that is bad. Such an equilibrium is located somewhere along the curve QB and is clearly inferior to the equilibrium that prevails in the absence of financial intermediation (point D).

The bad equilibrium can be eliminated by "the lender of the last resort." For instance, a government deposit insurance will nullify the possibility of a bank run. Note that such an insurance scheme is indeed feasible as there is no aggregate risk in the economy. In fact, the insurance will never be exercised (that is, a bank run will never occur) if everyone indeed believes that the government has sufficient resources to bail out the bank on which the depositors may run.

Nevertheless, in a more realistic setup there is some aggregate risk. For instance, the return of long-term investment (r_L) is typically risky. In this case, deposit insurance may be either infeasible (for instance, in a closed economy) or costly. It is also plagued by moral hazards, as the bank's investment strategy may be biased toward high-return, high-risk portfolio; in a "good" state of the world, it will reap the high return; in a "bad" state of the world, the government will bail it out.

The emergence of two different outcomes (good and bad) from the same action (deposit contracts) by the banks and the consumers is a serious drawback or inconsistency of the Diamond–Dybvig model. The bank is actually offering depositors contracts that may end up in a bank run without taking this possibility into account at all. Similarly, depositors accept such contracts that are not feasible in a state of a bank run without paying any attention to such a possibility of which they are fully aware at the time they make the deposits. Loosely speaking, the equilibrium in this model is not fully rational if the bank-run equilibrium has some positive probability. If all depositors believe that there will be no bank run and act accordingly, then there will not be one; if all believe that there will be a bank run and act accordingly, then there will indeed be a bank run. And, as described by Morris and Shin (2000), "The shift in beliefs which underpins the switch from one equilibrium to another is left unexplained."

The next section extends the Diamond–Dybvig model in a way that results in a fully rational equilibrium.

A RATIONAL-EXPECTATIONS BANK-RUN EQUILIBRIUM

We now assume that long-term investments are typically risky. Suppose then that $r_L = r_L(\theta)$, where θ is the state of the world; and assume, for concreteness, that r_L is strictly increasing in θ and that noone has any private information about the state of the world before deciding whether to withdraw her or his deposit in period two. Instead, θ is revealed to all at the same time (that is, the state of the world becomes common knowledge) after they decide whether or not to withdraw their deposits in period two.

We can verify [see, for instance, Goldstein and Pauzner (1999)] that this setup still lends itself to two outcomes with self-fulfilling beliefs: a "good" one with no bank runs and a "bad" one with bank runs, without any explanation for either the formation of each set of beliefs or for the switch from one set to another. As put by Morris and Shin (2000):

> "The apparent indeterminancy of beliefs can be seen as the consequence of two modelling assumptions. . . . First, the economic fundamentals are assumed to be common knowledge; Second, economic agents are assumed to be certain about others' behavior in equilibrium. . . . Both assumptions allow agents' actions and beliefs to be perfectly coordinated in a way that invites a multiplicity of equilibria."

They go on to explain what ingredients can be essential in rationalizing the model outcome. In their approach "agents have a small amount of idiosyncratic uncertainty about economic fundamentals. Even if this idiosyncratic uncertainty is small, agents will be uncertain about each other's behavior in equilibrium. This uncertainty allows us as modellers to pin down which set of self-fulfilling beliefs will prevail in equilibrium." They use this approach to tackle various issues such as bank runs [Morris and Shin (2000)] and currency crises [Morris and Shin (1998)].

Here we follow Goldstein and Pauzner (1999) in supposing that in period two, before agent i decides on whether or not to withdraw her or his deposit in period two, she or he receives an imperfect signal θ_i about the true value of θ, which is private to her or him. Given the state of the world (that is, the fundamental, θ), the signal is uniformly distributed over $[\theta - \varepsilon, \theta + \varepsilon]$. Knowing the distribution of the signal, if agent i receives a signal θ_i, then she or he knows that noone received a signal below $\theta_i - 2\varepsilon$ or above $\theta_i + 2\varepsilon$.

Goldstein and Pauzner (1999) elegantly show how, for a given fundamental θ [which uniquely determines the long-term rate of return $r_L(\theta)$], the indeterminancy between the two outcomes regarding bank runs is eliminated. This is shown in Fig. 7.2, in which the fraction of consumers withdrawing their deposits in period two is described by the solid line. Note that early consumers always withdraw their deposits in period two. Whether or not it pays a late consumer to withdraw her or his deposit in period two depends on d_S and on θ [because θ determines $d_L(\theta)$]. Given d_S, they show that there is a unique threshold level of the fundamental, denoted by $\theta^*(d_S)$, such that if the true value of the fundamental is below $\theta^*(d_S) - \varepsilon$, there will be a bank run; if $\theta > \theta^*(d_S) + \varepsilon$, there will be no bank run; and if $\theta^*(d_S) - \varepsilon < \theta < \theta^*(d_S) + \varepsilon$, only a fraction of the late consumers withdraw their deposits in period two.[4] As the signals are positively

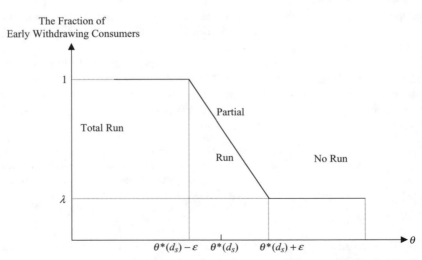

Fig. 7.2. The fraction of early-withdrawing consumers as a function of the fundamental. Note: This figure is adapted from Fig. III in Goldstein and Pauzner (1999).

correlated to the fundamental, this fraction (of consumers withdrawing their deposits in period two) is decreasing in the fundamental.

The rationale for this result is as follows. For a very large value of the fundamental θ, it is *assumed* that there will arise a lender of last resort that will guarantee the return $d_L(\theta)$. (Alternatively, for a very large value of the fundamental, the payoff of the long-term asset can arrive earlier in period two instead of in period three.) In this case, every consumer will receive a "high" level of the signal. Then no late consumer will withdraw early, no matter what she or he believes other late consumers may do. In this case, the fraction of early-withdrawing consumers is therefore equal to λ, the fraction of early consumers. On the other hand, for a very low level of the fundamental, each agent will receive a "low" level of the signal and will withdraw early, even if she or he believes that no other late consumer will do so.

Consider now "intermediate" values of the fundamental θ. An agent learns two things from the signal: First, the agent learns about the fundamental θ (and the long-term return). Second, the agent learns about the signals of other agents (which form their beliefs). The higher her or his signal θ_i, the more she or he expects to earn if she or he is a late consumer and decides not to withdraw early. Also, the higher θ_i, the higher the posterior expected value of θ and, consequently, the posterior expected value of other agents' signals. As a result, it becomes less likely that other agents will run on the bank. She or he then has less incentive for an early withdrawal. This consideration suggests how the indeterminancy between the two outcomes (of total bank run or no bank run) under common knowledge (more accurately, common ignorance) is eliminated. This is also why the fraction of early-withdrawing consumers is declining in θ.

As expected by this intuition, and actually shown by Goldstein and Pauzner (1999), the threshold $\theta^*(d_S)$ is equal to the level of the signal that equates the expected payoff of a late consumer from withdrawing her or his deposit in period two early or waiting until its planned maturity in period three. (This expected payoff is conditioned on the level of the signal that also reveals some information about the signals received by all consumers, which, in turn, affects the number of early-withdrawing consumers.) Evidently, the threshold θ^* is increasing in the deposit rate d_S.

Having eliminated the indeterminancy of the outcome of each deposit contract, the bank and the depositors can now assess the probability of a bank run, based on the underlined, exogenously given probability of the fundamental (θ). Therefore, the bank will take this probability into account in designing its deposit contracts, and depositors will do so in choosing their most preferred deposit contracts. In contrast to the Diamond–Dybvig model, in this model the bank now realizes that if it offers a higher short-term deposit rate (d_S), then it increases the probability of a bank run, that is, the solid line in Fig. 7.2 shifts to the right. The outcome of this extended model is a rational-expectations equilibrium of financial intermediation.

To sum up, if there is common knowledge about the fundamentals, there is a possibility of multiple equilibria. This means that at each realization of the fundamental, agents may coordinate on any one of these multiple equilibria. In contrast, with noisy signals, even with very small amount of "noise," the withdrawal action on which agents coordinate, for each realization of the fundamental, must be consistent with withdrawal actions they may take at adjacent values of the fundamentals. This places restrictions on their withdrawal behavior, which in this case brings about *unique* equilibrium.

BANK FAILURES AND BALANCE-OF-PAYMENTS CRISES

Formally speaking, the aforementioned analysis applies to economies that could be either isolated from or integrated into the world capital markets. However, a globalized economy is more vulnerable to bank runs. Furthermore, such episodes may be accompanied by (or interacting with) balance-of-payment crises, especially in emerging economies or in economies that recently underwent a capital market liberalization.[5] In this section, we highlight three possible mechanisms through which this interrelation takes place.

As already mentioned, a bank run can be averted by a credible lender of last resort or a credible government-sponsored deposit insurance. In either case, the government is essentially making a credible promise to bail out the creditors of the bank (that is, short- and long-term depositors, other banks extending credit to the said bank, etc.). However, although domestic politics may be sympathetic toward bailing out domestic creditors, it may be reluctant to bail out foreign creditors. Hypothetically, a government may distinguish between domestic and foreign creditors and provide insurance to the former only. In such a case, a bank with a high fraction of foreign creditors will be more vulnerable to a bank run. Such a bank run will generate a capital flight that may even reverse an otherwise inflow of capital, thereby creating a balance of payments crisis.

Such a distinction between foreign and domestic creditors may revoke international retaliation. Practically, it is also infeasible as foreign creditors may sell their claims to domestic residents. Nonetheless, domestic opposition to bailing out foreign creditors does not lessen. This makes it harder for the government altogether to implement a bail-out program. The credibility of a government-sponsored insurance scheme is eroded as the fraction of foreign credits out of all credits rises, thereby increasing the probability of a bank run. With a high fraction of foreign credits in the bank's total deposits, bank failures may coincide with capital-flow reversals and balance-of-payment crises.[6]

A second mechanism intertwining bank failures with capital-flow reversals in emerging and developing countries may work as follows. Foreign creditors in such economies may have better access to the world capital markets than domestic creditors have. (For example, domestic residents may still face legal restrictions on investing abroad.) In this case, when a late foreign depositor withdraws her or his deposit early, then she or he may face better reinvestment opportunities than her domestic counterpart. Therefore, foreign creditors may be more "trigger happy" in running on the bank than domestic creditors. Again, as the fraction of foreign credits out of all credits rises, the probability of a bank run, accompanied by a capital flight, increases.

A third mechanism that connects bank crises and currency crashes is rooted in currency mismatch of financial intermediaries' balance sheets [see Ratelet and Sachs (1999) and Goldstein (2000)], in addition to maturity mismatch. With short-term liabilities of the intermediaries denominated in foreign currency (the foreign deposits) and long-term assets (the financial intermediary loans) denominated in domestic currency (or bank obligants' assets denominated in domestic currency), a withdrawal of foreign deposits may lead to a bank crisis. Foreign-currency outflows put pressures on the currency peg. To the extent that the probability that the monetary authorities would be willing to defend the peg (when it becomes more costly to do so) rises, the likelihood of currency depreciation increases. However, when the probability that the currency will crash rises, the likelihood of early withdrawal of deposits from banks also increases, thereby raising the likelihood of bank runs. Therefore the currency mismatch in the financial intermediaries' balance sheet generates a circular interaction between currency crashes and bank crises.

8   Country Risk and Capital-Flow Reversals

INTRODUCTION

A remarkable feature of the 1997 crisis of the emerging economies in South and Southeast Asia is the lack of early warning of the traditional sort, such as budget deficits, external debts, slow capital formation, etc. Accordingly, the credit ratings of these economies were relatively sound. Nonetheless, the crises erupted.

In the preceding chapter, we focused on one kind of explanation: the vulnerability of the banking sector. In this chapter we offer another channel through which such crises can erupt. We present a classical model of credits with defaults, which is due to Townsend (1979), that will serve also in subsequent chapters. This model was later extended to macroeconomics by Bernanke and Gertler (1989). Here we use it to derive a sort of multiple-equilibria phenomena with self-fulfilling beliefs: one equilibrium with a steady inflow of capital, sound macroeconomic variables and a high credit rating, and another "bad" equilibrium with dried-up capital inflows, doomed growth prospects, and poor credit rating.

THE TOWNSEND MODEL OF CREDIT AND DEFAULT

Consider a two-period model of a small, capital-importing country. Capital imports are commonly classified as foreign direct investment (FDI), portfolio investment (equity and bonds), and credit. In this chapter, we focus on the latter; subsequent chapters will deal with other forms of capital imports.

Suppose then that capital imports are channeled solely through firms borrowing in the world capital markets. (The amount of direct retail credit is typically negligible.) As the economy is small, suppose initially that it faces a perfectly elastic supply of credit for *safe projects* at a given risk-free world rate of interest $-r^*$. The actual rate for any given firm will, of course, be higher depending on the riskiness of its investment plans, as we shall specify later. In the next section, we will introduce also an element of country risk.

Suppose there is a continuum of ex-ante identical domestic firms.[1] Each firm uses capital input (K) in the first period to produce a single composite good in the second period. We assume that capital depreciates at the rate δ. Output in the second period is equal to $F(K)(1 + \varepsilon)$, where $F(\cdot)$ is a production function exhibiting diminishing marginal productivity of capital and ε is a random productivity factor with zero mean that is independent across all firms. Factor ε is bounded from below by -1, so that output is always nonnegative. It is also assumed that it is bounded from above, say by one. We assume that ε is purely idiosyncratic, so that there is no aggregate uncertainty. For each ε, there will be exactly $N\Phi(\varepsilon)$ firms whose output in the second period will be below or equal to $F(K)(1 + \varepsilon)$, where $\Phi(\cdot)$ is the cummulation distribution function of ε and N is the number of firms. However, in the first period no one knows who these firms are. Thus, each firm faces a probability of $\Phi(\varepsilon)$ of having an output below or equal to $F(K)(1 + \varepsilon)$ in the second period. Following proper portfolio diversification, consumers–savers behave in a risk-neutral way. To simplify the notation we normalize the number of firms to one, that is, $N = 1$.

Investment decisions are made by the firms before the state of the world (ε) is known. Because all firms face the same probability distribution of ε, they all choose the same level of investment. They then seek funds to finance the investment, either at home or abroad. We denote the gross investment of the firm by I. Therefore, if its initial stock of capital in the first period, carried over from the preceding period, is $K_0(1 - \delta)$, then the stock of capital that the firm uses in the first period is $K = K_0(1 - \delta) + I$.

Because credit is extended ex-ante, before ε is revealed, firms cannot sign default-free loan contracts with the lenders. We therefore consider loan contracts that allow for the possibility of default. We adopt the "costly state verification" framework from Townsend (1979) in assuming that lenders make firm-specific loans, charging an interest rate of r^j to firm j. The interest and the principal payment commitment will be honored when the firm encounters a relatively good productivity shock and defaulted when it encounters a relatively bad shock. The loan contract is therefore characterized by a loan rate (r^j), with possible default, and a threshold value $(\bar{\varepsilon}^j)$ of the productivity parameter defined as follows:

$$F(K^j)(1 + \bar{\varepsilon}^j) + (1 - \delta)K^j = \left[K^j - (1 - \delta)K_0^j\right](1 + r^j), \tag{8.1}$$

$$[1 - \Phi(\bar{\varepsilon}^j)]\left[K^j - (1 - \delta)K_0^j\right](1 + r^j) + \Phi(\bar{\varepsilon}^j)(1 - \mu)\{F(K^j)[1 + e^-(\bar{\varepsilon}^j)]$$
$$+ (1 - \delta)K^j\} = \left[K^j - (1 - \delta)K_0^j\right](1 + r^*). \tag{8.2}$$

Equation (8.1) defines the value of the productivity shock for which the funds available to the firm just suffice to repay the principal of and the interest on the loan. These funds consist of the output of the firm plus the depreciated stock of capital. This is the expression on the left-hand side of Eq. (8.1). When the realized value of ε^j is larger than $\bar{\varepsilon}^j$, the firm is solvent and will thus pay the lenders the promised amount, consisting of the principal $K^j - (1 - \delta)K_0^j$, plus the interest $r^j[K^j - (1 - \delta)K_0^j]$, as given by the right-hand side of Eq. (8.1). If, however, ε^j is smaller than $\bar{\varepsilon}^j$, the firm will default. In the case of default, the lenders incur a cost in order to verify the true value of ε^j and to seize the residual value of the firm. This cost, interpretable as the cost of bankruptcy, is assumed to be proportional to the amount seized, $[F(K^j)(1 + \varepsilon^j) + (1 - \delta)K^j]$, where $0 < \mu \le 1$ is the factor of proportionality. As net of this cost, the lenders will receive $(1 - \mu)[F(K^j)(1 + \varepsilon^j) + (1 - \delta)K^j]$. The expected rate of return required by foreign lenders who are the marginal lenders in this capital-importing economy is r^*. Therefore, the "default" rate of interest, r^j, must offer a premium over and above the default-free rate, r^*, according to Eq. (8.2). The first term on the left-hand side of Eq. (8.2) is the contracted principal and interest payment, weighted by the no-default probability. The second term measures the amount seized by the creditors, net of the cost of bankrupcy, and weighted by the default probability, where $e^-(\bar{\varepsilon}^j) = E(\varepsilon/\varepsilon \le \bar{\varepsilon}^j)$ is the mean value of ε realized by the low-productivity firms.[2] The expression on the right-hand side of (8.2) is the no-default return required by foreign creditors.

Observe that Eqs. (8.1) and (8.2) together imply that

$$[1 - \Phi(\bar{\varepsilon}^j)] + \frac{\Phi(\bar{\varepsilon}^j)(1 - \mu)\{F(K^j)[1 + e^-(\bar{\varepsilon}^j)] + (1 - \delta)K^j\}}{F(K^j)(1 + \bar{\varepsilon}^j) + (1 - \delta)K^j} = \frac{1 + r^*}{1 + r^j}.$$

$$(8.3)$$

Because $\varepsilon^-(\bar{\varepsilon}^j) < \bar{\varepsilon}^j$ and $0 < \mu \le 1$, it follows that $r^j > r^*$, the difference being a default premium (which depends on, among other things, $K^j, \bar{\varepsilon}^j$, and μ).

The firm in this setup is competitive (that is, a price taker) only with respect to r^*, the international risk-free rate of return. This r^* cannot be influenced by the firm's actions. However, r^j, K^j, and $\bar{\varepsilon}^j$ are firm specific and must satisfy Eqs. (8.1) and (8.2). In making its investment [that is, $K^j - (1 - \delta)K_0^j$] and its financing (loan contract) decisions, the firm takes these constraints into account. Because these decisions are made before ε is known, that is, when all firms are (ex-ante) identical, they all make the same decision. Therefore, we henceforth drop the superscript j.

Consider now the investment-financing decision of the firm. Its objective is to maximize its net expected discounted value for its shareholders. Because consumers in this economy compete with foreign lenders in providing credits to the firms, they must, at equilibrium, earn the same rate of return as foreigners, namely, r^*. Hence, the net expected discounted value of the firm to its shareholders is

$$(1 + r^*)^{-1}[1 - \Phi(\bar{\varepsilon})]\{F(K)[1 + e^+(\bar{\varepsilon})] + (1 - \delta)K - [K - (1 - \delta)K_0](1 + r)\},$$

$$(8.4)$$

where $e^{+}(\bar{\varepsilon}) = E(\varepsilon/\varepsilon \geq \bar{\varepsilon})$ is the mean value of ε for the high-productivity firms. Note that the firm has a positive value in only the no-default states, that is, only when $\varepsilon \geq \bar{\varepsilon}$ and it fully repays the principal of and the interest (r) on the loan. The firm chooses K, $\bar{\varepsilon}$, and r so as to maximize Eq. (8.4), subject to Eqs. (8.1) and (8.2). Substituting Eq. (8.1) into the other constraint (8.2) and into objective function (8.4), we can eliminate the firm-specific interest rate r, and the optimization problem of the firm reduces to

$$\max_{\{K,\bar{\varepsilon}\}}\{(1 + r^{*})^{-1}[1 - \Phi(\bar{\varepsilon})]F(K)[e^{+}(\bar{\varepsilon}) - \bar{\varepsilon}]\}, \tag{8.5}$$

subject to

$$[1 - \Phi(\bar{\varepsilon})][F(K)(1 + \bar{\varepsilon}) + (1 - \delta)K] + \Phi(\bar{\varepsilon})(1 - \mu)\{F(K)$$
$$\times [1 + e^{-}(\bar{\varepsilon})] + (1 - \delta)K\} - [K - (1 - \delta)K_0](1 + r^{*}) \geq 0. \tag{8.6}$$

A solution of this problem defines an equal investment level for each firm $[I = K - (1 - \delta)K_0]$ and an equal firm-specific interest rate (r) and an equal default threshold $(\bar{\varepsilon})$. Note that $NI = I$ is also the total credit taken by all firms. The excess of this amount over national saving comprises the capital imports.

Note from either Eq. (8.4) or expression (8.5) that if a firm sets $\bar{\varepsilon} = 1$, then its net expected discounted value is zero. (Because in this case the firm will always default.) If the firm does not invest at all, then its net expected discounted value is $(1 + r^{*})^{-1}\{F[K_0(1 - \delta)] + K_0(1 - \delta)^2\}$, which is positive. Therefore, it always pays the firm to set a threshold level $\bar{\varepsilon}$ that would leave a positive probability of no default.

Note also that if the world rate of interest (r^{*}) is sufficiently high, then the firm will abstain from taking loans and making investments. This is because the firm-specific interest rate (r) must always include a default premium over r^{*}; see Eq. (8.3). However, at a sufficiently large interest on its loan, the firm will default in all states of nature (that is, values of ε). This contradicts our earlier conclusion that it does not pay the firm to default in all states of nature. A formal proof is provided in Appendix 8.1.

COUNTRY RISK

We have assumed so far that there is a fixed world rate of interest (r^{*}) at which foreign lenders are willing to extend credit to the domestic firms in the small economy. In reality, there are varities of world rates facing firms in different countries, depending on each country's credit rating. The credit rating is *external* to our (ex-ante) identical firms and depends on some aggregate (macro) economic variables or political factors.

Suppose, for instance, that the country's credit rating depends positively on its aggregate investment. Interpret now r^{*} as a basic interest rate (e.g., libor) and let π be a country-specific risk premium, so that firms borrow at $r^{*} + \pi$, where π is external to each individual firm. This π depends negatively on aggregate investment $NI = I$. That is, the more that a country invests (and the rosier its growth prospects look), then the lower the interest rate $(r^* + \pi)$ that it pays on its credits is.

Formally, the analysis now follows the same lines of the preceding section, except that $r^* + \pi$ replaces r^*. It is important to emphasize that although π depends on $NI = I$, this dependence is external to the firm. That is, when choosing $I = K - (1 - \delta)K_0$, the firm takes π as exogenously given in the same way that it views r^* as exogenous.

We turn now to the discussion of the equilibria in this case. Suppose that the equilibrium described in the preceding section involves a high level of aggregate investment. Then the country-specific risk premium introduced here would be very small (that is, the country gets a "flying-colors" credit rating). Hence the equilibrium will not change much now, and the country-specific risk premium would be hardly observable. This is referred to as a good equilibrium.

However, there may be another bad equilibrium with a very high π, no investment, and no foreign credit. (We have seen in the preceding section that if the world rate of interest is sufficiently large, investment is drawn down to zero). Thus a country may switch abruptly from the good equilibrium to the bad equilibrium, as its creditors may somehow, for reasons unexplained in the model, shift their beliefs about the country's credit worthiness. These new beliefs (that the country is at high credit risk) are self-fulfilling: Indeed, the country's investments dry out.

APPENDIX 8.1

From Eq. (8.1) we note that

$$1 + r \leqq \frac{F(K)(1 + 1) + (1 - \delta)K}{K - (1 - \delta)K_0}, \tag{A8.1}$$

because $\bar{\varepsilon} \leq 1$. Hence

$$1 + r \leqq \frac{2[F(K)/K] + (1 - \delta)}{1 - (1 - \delta)\frac{K_0}{K}} \equiv M(K). \tag{A8.2}$$

Because the average product of capital is assumed diminishing, it follows that

$$\lim_{K \to \infty} M(K) < 2\{F[K_0(1 - \delta)]/K_0(1 - \delta)\} + (1 - \delta).$$

Also,

$$\lim_{K \to K_0(1-\delta)} M(K) = 2\{F[K_0(1 - \delta)]/K_0(1 - \delta)\} + (1 - \delta).$$

Thus, there is an upper bound on the firm-specific interest rate (r) for which condition (8.1) can hold.

9   Foreign Portfolio Equity Investment and the Saving–Investment Correlation

INTRODUCTION

Even though financial markets today show a high degree of integration, with large amounts of capital flowing across international borders to take advantage of rates of return and risk-diversification benefits, there is still ample evidence of a home-bias portfolio. For instance, French and Poterba (1991) observed that Americans held roughly 94% of their equity wealth in the U.S. stock market. They also noted that the Japanese held roughly 98% of their equity wealth at home.

Similarly, Tesar and Werner (1995) found that despite the recent increase in U.S. equity investment abroad (including investment in emerging stock markets), the U.S. portfolio remains strongly biased toward domestic equity. They reported that equity-portfolio flows to Western Europe, as a fraction of the capitalized value of the U.S. equity markets, rose from only 0.3% in 1976 to approximately 2.2% in 1990. The share invested in Canada remained fairly constant, at less than 1%. More recently, Capital Asset Pricing Model (CAPM)-based portfolios are found to be much more diversified worldwide than is actually the case; see Lewis (1999) for a good survey.

Furthermore, this home bias is even noticeable among states within the U.S.: For instance, Huberman (1997) found that American investors have strong preferences toward firms located in their states over out-of-state firms.

Relatedly, when we consider total capital flows (including not only equity-portfolio flows, but also FDI, debt, and loan flows, etc.), the Feldstein–Horioka puzzle arises; see Feldstein and Horioka (1980). They demonstrated that long-term averages of national savings are highly correlated with the same averages of domestic investments in the OECD countries, despite the presumed capital openness of these countries. Recall that free capital mobility allows foreign funds to finance domestic investment, thereby eliminating the closed-economy tight identity (unitary correlation coefficient) between savings and investments.

Thus the high correlation between national savings and domestic investments is puzzling; see also Obstfeld (1995) and Baxter (1995).

In this chapter, we provide a theoretical explanation for the two puzzles, based on informational home bias; for a recent empirical application of this idea, see Portes and Rey (1999).

THE GORDON–BOVENBERG MODEL
OF HOME-BIAS INFORMATION

Suppose, for simplicity, that foreign portfolio equity investment (FPEI) is the sole channel through which foreign capital flows into the country. Officially, FPEI is defined as buying less than a certain small fraction (say, 10%–20%) of shares of a firm. However, from an economic point of view, the critical feature of FPEI is the lack of control of the foreign investor over the management of the domestic firm because of the absence of foreign managerial inputs. For our purposes, we shall simply assume that foreign investors buy shares in existing firms without exercising any form of control or applying their own managerial input.

In the next chapter, we introduce FDI in which foreign control and, perhaps, also management is exercised. This lack of control and management associated with portfolio investment and the distance from where the "action" takes place give rise to a home bias in information.

We model the uncertainty in the economy by following Gordon and Bovenberg (1996), as in the preceding chapter. Suppose again that there is a continuum of ex-ante identical domestic firms. Each firm uses capital input (K) in the first period to produce a single composite good in the second period. We continue to assume that capital depreciates at the rate δ. Output in the second period is equal to $F(K)(1 + \varepsilon)$, where $F(\cdot)$ is a production function exhibiting diminishing marginal productivity of capital and ε is a random productivity factor with zero mean that is independent across all firms. Factor ε is bounded from below by -1, so that output is always nonnegative. As before, ε is purely idiosyncratic, so that there is no aggregate uncertainty. For each ε, there will be exactly $N\Phi(\varepsilon)$ firms whose output in the second period will be less than or equal to $F(K)(1 + \varepsilon)$, where $\Phi(\cdot)$ is the cumulation distribution function of ε and N is the number of firms. Again, no one in the first period knows who these firms are. Thus, each firm faces a probability of $\Phi(\varepsilon)$ of having an output less than or equal to $F(K)(1 + \varepsilon)$ in the second period. As before, we assume that through proper portfolio diversification, consumers–savers behave in a risk-neutral way. We also normalize the number of firms to one, that is, $N = 1$.

Investment decisions are made by the firms before the state of the world (ε) is known. Because all firms face the same probability distribution of ε, they all choose the same level of investment. Denote the gross investment of the firm by I. Therefore, if its initial stock of capital in the first period, carried over from the preceding period, is $K_0(1 - \delta)$, then the stock of capital the firm uses in the first period is $K = (1 - \delta)K_0 + I$.

All firms are originally owned by domestic investors who equity finance their capital investment I. After this capital investment is made, the value of ε is revealed to domestic savers–investors, but not to foreign portfolio investors. The latter buy shares in the existing firms. The rationale for this informational asymmetry – the informational home bias – is the very reference to the foreigners as portfolio investors who are "far from the action" and therefore informationally handicapped.

Being unable to observe ε, foreign investors will offer the same price for all firms, reflecting the average productivity of the firms they purchase. On the other hand, domestic investors who do observe ε will not be willing to sell at that price the firms that have experienced higher than average values of ε. (Equivalently, domestic investors will outbid foreign investors for these firms.) Therefore, there will be a cutoff level of ε, say ε_0, such that all firms that experience a value of ε lower than the cutoff level will be purchased by foreigners. All other firms will be retained by domestic savers–investors. The cutoff level of ε is then defined by

$$\frac{F(K)[1 + e^-(\varepsilon_0)] + (1 - \delta)K}{1 + r^*} = \frac{F(K)(1 + \varepsilon_0) + (1 - \delta)K}{1 + \bar{r}}, \quad (9.1)$$

where

$$e^-(\varepsilon_0) = E(\varepsilon/\varepsilon \leq \varepsilon_0), \quad (9.2a)$$

and for later use we also define

$$e^+(\varepsilon_0) = E(\varepsilon/\varepsilon \geq \varepsilon_0), \quad (9.2b)$$

and, as in the preceding chapter,

$$\Phi(\varepsilon_0)e^-(\varepsilon_0) + [1 - \Phi(\varepsilon_0)]e^+(\varepsilon_0) = E(\varepsilon) = 0. \quad (9.3)$$

The value of a typical domestic firm in the second period is equal to its expected output plus its residual stock of capital, that is, $F(K)[1 + e^-(\varepsilon_0)] + (1 - \delta)K$. Because foreign portfolio investors will buy only those firms with $\varepsilon \leq \varepsilon_0$, the expected second-period value of a firm they buy is $F(K)[1 + e^-(\varepsilon_0)] + (1 - \delta)K$, which they then discount by the factor $1 + r^*$ to determine the price they are willing to pay for it in the first period, where r^* is the world rate of interest. At equilibrium, this price is equal to the price that a domestic investor is willing to pay for the firm that experiences a productivity value of ε_0. The cutoff price is equal to the output of the firm plus its residual capital, discounted at the domestic rate of interest $\bar{r}$. This explains equilibrium condition (9.1).

As $e^-(\varepsilon_0) < \varepsilon_0$, an interior equilibrium with both foreigners and residents having nonzero holdings in domestic firms requires that the foreigners' rate of return (r^*) be lower than the residents' rate of return ($\bar{r}$). In some sense, this means that foreign investors are overcharged for their purchases of domestic firms. They outbid domestic investors who are willing to pay *on average* only a price of $\{F(K)[1 + e^-(\varepsilon_0)] + (1 - \delta)K\}/(1 + \bar{r})$ for the low-productivity firms.

Consider now the capital investment decision of the firm that is made before ε becomes known. The firm seeks to maximize its market value, net of the original investment $[K - (1 - \delta)K_0]$. There is a probability $\Phi(\varepsilon_0)$ that it will be sold to foreign portfolio investors, who will pay $\{F(K)[1 + e^-(\varepsilon_0)] + (1 - \delta)K\}/(1 + r^*)$. There is a probability $[1 - \Phi(\varepsilon_0)]$ that it will be sold to domestic investors, who will pay, on average, $\{F(K)[1 + e^+(\varepsilon_0)] + (1 - \delta)K\}/(1 + \bar{r})$. Hence, the firm's expected market value, net of the original capital investment, is

$$-[K - (1 - \delta)K_0] + \frac{\Phi(\varepsilon_0)\{F(K)[1 + e^-(\varepsilon_0)] + (1 - \delta)K\}}{1 + r^*}$$
$$+ \frac{[1 - \Phi(\varepsilon_0)]\{F(K)[1 + e^+(\varepsilon_0)] + (1 - \delta)K\}}{1 + \bar{r}}. \tag{9.4}$$

Maximizing this expression with respect to K yields the following first-order condition:

$$-1 + \frac{\Phi(\varepsilon_0)\{F'(K)[1 + e^-(\varepsilon_0)] + (1 - \delta)\}}{1 + r^*}$$
$$+ \frac{[1 - \Phi(\varepsilon_0)]\{F'(K)[1 + e^+(\varepsilon_0)] + (1 - \delta)\}}{1 + \bar{r}} = 0. \tag{9.5}$$

Because the firm knows when making its capital investment decision that it will be sold to foreign portfolio investors at a "premium" if faced with low-productivity events, it tends to overinvest relative to the domestic rate of return ($\bar{r}$) and underinvest relative to the world rate of return (r^*):

$$r^* < F'(K) - \delta < \bar{r}. \tag{9.6}$$

(A formal proof of these inequalities is provided in Appendix 9.1.)

THE HOME-BIASED PORTFOLIO
AND THE SAVING–INVESTMENT CORRELATION

Note that relation (9.6) implies that the net return to domestic capital [namely, $F'(K) - \delta$] exceeds the world rate of interest. This means that the country in question does not attract enough foreign portfolio equity investment. Put differently, foreign portfolio investors are biased away from this country's equity toward their own countries' equity – the so-called home-bias portfolio.

Relatedly, foreign sources do not provide adequate financing for domestic investment. That is, national saving must play a larger role of financing domestic investment. Recall that in the full-information, frictionless capital mobility benchmark case there is a separation between savings and investments decisions: Domestic capital accumulates up to that level where its net marginal is equated to the world interest rate, no matter whether national saving falls short or exceeds the investment needed to let domestic capital reach this level. The difference between national saving and this investment is absorbed by current account imbalances. In the informational asymmetry case described in this chapter, foreign sources play a more limited role in financing domestic investment, thereby strengthening the correlation between national saving and domestic investment. This model helps provide a theoretical explanation for the Feldstein–Horioka (1980) puzzle about the strong correlation between national saving and domestic investment in the OECD countries, which are fairly open to capital flows.

Note that the home-bias portfolio and the related correlation between national saving and domestic investment in this chapter stem from the asymmetry in information between foreign portfolio investors and domestic savers–investors. Specifically, the latter are better informed than the former about the productivity (ε) of domestic firms. For this asymmetry to persist, it must be that the foreign portfolio investors cannot infer the productivity factor (ε) from the price of the firms retained by the domestic savers–investors. This may happen when, for instance, the high-ε firms are retained by their original domestic owners, so that they are not traded and thus not priced. Were foreign portfolio investors able to infer the true productivity of the high-ε firms from their market price, then, as long as $r^* < \bar{r}$, they would be able to bid up domestic savers–investors for all domestic firms; or, alternatively, $\bar{r}$ converges to r^*. In both cases, the net marginal product of capital will be driven down to r^*, in which case the home-bias portfolio disappears and the correlation between national saving and domestic investment is weakened. Nevertheless, markets with such fully revealing prices seldom exist.

CONCLUSION

We used a model of informational home bias to explain two related puzzles: The home-bias portfolio and the high correlation between national saving and domestic investment. The informational asymmetry gives rise to a market failure that is expressed in two types of inefficiency. First, there is foreign underinvestment: The net marginal product of domestic capital exceeds the world rate of interest. Second, there is domestic oversaving: The domestic rate of return to domestic savers exceeds the net marginal product of domestic capital. These two inefficiencies may be mitigated by a corrective (Pigouvian) tax policy; see Gordon and Bovenberg (1996) and Razin, Sadka, and Yuen (1998).

APPENDIX 9.1: A PROOF OF RELATION (9.6)

From Eq. (9.1) we conclude that

$$1 + r^* = \frac{F(K)[1 + e^-(\varepsilon_0)] + (1 - \delta)K}{F(K)(1 + \varepsilon_0) + (1 - \delta)K} \cdot (1 + \bar{r}) \qquad (A9.1)$$

or that

$$1 + \bar{r} = \frac{F(K)(1 + \varepsilon_0) + (1 - \delta)K}{F(K)[1 + e^-(\varepsilon_0)] + (1 - \delta)K} \cdot (1 + r^*). \qquad (A9.2)$$

Now, substituting Eq. (A9.1) into first-order condition (9.5) yields

$$1 + \bar{r} = \frac{\Phi(\varepsilon_0)\{F'(K)[1 + e^-(\varepsilon_0)] + (1 - \delta)\}\{F(K)(1 + \varepsilon_0) + (1 - \delta)K\}}{F(K)[1 + e^-(\varepsilon_0)] + (1 - \delta)K}$$
$$+ [1 - \Phi(\varepsilon_0)]\{F'(K)[1 + e^+(\varepsilon_0)] + (1 - \delta)\}. \qquad (A9.3)$$

Because $e^-(\varepsilon_0) < \varepsilon_0$, it follows that

$$\frac{F(K)(1 + \varepsilon_0) + (1 - \delta)K}{F(K)[1 + e^-(\varepsilon_0)] + (1 - \delta)K} > 1,$$

and hence, by Eq. (A9.3),

$$1 + \bar{r} > \Phi(\varepsilon_0)\{F'(K)[1 + e^-(\varepsilon_0)] + (1 - \delta)\}$$
$$+ [1 - \Phi(\varepsilon_0)]\{F'(K)[1 + e^+(\varepsilon_0)] + (1 - \delta)\}$$
$$= F'(K) + (1 - \delta),$$

where use is made of Eq. (9.3). This proves that

$$F'(K) - \delta < \bar{r}.$$

Similarly, we substitute Eq. (A9.2) into the first-order condition (9.5) to get

$$1 + r^* = \Phi(\varepsilon_0)\{F'(K)[1 + e^-(\varepsilon_0)] + (1 - \delta)\}$$
$$+ \frac{[1 - \Phi(\varepsilon_0)]\{F'(K)[1 + e^+(\varepsilon_0)] + (1 - \delta)\}\{F(K)[1 + e^-(\varepsilon_0)] + (1 - \delta)K\}}{F(K)(1 + \varepsilon_0) + (1 - \delta)K}.$$
$$\qquad (A9.4)$$

Because $e^-(\varepsilon_0) < \varepsilon_0$, it follows that

$$\frac{F(K)[1 + e^-(\varepsilon_0)] + (1 - \delta)K}{F(K)(1 + \varepsilon_0) + (1 - \delta)K} < 1,$$

and hence, by Eq. (A9.4),

$$
\begin{aligned}
1 + r^* &< \Phi(\varepsilon_0)\{F'(K)[1 + e^-(\varepsilon_0)] + (1-\delta)\} \\
&\quad + [1 - \Phi(\varepsilon_0)]\{F'(K)[1 + e^+(\varepsilon_0)] + (1-\delta)\} \\
&= F'(K) + (1-\delta),
\end{aligned}
$$

where use is made again of Eq. (9.3). This proves that $r^* < F'(K) - \delta$.

10 Foreign Direct Investment: A Challenge for Control of Domestic Capital

INTRODUCTION

In the preceding chapter, we considered portfolio equity flows. Formally, these are defined as purchases of insignificant shares in domestic firms. From an economic point of view, the distinctive feature of portfolio flows is the lack of control and management. However, FDI is different from foreign portfolio investment, concerning control and management of the domestic firm.

FDI has proven to be resilient during financial crises. In situations of international illiquidity, when the country's consolidated financial system has short-term obligations in foreign currency in excess of foreign currency that the country has access to on short notice, FDI flows provide the only direct link between the domestic capital market in the host country and the world capital market at large. For instance, FDI flows to the East Asian countries were remarkably stable during the global financial crises of 1997–98. In sharp contrast, portfolio equity and debt flows as well as bank loans dried up almost completely during the same period. The resilience of FDI to financial crises was also evident in the Mexican crisis of 1994 and the Latin American debt crisis of the early 1980s. This may reflect a unique characteristic of FDI, which is determined by considerations of ownership and control by multinationals of domestic activities that are more long term in nature.[1] In contrast, portfolio flows may be influenced to a greater extent by short-term fluctuations in the value of domestic currency and the availability of credit and liquidity.

In this chapter, we develop an information-based model of FDI that could explain the relatively large flows of FDI. The model features a built-in flip side, especially when FDI is leveraged domestically, as is often the case in the real world.[2] In the next chapter we discuss some positive externalities brought about by FDI flows. Note, nevertheless, that the model presented in this chapter is not intended to explain sudden reversals of flows and therefore does not attempt to explain the emergence of financial crises; see Chaps. 7 and 8 for some possible explanations for such crises.

AN INFORMATION-BASED MODEL OF FDI FLOWS

Conventionally, portfolio equity flows (discussed in the preceding chapter) are formally defined as purchases of small stakes (usually less than 10%) in domestic firms. However, we emphasized that, from an economic point of view, the distinctive feature of portfolio equity flows is that the foreign investors remain "silent" in the sense that they do not gain control of the domestic firm and do not put any managerial value added. An FDI, on the other hand, has a distinctive feature of gaining control and applying managerial value added to the domestic firm. This value added may attribute some positive externality to FDI – an issue that we shall address in the next chapter. In this chapter, we focus on the control aspect that may render "inside" information to the foreign investor, possibly to the disadvantage of the FDI-recipient country.

To reemphasize, FDI is not only an exchange of the ownership of domestic investment sites from domestic residents to foreign residents, but also a corporate governance mechanism in which the foreign investors exercise management and control over the host country firm. In so doing, the foreign direct investors gain crucial inside information about the productivity of the firm under their control – an obvious advantage over the uninformed domestic savers who are offering to buy shares in the firm. Taking advantage of their superior information, the foreign direct investors will tend to retain the high-productivity firms under their ownership and control and sell the low-productivity firms to these uninformed savers.

We follow the preceding chapter in modeling the risk in this economy. Suppose there is a very large number (N) of ex-ante identical domestic firms. Each firm uses capital input (K) in the first period to produce a single composite good in the second period. We assume that capital depreciates at the rate δ. Output in the second period is equal to $F(K)(1 + \varepsilon)$, where $F(\cdot)$ is a production function exhibiting diminishing marginal productivity of capital and ε is a random productivity factor with zero mean and is independent across all firms. We normalize the number of firms to be one: $N = 1$.

As before, capital investment decisions are made by the firms before the state of the world (ε) is known. Because all firms face the same probability distribution of ε, they all choose the same level of investment. They then seek funds to finance the investment. At this stage, the owners–managers of the firms are better informed than the outside fund suppliers. Specifically, we assume that the owners–managers, being "close to the action," observe ε before they make their financing decisions; but the fund providers, being "far away from the action," do not.

When investment is equity financed, the original owners–managers observe ε while the new potential shareholders of the firm do not. The market will be trapped in the "lemons" situation described by Akerlof (1970). At the price offered by the new (uninformed) potential equity buyers, which reflects the

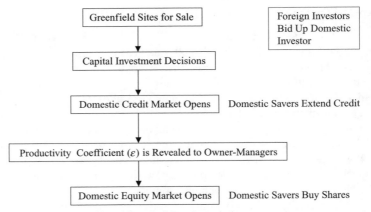

Fig. 10.1. Sequencing of firm decisions in period one.

average productivity of all firms (that is, the average level of ε) in the market, the owner–manager of a firm experiencing a higher-than-average value of ε will not be willing to sell its shares and will pull out of the market completely. In the absence of FDI, the equity market will fail.

However, a domestic credit market can do a better job of channeling domestic savings into domestic investment. Even FDI can utilize this market. In fact, it is often observed that FDI is highly leveraged domestically. After gaining control of the domestic firm, a foreign direct investor typically resorts to the domestic credit market to finance new investments and possibly sell (shares of) the firm in the domestic equity market later on.

The sequencing of firm decisions, all conducted in period one, is as follows (see Fig. 10.1). Before ε is revealed to anyone (that is, under effectively symmetric information), foreign investors bid up domestic firms from their original domestic owners; then investment decisions are made; and finally, full financing through domestic credit is secured. Then, ε is revealed to the owners–managers (who are all foreigners), but not also to domestic portfolio equity investors. At this stage, shares are offered in the domestic equity market and the ownership in some of the firms is transferred to the domestic investors. In the initial stage (that is, when ε is revealed to no one), the foreign direct investors are able to outbid the domestic savers because the latter are assumed to lack access to amounts of funds large enough to seize control of the firms; whereas the former, by assumption, are not liquidity constrained.[3]

The domestic credit market operates as described in Chap. 8. Because credit is extended ex-ante, before ε is revealed, firms cannot sign default-free loan contracts with the lenders. We therefore consider loan contracts that allow for the possibility of default. The loan contract is characterized by a loan rate (r), with possible default, and a threshold value ($\bar{\varepsilon}$) of the productivity parameter as follows:

$$F(K)(1 + \bar{\varepsilon}) + (1 - \delta)K = [K - (1 - \delta)K_0](1 + r). \tag{10.1}$$

When the realized value of ε is larger than $\bar{\varepsilon}$, the firm is solvent and will thus pay the lenders the promised amount, consisting of the principal $K - (1 - \delta)K_0$, plus the interest $r[K - (1 - \delta)K_0]$, as given by the right-hand side of Eq. (10.1). If, however, ε is smaller than $\bar{\varepsilon}$, the firm will default. In the case of default, the lenders must incur a cost in order to verify the true value of ε and to seize the residual value of the firm. This cost, interpretable as the cost of bankruptcy, is assumed, as before, to be proportional to the firm's realized gross return, $\mu[F(K)(1 + \varepsilon) + (1 - \delta)K]$, where $\mu \leq 1$ is the factor of proportionality. Net of this cost, the lenders will receive $(1 - \mu)[F(K)(1 + \varepsilon) + (1 - \delta)K]$.

Because there is no aggregate risk, the expected rate of return required by domestic consumers–savers, denoted by $\bar{r}$, can be secured by sufficient diversification. Therefore the default rate of interest, r, must offer a premium over and above the default-free rate, $\bar{r}$, according to

$$[1 - \Phi(\bar{\varepsilon})][K - (1 - \delta)K_0](1 + r) + \Phi(\bar{\varepsilon})(1 - \mu)\{F(K)[1 + e^-(\bar{\varepsilon})]$$
$$+ (1 - \delta)K\} = [K - (1 - \delta)K_0](1 + \bar{r}), \tag{10.2'}$$

where $\Phi(\cdot)$ is the cumulative probability distribution of ε and $e^-(\bar{\varepsilon})$ is the mean value of ε realized by the low-productivity firms (see Chap. 8 or Chap. 9). The first term on the left-hand side of Eq. (10.2') is the contracted principal and interest payment, weighted by the no-default probability. The second term measures the net residual value of the firm, weighted by the default probability. The right-hand side is the no-default return required by the domestic lender.

The firm in this setup is competitive (that is, a price taker) only with respect to $\bar{r}$, the market default-free rate of return. This $\bar{r}$ cannot be influenced by the firm's actions. However, r, K, and $\bar{\varepsilon}$ are firm specific and must satisfy Eqs. (10.1) and (10.2'). As before, the firm takes these constraints into account in making its investment [that is, in choosing $K - (1 - \delta)K_0$] and its financing (loan contract) decisions.

In the equity market, which opens after ε is revealed to the (foreign) owners–managers, there is a cutoff level of ε, denoted by ε_0, such that all firms experiencing a value of ε above ε_0 will be retained by the foreign direct investors and all other firms (with ε below ε_0) will be sold to domestic savers; see also Chap. 9. This cutoff level of ε is given by

$$\frac{F(K)(1 + \varepsilon_0) + (1 - \delta)K - [K - (1 - \delta)K_0](1 + r)}{1 + r^*}$$
$$= \left[\frac{\Phi(\bar{\varepsilon})}{\Phi(\varepsilon_0)}\right] \cdot 0 + \left[\frac{\Phi(\varepsilon_0) - \Phi(\bar{\varepsilon})}{\Phi(\varepsilon_0)}\right]$$
$$\times \left\{\frac{F(K)[1 + \hat{e}(\bar{\varepsilon}, \varepsilon_0)] + (1 - \delta)K - [K - (1 - \delta)K_0](1 + r)}{1 + \bar{r}}\right\}, \tag{10.3'}$$

where $\hat{e}(\bar{\varepsilon}, \varepsilon_0) \equiv E(\varepsilon/\bar{\varepsilon} \leq \varepsilon \leq \varepsilon_0)$ is the conditional expectation of ε given that ε lies between $\bar{\varepsilon}$ and ε_0.

Note that firms that experience a value of ε below $\bar{\varepsilon}$ default and have zero value. These firms are not retained by the foreign direct investors; hence $\varepsilon_0 \geq \bar{\varepsilon}$. All other firms generate in the second period a *net* cash flow of $F(K)(1 + \varepsilon) + (1 - \delta)K - [K - (1 - \delta)K_0](1 + r)$. The left-hand side of Eq. (10.3′) represents the marginal (from the top of the distribution) firm retained by foreign investors. The right-hand side of Eq. (10.3′) is the expected value of the firms that are purchased by domestic savers. With a conditional probability of $[\Phi(\varepsilon_0) - \Phi(\bar{\varepsilon})]/\Phi(\varepsilon_0)$, they generate a net expected cash flow of $F(K)[1 + \hat{e}(\bar{\varepsilon}, \varepsilon_0)] + (1 - \delta)K - [K - (1 - \delta)K_0](1 + r)$; and with a probability of $\Phi(\bar{\varepsilon})/\Phi(\varepsilon_0)$, they generate a zero net cash flow. This explains Eq. (10.3′).[4]

We can substitute Eq. (10.1) into Eqs. (10.2′) and (10.3′) to eliminate r and then rearrange terms to obtain

$$[1 - \Phi(\bar{\varepsilon})] F(K)(1 + \bar{\varepsilon}) + \Phi(\bar{\varepsilon})(1 - \mu)F(K)[1 + e^-(\bar{\varepsilon})]$$
$$+ [1 - \Phi(\bar{\varepsilon})\mu](1 - \delta)K = [K - (1 - \delta)K_0](1 + \bar{r}), \qquad (10.2)$$

$$\frac{\varepsilon^0 - \bar{\varepsilon}}{1 + r^*} = \left[\frac{\Phi(\varepsilon_0) - \Phi(\bar{\varepsilon})}{\Phi(\varepsilon_0)} \right] \cdot \left[\frac{\hat{e}(\bar{\varepsilon}, \varepsilon_0) - \bar{\varepsilon}}{1 + \bar{r}} \right]. \qquad (10.3)$$

Consider now the capital investment decision of the firm that is made before ε becomes known, while it is still owned by foreign direct investors. With a probability of $\Phi(\varepsilon_0) - \Phi(\bar{\varepsilon})$, it will be sold to domestic savers who pay a positive price equaling

$$\{F(K)[1 + \hat{e}(\bar{\varepsilon}, \varepsilon_0)] + (1 - \delta)K - [K - (1 - \delta)K_0](1 + r)\}/(1 + \bar{r})$$
$$= F(K)[\hat{e}(\bar{\varepsilon}, \varepsilon_0) - \bar{\varepsilon}]/(1 + \bar{r})$$

by use of Eq. (10.1). With a probability of $1 - \Phi(\varepsilon_0)$, it will be retained by the foreign investors for whom it is worth

$$\{F(K)[1 + e^+(\varepsilon_0)] + (1 - \delta)K - [K - (1 - \delta)K_0](1 + r)\}/(1 + r^*)$$
$$= F(K)[e^+(\varepsilon_0) - \bar{\varepsilon}]/(1 + r^*),$$

by use of Eq. (10.1), where $e^+(\varepsilon_0)$ is the mean value of the high-productivity firms. Hence the firm seeks to maximize

$$V = [1 - \Phi(\varepsilon_0)] \cdot \left\{ \frac{F(K)[e^+(\varepsilon_0) - \bar{\varepsilon}]}{1 + r^*} \right\}$$
$$+ \Phi(\bar{\varepsilon}) \cdot 0 + [\Phi(\varepsilon_0) - \Phi(\bar{\varepsilon})] \cdot \left\{ \frac{F(K)[\hat{e}(\bar{\varepsilon}, \varepsilon_0) - \bar{\varepsilon}]}{1 + \bar{r}} \right\}, \qquad (10.4)$$

subject to constraint (10.2), by choice of K and $\bar{\varepsilon}$, given ε_0.[5] The first-order conditions are given in Appendix 10.1.

The (maximized) value of V in Eq. (10.4) is also the price paid by the foreign direct investors at the greenfield stage of investment, or through merger and acquisition prior to the implementation of a significant investment project. Because the value of ε is not known at this point, the same price is paid for all firms. After ε is revealed to the foreign direct investors, the low-ε firms are then resold to domestic savers, all at the same price, because ε is not observed by these savers. Net capital inflows through FDI therefore are given by

$$\text{FDI} = N[1 - \Phi(\varepsilon_0)]F(K)[e^+(\varepsilon_0) - \bar{\varepsilon}]/(1 + r^*) \tag{10.5}$$

[see Eq. (10.4)].

The remainder of the equilibrium conditions are standard. Let there be a representative consumer with a utility function $u(c_1, c_2)$, where c_i is consumption in period $i = 1, 2$. The first-period resource constraint is given by

$$\text{FDI} = N[K - (1 - \delta)K_0] - [NF(K_0) - c_1]. \tag{10.6}$$

The second-period resource constraint is

$$\begin{aligned} c_2 = {}& N[F(K) + (1 - \delta)K] - \text{FDI}(1 + r^*) - N\mu\Phi(\bar{\varepsilon}) \\ & \times \{F(K)[1 + e^-(\bar{\varepsilon})] + (1 - \delta)K\}. \end{aligned} \tag{10.7}$$

Finally, the consumers–savers do not have access to the world capital market and can only borrow/lend from the domestic market. As a result, in maximizing utility, the representative consumers–saver will equate her or his intertemporal marginal rate of substitution to the domestic risk-free rate of return,

$$\frac{u_1(c_1, c_2)}{u_2(c_1, c_2)} = 1 + \bar{r}, \tag{10.8}$$

where u_i is the marginal utility of c_i, $i = 1, 2$.

In this model, the eight equations [that is, Eqs. (10.2), (10.3), and (10.5)–(10.8), together with the two first-order conditions associated with the choice of K and $\bar{\varepsilon}$ derived in Appendix 10.1] determine the eight endogenous variables, that is, K, $\bar{r}$, $\bar{\varepsilon}$, ε_0, c_1, c_2, FDI, and the Lagrange multipler λ associated with constraint (10.2).

GAINS (LOSSES) FROM FDI FLOWS

To flash out in a simplified manner the kind of gains or losses brought about by FDI, we compare the equilibrium allocation in the presence of FDI with the closed-economy equilibrium allocation. The latter economy is referred to as a financial autarky.

Financial Autarky

In the financial autarky case, the "lemons" problem will drive the equity market out of existence. Firms will have to rely solely on the provision of domestic credit in financing their investment projects. The firm-specific debt contract continues to be characterized by a default-risk interest rate (r) and a threshold productivity level $(\bar{\varepsilon})$ that satisfy cutoff condition (10.1). The default-free interest rate $(\bar{r})$ is still defined implicitly by Eq. (10.2'). The firm's investment decision is to choose K, r, and $\bar{\varepsilon}$ to solve the following problem:

$$\max_{\{K,r,\bar{\varepsilon}\}} (F(K) - \Phi(\bar{\varepsilon})\{F(K)[1 + e^-(\bar{\varepsilon})] + (1 - \delta)K\}$$
$$- [1 - \Phi(\bar{\varepsilon})][K - (1 - \delta)K_0](1 + r)), \qquad (10.4')$$

subject to Eqs. (10.1) and (10.2'). We can again use Eq. (10.1) to substitute out the risky interest rate (r) in (10.2') as well as in the objective function above. The first-order conditions with respect to K and $\bar{\varepsilon}$ for this reduced problem are laid out in Appendix 10.1. Utility maximization by the consumers–savers continues to yield the same intertemporal condition (10.8). In the absence of capital flows, FDI $\equiv 0$ in the two resource constraints (10.6) and (10.7). The three equations (10.2), (10.6), and (10.7) and the two first-order conditions for K and $\bar{\varepsilon}$ (laid out in Appendix 10.1) determine the five endogenous variables K^A, $\bar{r}^A$, $\bar{\varepsilon}^A$, c_1^A, and c_2^A.

Numerical Simulations

We use numerical simulations to compare the FDI case with the autarky case. In the simulation, we consider a logarithmic utility function $[u(c_1, c_2) = \ln(c_1) + \gamma \ln(c_2)]$, with a subjective discount factor γ, a Cobb–Douglas production function $[F(K) = AK^\alpha]$, and a uniform distribution of ε defined over the interval $[-\beta, \beta]$. We set the parameter values as follows: $\gamma = 0.28$, $\alpha = 0.33$, $\delta = 0.56$, $N = 1$, $A = 0.9$, $K_0 = 0.03$, $\beta = 0.84$, and $\mu = 0.05$. Because we think of each period as constituting half of the lifetime of a generation (that is, approximately 25 years), the values of γ and δ are chosen in such a way as to reflect an annual time preference rate of approximately 3% and an annual depreciation rate of approximately 3%. We calculate also the welfare level of the representative consumer in the two cases.

The welfare gain (loss) from FDI is measured by the uniform percentage change in c_1 and c_2 that is needed to lift the autarkic utility level to the FDI utility level. FDI is beneficial when, and only when, this percentage change is positive; FDI entails a loss to the host economy if and only if this percentage change is negative.

The Welfare Effects of FDI

FDI flows have two possibly conflicting effects on welfare. The first effect is to allow foreign sources to add to the resources available to finance domestic investment. Traditionally, this effect is welfare enhancing. However, in our model there are two factors that mitigate this effect: (i) FDI is domestically leveraged and the initial amount is pulled out partially after a short while by a resale of some firms (the low-productivity firms) to domestic residents. Therefore foreign savings finance a relatively small portion of the capital accumulation generated by FDI.[6] (ii) The informational asymmetry associated with the control of the firm generates a market failure: The net marginal product of capital, as in Chap. 9, is not equated to the world rate of interest even though the latter is equal to the social cost of capital. Thus, the amount of FDI flows may not be efficient. For instance, as we shall see in the simulations, capital may flow in even when the net marginal product of capital under autarky is lower than the world rate of interest. Thus the aforementioned effect of FDI on welfare is not clear cut.

The second effect of FDI is to facilitate the channeling of domestic saving into domestic investment by getting around a "lemons" problem in the autarkic economy. With FDI a domestic equity market is sustainable, whereas without FDI the market collapses. However, here again there is a mitigating effect that is due to the informational asymmetry that creates a market failure. Therefore once again we cannot ascertain that this effect is always welfare enhancing; it may well reduce welfare.

As explained above, the first effect is potentially positive. The magnitude of its contribution to welfare depends on the size of the gap between the net marginal product of domestic capital under autarky and the world rate of interest, as elementary trade theory teaches us; see, for instance, Caves, Frankel, and Jones (1996). If this return gap is not large, the first effect should not be expected to be sizable. In addition, in our case there are also two mitigating factors that reduce its benefit and could even turn it negative. Similarly, the second potentially positive effect is also mitigated by an adverse-selection distortion. Hence, international openness, which takes the form of FDI inflows in our context, is not necessarily beneficial.

This point is illustrated in Fig. 10.2, in which the FDI equilibrium is plotted for alternative levels of the world rate of interest. We compare the utility of the representative consumer, generated by free flows of FDI for different world rates of interest (r^*), with the utility entailed under financial autarky. Naturally, the autarky utility level does not depend on the world rate of interest (r^*). We then measure the benefit (possibly negative) of FDI by calculating the percentage of change in lifetime consumption under autarky (that is, the uniform change in c_1 and c_2) that will lift autarkic utility to the corresponding utility level in the presence of FDI. When this percentage of change is negative it means that

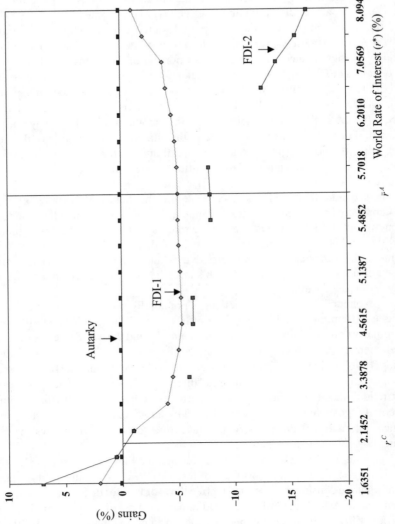

Fig. 10.2. Welfare gains from FDI relative to financial autarky.

autarkic utility is higher than the corresponding utility level under FDI, that is, free FDI flows actually *reduce* welfare!

Note that there is a strong element of *circularity* involved in two credit-market relationships, Eqs. (10.1) and (10.2′). To see this, note that, on the one hand, a rise in the firm-specific rate of interest (including the risk premium) r implies that the cutoff productivity level (which determines the number of solvent firms and the number of insolvent firms in equilibrium) $\bar{\varepsilon}$ must rise. This is because more firms are expected to default with the rise in the rate of interest [see Eq. (10.1)]. On the other hand, when the cutoff productivity level $\bar{\varepsilon}$ rises, the return on risky credit must rise, and therefore $\bar{r}$ should rise as well. The increase in r is needed to restore the balance between the risky return and the alternative return on the risk-free credit, governed by the risk-free rate of interest, $\bar{r}$ [see Eq. (10.2′)]. Interacting with the adverse-selection effect of FDI, the circularity property leads, under some parameter configurations, to a multiplicity of equilibria.

The first equilibrium, represented by the curve with squares in Fig. 10.2, is characterized by a relatively high rate of default on credit ($\bar{\varepsilon}$) and a high firm-specific interest rate (r), whereas the second, indicated by diamonds, is characterized by a low default rate ($\bar{\varepsilon}$) and a low firm-specific interest rate (r). Evidently, a sudden shift from the bad equilibria to the good equilibria, triggered by a switch in expectations, can have significant effect on the economy. For example, as shown in Figs. 10.2 and 10.3, at the world interest rate of 7.8%, a shift from the good equilibrium to the bad equilibrium leads to a rise in the FDI from a medium fraction of the GDP (approximately 8%) to a large fraction (approximately 13%) of the GDP. At the same time, the capital stock rises, the risk-free rate of interest falls, first-period consumption rises while second-period consumption declines, the solvency/insolvency cutoff productivity level $\bar{\varepsilon}$ rises, and the productivity cutoff level ε_0 that determines the number of low-productivity firms that the foreign direct investors sell in the domestic stock market declines.

A critical value of the rate of interest, which implies that the inflows of capital are neither welfare improving nor welfare reducing, is denoted by r^c. If the world rate of interest is equal to this rate, the beneficial effect of FDI, being the flow of foreign saving that complements domestic saving in the financing of domestic investment (when the world rate of interest is still below the autarkic domestic rate of interest) is offset by the adverse-selection effect of FDI on the domestic stock market. When $r^* < r^c$, FDI is beneficial; when $r^* > r^c$, FDI flows reduce welfare. The rate r^c is shown in Fig. 10.2 by the intersection between the two curves representing the FDI equilibria (overlapping at this point) with the horizontal axis. This r^c is equal to 2%, below the autarkic rate of interest ($\bar{r}^A$), which is 5.6%.

Consider first the case where the world rate of interest (r^*) is below the critical rate of interest (r^c), which, in turn, is smaller than the autarkic rate of interest ($\bar{r}^A$). Recall that in a distortion-free, perfectly competitive setup,

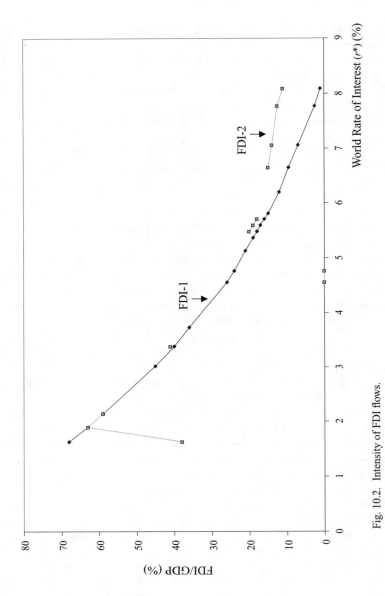

Fig. 10.2. Intensity of FDI flows.

the autarkic rate of interest is the benchmark rate for predicting the direction of capital movements. If the world rate of interest falls short of the benchmark rate, capital flows in, and the larger the difference between the rates, the larger the gains from capital mobility. (When the world rate of interest exceeds the benchmark rate, capital should efficiently flow out.) Therefore we expect the positive (traditional) welfare effect of FDI, which allows foreign-saving financing of domestic investment in addition to the domestic-saving finance, to dominate the adverse-selection negative effect of FDI on the domestic equity market. One of the two equilibria (described by the curve with squares) delivers utility levels above the autarkic level of utility, in accordance with the traditional gains-from-trade theorem. This good equilibrium is associated also with low-FDI flows. The bad equilibrium (relative to the good equilibrium) is associated with high-FDI flows; see Fig. 10.3. FDI flows may be excessive. To sustain the good low-FDI equilibrium, policymakers may resort to a ceiling on FDI flows. Interestingly, the good equilibrium is associated with a high default rate ($\bar{\varepsilon}$) and a high firm-specific rate of interest (r).

Consider next the other case in which the world rate of interest (r^*) is above the critical rate of interest, that is, $r^* > r^c$. Our simulations show that FDI flows are clearly welfare reducing. Among the two FDI equilibria depicted in Fig. 10.2, the equilibrium associated with the high FDI delivers low utility, whereas the equilibrium associated with the low FDI generates relatively high level of utility. However, the utility levels that are associated with low- and high-FDI equilibria both fall short of the level of utility under financial autarky in the absence of FDI. Therefore the adverse-selection feature of FDI dominates, and the host economy loses from the excessive FDI inflows. Of particular interest in this case is when r^* is also above $\bar{r}^A$. In this subcase, in a distortion-free environment, FDI should have not efficiently flown in at all. Nevertheless, FDI does flow in and is therefore detrimental to welfare. The prescription policy is straightforward: A total ban on FDI inflows is warranted whenever the world rate of interest (r^*) exceeds a critical level (r^c).

CONCLUSION

In this chapter, we explored the welfare implications of FDI, which is a major form of capital flows to developing countries. FDI flows, like other types of capital flows, are presumed traditionally to raise welfare in the host country when the marginal product of its domestic capital is higher than the opportunity rate of return (the world rate of interest). We alluded to two pitfalls. First, FDI may be heavily leveraged domestically and also partially resold to domestic savers. In such a case the resulting *net* capital flow is substantially smaller than the initial *gross* amount recorded as FDI in the balance-of-payments statistics. Second, there typically exists an informational asymmetry between the "insiders" and the "outsiders" of a firm. This asymmetry happens to promote FDI flows. It enables the foreign investors who command large funds to gain access to the firm's "inside" – a flip side of FDI flows from the point of view of the host country.

APPENDIX 10.1: DERIVATION OF FIRST-ORDER CONDITIONS FOR THE FIRM'S INVESTMENT PROBLEM

In the presence of FDI-open-economy case, the maximization of the firm value, V, as specified in Eq. (10.4), with respect to K and $\bar{\varepsilon}$ yields the following first-order conditions:

$$
0 = \left\{ \frac{[1 - \Phi(\varepsilon^o)][e^+(\varepsilon^o) - \bar{\varepsilon}]}{1 + r^*} + \frac{[\Phi(\varepsilon^o) - \Phi(\bar{\varepsilon})][\hat{e}(\bar{\varepsilon}, \varepsilon^o) - \bar{\varepsilon}]}{1 + \bar{r}} \right\} F'(K)
$$
$$
+ \lambda\{[1 - \Phi(\bar{\varepsilon})](1 + \bar{\varepsilon}) + \Phi(\bar{\varepsilon})(1 - \mu)[1 + e^-(\bar{\varepsilon})]\} F'(K)
$$
$$
- \lambda(\bar{r} + \delta) - \lambda\Phi(\bar{\varepsilon})\mu(1 - \delta), \qquad (A10.1)
$$

and

$$
0 = -\frac{1 - \Phi(\varepsilon^o)}{1 + r^*} - \frac{\Phi'(\bar{\varepsilon})[\hat{e}(\bar{\varepsilon}, \varepsilon^o) - \bar{\varepsilon}]}{1 + \bar{r}}
$$
$$
+ \frac{[\Phi(\varepsilon^o) - \Phi(\bar{\varepsilon})]\left[\dfrac{\partial \hat{e}}{\partial \bar{\varepsilon}}(\bar{\varepsilon}, \varepsilon^o) - 1\right]}{1 + \bar{r}} - \lambda\Phi'(\bar{\varepsilon})(1 + \bar{\varepsilon})
$$
$$
+ \lambda[1 - \Phi(\bar{\varepsilon})] + \lambda\Phi'(\bar{\varepsilon})(1 - \mu)[1 + e^-(\bar{\varepsilon})]
$$
$$
+ \lambda\Phi(\bar{\varepsilon})(1 - \mu)\frac{de^-(\bar{\varepsilon})}{d\bar{\varepsilon}}F(K) - \lambda\mu\Phi'(\bar{\varepsilon})(1 - \delta)K, \qquad (A10.2)
$$

where λ is a Lagrange multiplier. Our numerical simulations suggest that there will be domestic under-saving and foreign over-investment, i.e., $\bar{r} < F'(K) - \delta < r^*$. In the absence of FDI, the first-order conditions for the maximization problem as stated in (10.4') with respect to K and $\bar{\varepsilon}$ are:

$$
0 = F'(K) - \Phi(\bar{\varepsilon})\{F'(K)[1 + e^-(\bar{\varepsilon})] + (1 - \delta)\}
$$
$$
- [1 - \Phi(\bar{\varepsilon})][F'(K)(1 + \bar{\varepsilon}) + (1 - \delta)]
$$
$$
+ \lambda[1 - \Phi(\bar{\varepsilon})][F'(K)(1 + \bar{\varepsilon}) + (1 - \delta)]
$$
$$
+ \lambda\Phi(\bar{\varepsilon})(1 - \mu)\{F'(K)[1 + e^-(\bar{\varepsilon})] + (1 - \delta)\}
$$
$$
- \lambda(1 + \bar{r}), \qquad (A10.1')
$$

and

$$
0 = -\Phi'(\bar{\varepsilon})\{F(K)[1 + e^-(\bar{\varepsilon})] + (1 - \delta)K\}
$$
$$
- \Phi(\bar{\varepsilon})F(K)[de^-(\bar{\varepsilon})/d\bar{\varepsilon}] - [1 - \Phi(\bar{\varepsilon})]F(K)
$$
$$
+ \Phi'(\bar{\varepsilon})[F(K)(1 + \bar{\varepsilon}) + (1 - \delta)K] + \lambda[1 - \Phi(\bar{\varepsilon})]F(K)
$$
$$
- \lambda\Phi'(\bar{\varepsilon})[F(K)(1 + \bar{\varepsilon}) + (1 - \delta)K]
$$
$$
+ \lambda\Phi'(\bar{\varepsilon})(1 - \mu)\{F(K)[1 + e^-(\bar{\varepsilon})] + (1 - \delta)K\}
$$
$$
+ \lambda\Phi(\bar{\varepsilon})(1 - \mu)\{F(K)[de^-(\bar{\varepsilon})/d\bar{\varepsilon}]. \qquad (A10.2')
$$

11 Foreign Direct Investment: A Vehicle for Technology Transfer and Increased Competition

INTRODUCTION

Foreign direct investment is not merely just another form of capital flows. We pointed out in the preceding chapter a distinctive feature of FDI – control and management – and discussed its potential pitfalls. Nevertheless, it is common-place for governments in developing and emerging countries to woo FDI. Indeed FDI often offers significant advantages to the host countries, over and beyond the very flow of additional capital. In this chapter, we analyze two nontraditional benefits of FDI: The promotion of competition and the international transfer of technology.[1]

We start with an elementary view of certain advantages of FDI. Consider an autarkic situation in the host country in which only traditional inputs are used for domestic production and domestic input markets are plagued by perils of imperfect competition. We now open the economy to FDI flows. Suppose that FDI can bring new inputs to an economy and can promote competition in the domestic input market. We view technology transfer as the introduction of new inputs brought in by the foreign direct investors in the sense that total factor productivity can be raised by the addition of more varieties of inputs.

Consider, first, an elementary *partial* equilibrium setting. The gain from increased competition in the use of traditional inputs is illustrated in Fig. 11.1. Suppose that the autarkic (noncompetitive) price for a typical traditional input is w whereas its average (=marginal) cost is unity. Total economic surplus is the area $CABE$, consisting of a consumer's surplus of FAB and a producer's surplus of $CFBE$. Now, suppose that FDI flows that also bring new inputs increase competition in the traditional input market to the level of perfect competition, so that the input price falls to unity. Economic surplus rises to be the area CAG, consisting wholly of a consumer's surplus. The economic gain from increased competition in the domestic input market is therefore measured by the area EBG.

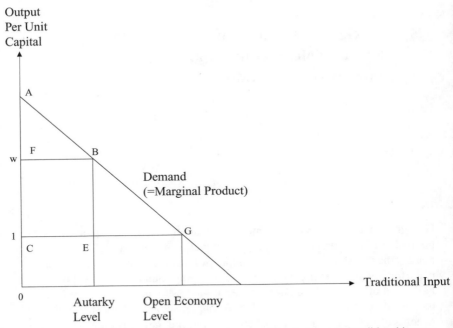

Fig. 11.1. Gains from an increase in competition in the use of traditional inputs.

Similarly, the gain from the introduction of a new input is illustrated in Fig. 11.2. Suppose that the new input is sold in the domestic market at a price of unity. Then the technology-transfer gain is measured by the area ABC.

A SECOND LOOK

The partial-equilibrium analysis of the preceding section is now extended in a straightforward manner into a general equilibrium setting in order to evaluate the importance of increased competition and the transfer of technology in the next section. Suppose, as before, that the economy produces a single all-purpose (consumption and capital) good. However, this time capital is a composite good consisting originally (under autarky) of M inputs $(k_1, k_2, \ldots, k_M)$ as follows:

$$K = \left(\sum_{j=1}^{M} k_j^{\theta}\right)^{1/\theta}, \tag{11.1}$$

where $0 < \theta < 1$. The production function is of the Cobb–Douglas type:

$$Y = AK^{\alpha}, \tag{11.2}$$

where $0 < \alpha < 1$. The elasticity of substitution in production between any two inputs is $(1 - \theta)^{-1}$.

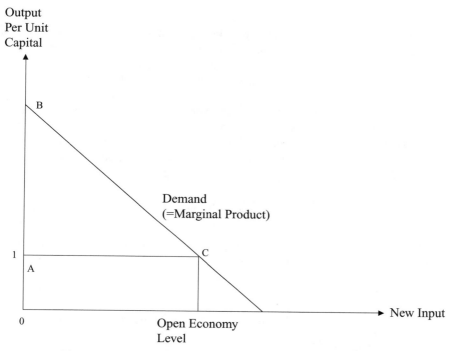

Fig. 11.2. Technological transfer: gains from the introduction of new inputs.

When the cost of production is held constant, a mere increase in the number of inputs can generate more output. To see this, suppose that either $\hat{k}$ units each of M kinds of inputs or $\tilde{k}$ units each of $M + m$ kinds of inputs can be used to comprise the same aggregate level of capital stock $(\bar{K})$, that is, $M\hat{k} = (M + m)\tilde{k} = \bar{K}$. If these inputs command the same price, then in each case the cost of production is the same. Then,

$$Y(M, \hat{k}) = A \left(\sum_{j=1}^{M} \hat{k}^{\theta} \right)^{\alpha/\theta} = A[M(\bar{K}/M)^{\theta}]^{\alpha/\theta} = AM^{\alpha(1-\theta)/\theta} \bar{K}^{\alpha},$$

$$Y(M + m, \tilde{k}) = A \left(\sum_{j=1}^{M} \tilde{k}^{\theta} \right)^{\alpha/\theta} = A\{(M + m)[\bar{K}/(M + m)]^{\theta}\}^{\alpha/\theta}$$

$$= A(M + m)^{\alpha(1-\theta)/\theta} \bar{K}^{\alpha}.$$

Obviously, $Y(M + m, \tilde{k}) > Y(M, \hat{k})$ for $m > 0$, that is, there exist productivity gains from an increase in the variety of inputs. From the growth-accounting perspective, a 1% growth in the variety of inputs will translate into an $\alpha(1 - \theta)/\theta$ percent growth in total output.

Autarky

We view the market structure for capital inputs as monopolistically competitive. There are M symmetric input-coordinating firms. Each firm buys each specific input (k_i) from the households at the competitive price of unity and sells the aggregate stock to the final producers at a monopolistically competitive price of w_i.

We follow the same two-period framework used in the preceding chapter: Output is attained in the second period, and each capital input depreciates at the uniform rate δ. Taking input prices w_i and the interest rate $\bar{r}^A$ as given, the producer of the final good chooses its quantities demanded for the capital inputs (k_i) by solving the following optimization problem:

$$\max_{\{k_i\}} \left\{ \frac{Y + (1-\delta)\sum_{j=1}^{M} k_j}{1 + \bar{r}^A} - \sum_{j=1}^{M} w_j k_j \right\}, \tag{11.3}$$

subject to Eqs. (11.1) and (11.2). The solution to this problem yields the following inverse demand function:

$$w_i(k_i) = \frac{mpk_i + (1-\delta)}{1 + \bar{r}^A}, \tag{11.4}$$

where mpk_i is the marginal product of the ith capital input, defined as

$$mpk_i \equiv \alpha A K^{\alpha-\theta} k_i^{\theta-1}. \tag{11.5}$$

As a monopoly supplier of capital inputs to the final producers, the ith-input firm will take the inverse demand functions $w_i(k_i)$ (and the competitive return of unity to be paid to the households) as given and choose the quantities supplied of capital inputs k_i so as to maximize its profit:

$$\max_{\{k_i\}} \pi_i(k_i) \equiv [w_i(k_i) - 1]k_i.$$

The solution to this problem yields the following markup condition:

$$w_i(k_i)[1 - \eta_i(k_i)] = 1, \tag{11.6}$$

where $\eta_i(k_i)$ is the reciprocal of the elasticity of the inverse demand function, defined as

$$\eta_i(k_i) \equiv -\frac{w_i'(k_i)k_i}{w_i(k_i)} = -\left[\frac{mpk_i}{mpk_i + (1-\delta)} \right]$$

$$\times \left[(\theta-1) + (\alpha-\theta)\left(\frac{k_i^{\theta}}{\sum_{j=1}^{M} k_j^{\theta}} \right) \right]. \tag{11.7}$$

[Recall that the marginal cost to the firm on purchasing the input from the household is unity, the right-hand side of Eq. (11.6)].

Note that with full depreciation ($\delta = 1$) and when the number of capital inputs is infinitely large ($M \to \infty$), $\eta_i(k_i) \to \theta - 1$, so that the markup, $-1 + 1/[1 - \eta_i(k_i)]$, converges to a constant equaling $\theta^{-1} - 1$ (> 0). Note also that the markup does not converge to zero (when $M \to \infty$) because there is no perfect substitution between the inputs, which are each supplied by a monopoly [$(1 - \theta)^{-1} < \infty$].

The problem of the consumer–saver (competitive supplier of domestic savings) is the same as the one described in Chap. 10 except that, instead of K_0 she or he now takes $\sum_{j=1}^{M} k_{j0}$ as the initial endowment. The solution to her or his utility maximization problem yields the standard intertemporal condition

$$\frac{u_1(c_1, c_2)}{u_2(c_1, c_2)} = 1 + \bar{r}^A. \tag{11.8}$$

Assuming symmetry in the capital inputs across firms, we put $k_i = k$ and $w_i = w$. The economy-wide resource constraints are given, as in the preceding chapter, by

$$c_1 = N\{AM^{\alpha/\theta}k_0^\alpha - M[k - (1 - \delta)k_0]\}, \tag{11.9}$$

$$c_2 = N[AM^{\alpha/\theta}k^\alpha + (1 - \delta)Mk]. \tag{11.10}$$

In this model, the five equations [Eqs. (11.4), (11.6), and (11.8)–(11.10)] determine the five endogenous variables: c_1, c_2, k, w, and $\bar{r}^A$.

FDI with New Inputs and Increased Competition

The opening up of the economy involves three features. First, because of the difference between the world rate of interest r^* and the autarky interest rate $\bar{r}^A$, capital tends to flow in. Second, bundled with FDI, m new types of capital inputs will be imported.[2] Third, we assume that the increase in competition (given the perfectly elastic supply of inputs from abroad) will drive w_i to its competitive level of unity.

In the presence of imported capital inputs and under a competitive input market structure, the maximization problem facing the producers–investors becomes the following:

$$\max_{\{k_i\}} \left\{ \frac{Y + (1 - \delta)\sum_{j=1}^{M+m} k_j}{1 + r^*} - \sum_{j=1}^{M+m} k_j \right\}, \tag{11.3'}$$

subject to

$$K = \left(\sum_{j=1}^{M+m} k_j^\theta\right)^{1/\theta}, \tag{11.1'}$$

$$Y = AK^\alpha. \tag{11.2'}$$

The solution to the problem yields the standard marginal productivity condition,

$$mpk_i = r^* + \delta, \tag{11.4'}$$

where r^* is, as before, the world rate of interest, and where, as in Eq. (11.5), $mpk_i \equiv \alpha A K^{\alpha-\theta} k_i^{\theta-1}$, except that K now includes both traditional and new inputs.

The consumer–saver's problem remains unchanged, except that the autarky interest rate $\bar{r}^A$ is now replaced with the world rate of interest r^*. As a result, the intertemporal condition becomes

$$\frac{u_1(c_1, c_2)}{u_2(c_1, c_2)} = 1 + r^*. \tag{11.8'}$$

The two economy-wide resource constraints are modified as follows:

$$FDI = N[(M+m)k - (1-\delta)Mk_0] - (NAM^{\alpha/\theta}k_0^\alpha - c_1), \tag{11.9'}$$

$$c_2 = N[A(M+m)^{\alpha/\theta}k^\alpha + (1-\delta)(M+m)k] - FDI(1+r^*). \tag{11.10'}$$

In this model, the four equations [Eqs. (11.4'), (11.8'), (11.9'), and (11.10')] determine the four endogenous variables: $c_1, c_2, k,$ and FDI.

Gains from FDI

As discussed above, there are three possible sources of gains from FDI flows: (i) traditional capital mobility gains (from the use of foreign savings to augment the domestic capital stock), (ii) gains from technology transfer, and (iii) gains from the promotion of competition in the input market.

The two FDI-specific types (ii) and (iii) both result from the import of an increased variety of capital inputs. We now resort to numerical simulations to evaluate these gains. We assume that the utility of the representative consumer is $u(c_1, c_2) = \ln c_1 + \gamma \ln c_2$. In the simulations, we choose the following set of parameter values: $\gamma = 0.295$, $\alpha = 0.333$, $\delta = 0.723$, $N = 1$, and $K_0 = 1$. Assuming that each of the two periods last 25 years, the aforementioned parameter values of γ and δ represent an annual subjective discount rate of 5% and an annual depreciation rate of 5%, respectively. In the baseline model with both the technology-transfer and the competition-promotion features, we set $\theta = 0.314$, $M = 0.05$, and $m/M = 0.1$. The value of the production coefficient A is set equal to 1 so as to generate a normalized output level of unity in the first period in the presence of input variety M. The values of θ and M are chosen in such a way as to produce a markup of input price over its marginal cost of 40% as in Rotemberg and Woodford (1995). Our values of α and θ also imply a contribution of input variety to output growth $[\partial \ln(Y)/\partial \ln(M) = \alpha(1-\theta)/\theta$ of 0.728].

The welfare gain from FDI is illustrated in Fig. 11.3 as a function of the gap between the world rate of interest (r^*) and the autarkic rate of interest $(\bar{r}^A)$.

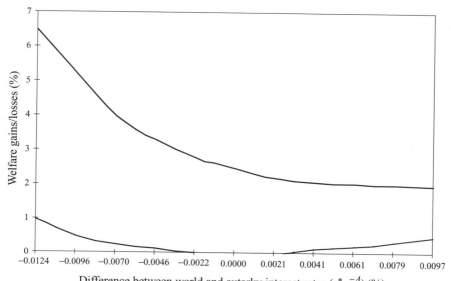

Fig. 11.3. Welfare gains from FDI with technology transfer and competition promotion versus traditional gains from FDI.

The upper curve describes the total gain (that is, the sum of all three types of gains) from FDI. The gain is measured by the percentage increase in lifetime consumption (c_1, c_2) under autarky, which is needed to lift utility under autarky to the level of utility attained with FDI. Interestingly, the gain is positive even when $r^* - \bar{r}^A > 0$, that is, $r^* > \bar{r}^A$. Note that in this case the traditional gains-from-trade hypothesis predicts no FDI flows and no gains from FDI. However, in our case, because of technology transfer and increased competition, there are still gains [of types (ii) and (iii)] from FDI. Note also that the gains from FDI are declining in the rate-of-return gap ($r^* - \bar{r}^A$), in accordance with the traditional hypothesis.

Also note that our simulations suggest that the nontraditional effects [(ii) and (iii)] constitute the major share of the gains from FDI. The lower curve in Fig. 11.3 illustrates the traditional gains stemming from the rate-of-return differential. We derived this curve by assuming perfectly competitive input markets and allowing no technology transfer. We set $\theta = 0.298$ and $m/M = 0$ so as to yield a zero markup. Also, in order not to change overall productivity, the production coefficient A was reset from 1 to 24, so as to maintain a normalized output level of unity in the first period. As one can see from Fig. 11.3, the traditional gains constitute a small share of the total gains from FDI. For instance, when $r^* = \bar{r}^A$ (and the traditional gains are absent), we still have a positive *FDI/GDP* ratio of 9%, producing a gain of 2.6% that measures the nontraditional gains.

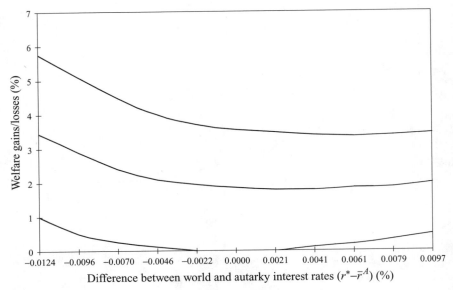

Fig. 11.4. Welfare gains from FDI with technology transfer.

To disentangle the two nontraditional effects [(ii) and (iii)], we conducted some sensitivity analyses, described in Figs. 11.4 and 11.5. In Fig. 11.4 we examine the relevance of the technology-transfer effect by varying the m/M ratio from 0% (the lower curve) to the baseline 10% (the middle curve), to 20% (the upper curve), while shutting off the competition-promotion channel (by setting the markup at zero). Compared with the traditional gains, which range from 0.5% to 1% in our simulations, the technology-transfer gains range from 3% to 6% as the rate-of-return differential (that is, $r^* - \bar{r}^A$) varies from -1% to $+1\%$. Similarly, in Fig. 11.5 we examine the competition-promotion effect. We do this by setting $m = 0$ and varying the markup from the competitive level of zero (the lower curve) to the baseline level of 40% (the middle curve), to the level of 100% [the upper curve, based on Hall's (1986) estimate]. The competition-promotion effect is quite sizable in our simulations: It ranges from a gain of 1.5% to 8% over and above the traditional gain, as the rate-of-return differential varies from -1% to $+1\%$.

The two nontraditional effects can generate large welfare gains through FDI inflows even in the absence of traditional gains from FDI. For instance, when $r^* = \bar{r}^A$ (and the traditional gain is nil), the technology-transfer effect delivers a welfare gain of 1.9% when the m/M ratio equals the baseline value of 10%, whereas the competition-promotion effect induces a gain of 0.7% when the markup equals the baseline value of 40%. These two welfare numbers together make up the overall nontraditional gains of 2.6% found in the all-inclusive case depicted by Fig. 11.3.

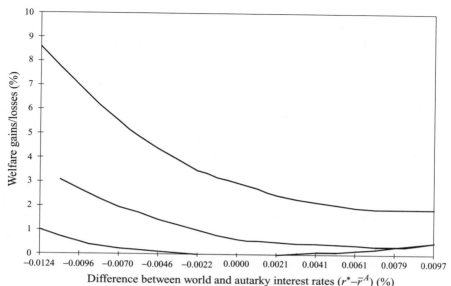

Fig. 11.5. Welfare gains from FDI with promotion of competition.

CONCLUSION

FDI inflows, like other forms of capital inflows that take advantage of rate-of-return differentials, deliver the traditional gains from trade. We emphasize in this chapter two distinctive features that occasionally characterize FDI flows: Facilitating the transfer of new technologies through the import of new varieties of factor inputs and promoting competition in the input markets. To do so, we blend the traditional and the nontraditional effects of FDI into a calibrated model and use numerical simulations to reassess the welfare gains of FDI inflows. In accordance with the literature, the traditional gains were found to be relatively small, but the nontraditional gains were found to be sizable. Furthermore, even when the net marginal product of capital under autarky is equal to the world rate of interest and the traditional gain is nil, the nontraditional gains are still there in full force.

12   Episodes of Capital-Flow Reversals

> Happy families are all alike; every unhappy family is unhappy in its own way.
>
> Leo Tolstoy, *Anna Karenina* (1875–1877, Part I, Chap. 1)

INTRODUCTION

External crises, like the misery of a family in Tolstoy's *Anna Karenina*, are different from each other. They are caused by different factors and erupt or evolve in different political-economic backgrounds. Therefore, it is difficult to pin down a common framework for their empirical analysis. This chapter attempts to merely provide some empirical regularities that are common to most external crises.

Three waves of external crises have swept international capital markets during the 1990s: the European Monetary System (EMS) crisis in 1992–1993, the collapse of the Mexican peso with its induced "tequila effects" and, most recently, the financial crisis in East Asia. In Italy (a member of the former EMS) and Mexico, the currency crisis was followed by a sharp reversal in the capital flows and the current account[1]; Italy went from a current account deficit of 2.4% in 1992 to an average surplus of close to 2% in 1993–1996, and Mexico went from a deficit of 7% in 1993–1994 to a virtual balance in 1995–1996, reflecting a capital outflow of similar magnitude (including reserve depletions). A similar outcome has occurred in East Asia after the 1997 baht crisis and its aftermath, as the table below shows.

	Indonesia	Korea	Malaysia	Philippines	Thailand
Current account reversal[2]	6.8	15.1	19.6	6.8	18.8
Real depreciation[3]	40.5	21.9	18.0	14.1	19.6

Are external crises characterized by large nominal devaluations invariably followed by sharp reductions in current account deficits? And what is the impact of crises and reversals in current account imbalances on economic performance? This chapter addresses these questions by characterizing real and nominal aspects of sharp external adjustments in low- and middle-income countries. It presents stylized facts associated with sharp reductions in current account deficits (reversals) and with large nominal devaluations (currency crises), and examines what precrisis event factors are associated with macroeconomic performance after such events occur.

Recent episodes of external instability have stimulated new theoretical and empirical research on crises in an attempt to provide a conceptual framework that helps us to understand these traumatic events and, possibly, to improve policy design so as to minimize the likelihood of their occurrence. In principle, a reversal in capital flows can cause a currency crisis and force a reduction in current account deficits because of the drying up of sources of external financing. However, a reversal can also occur in response to a change in macroeconomic policy designed to forestall the possibility of future speculative attacks or capital-flow reversals or as a consequence of favorable terms-of-trade shocks. Speculative attacks leading to currency crises can follow a collapse in domestic assets markets (as seems to have been the case in recent events in Asia), accumulation of short-term debt denominated in foreign currency, a persistent real appreciation and deterioration of the current account (as was the case of Mexico), or a political choice to abandon a rigid-exchange-rate system (as in the case of the U.K. in 1992).

FIRST-, SECOND-, AND THIRD-GENERATION MODELS OF EXTERNAL CRISES

How well does theory match the variety of these different experiences? So-called first-generation models of currency crises [e.g., Krugman (1979) and Flood and Garber (1984)] are built on an inevitable collapse of a fixed-exchange-rate system, in which the central bank mechanically expands domestic credit, for example by monetizing a persistent fiscal deficit. After a period of gradual reserve losses, a perfectly foreseen speculative attack wipes out the remaining reserves of the Central Bank and forces the abandonment of the fixed exchange rate. The main insight from these models is about the mechanics and timing of the sudden collapse in the context of a national expectations framework.

Second-generation models of currency crises [e.g., Obstfeld (1994)] endogenize government policy. Private agents forecast the government choice as to whether or not to defend the peg, based on trading off short-term flexibility and long-term credibility. The peg is abandoned either as a result of deteriorating fundamentals, as in first-generation models, or following a speculative attack driven by self-fulfilling expectations. Note that a self-fulfilling attack can (but need not) occur only with "vulnerable" fundamentals.

The latest waves of currency crises referred to above have brought the second-generation explanations of crises based on multiple equilibria and/or on contagion effects to the forefront [on the former see, for example, Eichengreen, Rose, and Wyplosz (1995), among others; on the latter, Eichengreen, Rose, and Wyplosz (1996), Calvo and Mendoza (1996), Jeanne (1997) and Masson (1998)].[4] Empirical tests of crisis models use various indicators of fundamentals, such as reserves-to-money ratio, fiscal balance, and the rate of domestic credit creation. The issue is whether (some) fundamentals are steadily deteriorating in the period, leading up to a speculative attack or not. However, it is difficult to infer from the data whether the collapse of the peg is a result of deteriorating fundamentals or self-fulfilling prophecies [see, for example, Eichengreen, Rose, and Wyplosz (1995) and Krugman (1996)].

The third-generation models [e.g., Morris and Shin (1998), and Goldstein (2000)] depart from the common-knowledge assumption concerning the fundamentals. With noisy signals, the actions of agents are coordinated (not through a market leader but through market participants' own expectations) on a unique fundamentals-based crisis equilibrium. Morris and Shin (1998) generalize Obstfeld's (1994) model to a model with a continuum of investors deciding whether or not to attack a currency with a fixed peg. Higher-order beliefs are a key determinant of investors' ability to coordinate their behavior, and thus a key factor in determining when the fundamental is sufficiently weak so as to uniquely trigger a currency attack.

A growing body of empirical research is devoted to studying the mechanics of crises in developing countries. Edwards (1989) studied the link between devaluation, the current account and output behavior. Kaminsky and Reinhart (1999), Kaminsky, Lizondo, and Reinhart (1998) and Demirgüç-Kunt and Detragiache (1998) focus on leading indicators of balance-of-payments and banking crises; Sachs, Tornell, and Velasco (1996) explore the spillover effects of the Mexican crisis on other emerging markets; and Frankel and Rose (1996) undertake a cross-country study of currency crashes in low- and middle-income countries.

The focus of the literature on the intertemporal aspects of the current account goes back to the theoretical work by Sachs (1981, 1982), Obstfeld (1982), and Svensson and Razin (1983). They were followed by empirical research on current account sustainability [e.g., Milesi-Ferretti and Razin (1996a, 1996b)] and on current account reversals [e.g., Milesi-Ferretti and Razin (1998)]. Empirical research in this area includes also that Debelle and Faruqee (1996), who undertake a cross-country study of determinants of the current account, Kraay and Ventura (1997), who argue that debtor and creditor countries respond asymmetrically to income shocks, and Lane and Perotti (1998), who investigate the impact of fiscal policy on the trade balance in OECD countries. A number of authors have focused on capital account developments, and in particular on capital flows to emerging markets, underlining the importance of both push and pull factors in explaining capital flows [see, for example, Calvo, Leiderman, and

Reinhart (1993), Corbo and Hernández (1996), Fernández-Arias (1996), Fernández-Arias and Montiel (1996), and Dornbusch, Goldfajn, and Valdes (1995)].

In this chapter, we put together these related strands of literature and describe some evidence pertaining to indicators and consequences of current account reversals and currency crises in a large sample of low- and middle-income countries over the period 1970–1996. The list of these countries is presented in Appendix 12.1.

In reporting this empirical evidence, we attempt to characterize a broad set of stylized facts associated with reversals and crises. However, caution must be exercised in interpreting these regularities as a reliable predictive model. The burgeoning analytical literature of financial crises has highlighted several mechanisms that can generate such an outcome: inconsistency between deteriorating fundamentals and the maintenance of a fixed exchange rate [Krugman (1979)], self-fulfilling crises à la Obstfeld (1994), and models of crises based on bank runs à la Diamond and Dybvig (1983) [e.g., Goldfajn and Valdés (1997) and Chang and Velasco (1998)]. Although these mechanisms that generate crises are different, the models point to an overlapping set of indicators (e.g., the level of reserves, the rate of growth in domestic credit, world interest rates, etc.). Hence, empirical exercises relating the probability of a crisis to a large set of indicators cannot discriminate between different explanations for crises. Failure to identify the alternative (potentially different) mechanisms underlying crises limits the usefulness of these exercises as predictive tools because the reduced-form relationship between crisis events and indicators averages the particular pattern of crises prevailing in the sample, which may not be repeated in the future (as in the standard Lucas critique). In addition, policy inference is hindered by the fact that the crisis-generating mechanisms, which we cannot disentangle, can have different policy implications (e.g., tight monetary policy is called on in a standard Krugman-type crisis, whereas a more flexible monetary policy is called on in the event of bank runs of the Diamond–Dybvig type).

DETERMINANTS OF REVERSALS AND CURRENCY CRISES: THEORETICAL EXAMPLES

Example One

The first-generation theoretical framework that describes currency crises was provided by Krugman (1979) and Flood and Garber (1984); see Obstfeld and Rogoff (1996) for a comprehensive analysis. In this framework, the source of the crisis is an inconsistency between the exchange-rate peg and the rate of domestic credit expansion, which leads to a gradual depletion of foreign exchange reserves, culminating in a speculative attack in which the remaining reserves are wiped out instantly. The attack takes place once the shadow exchange rate e^s, defined as the implicit floating exchange rate that would prevail whenever reserves are exhausted, equals the pegged rate e. In the simple monetary model on which this analysis is based, a measure of the vulnerability to speculative attacks is usefully given by

$$\frac{e^s}{e} = \frac{1 - \mu(eR)/M_2)}{1 - \eta\pi},$$

where μ is the base money multiplier, M_2 is broad money, R is the level of foreign exchange reserves, η is the interest semielasticity of the demand for money, and π is the rate of credit expansion. As this expression reveals, the ratio e^s/e is positively related to the rate of deterioration in the fundamental π. Thus, the likelihood of a crisis (which occurs whenever the ratio e^s/e reaches one) rises with π. Similarly, Calvo (1997) emphasizes the importance of the ratio eR/M_2 (and of the related ratio of reserves to short-term debt) as a measure of the adequacy of international reserves. This class of models does not yield clear predictions with regard to the link between exchange-rate crises and the behavior of the trade balance. However, if the model is amended to allow for capital controls [as in Wyplosz (1986)], reserve depletion can take place through the current account as well, with trade deficits eventually leading to an exhaustion of reserves and a collapse of the peg.

Example Two

We can cast the analysis of sharp reversals in the current account in terms of the standard transfer problem, which is illustrated in the second-generation model of Krugman (1999). Consider a small open economy producing goods that are imperfect substitutes for traded goods produced abroad. Assume that the world marginal propensity to spend on the country's product (set to zero for simplicity) is smaller than the country's marginal propensity to spend on domestic goods, $1 - \mu$. World demand for domestic exports is fixed at X. A share μ of both consumption and investment demand (C and I) falls on foreign goods. Market clearing for GDP Y implies that

$$Y \equiv (1-\mu)I + (1-\mu)C + pX = (1-\mu)I + (1-\mu)(1-s)Y + pX,$$

where s is the marginal propensity to save and p is the relative price of foreign goods in terms of domestic goods (a measure of the real exchange rate). For given Y and X, it is possible to solve for p as a function of investment:

$$p = \frac{1}{X}\{[1 - (1-\mu)(1-s)]Y - (1-\mu)I\}.$$

Suppose that investment financing depends on external capital flows. A reversal in capital flows will cause a decline in investment and, for given output, a real depreciation. In terms of the transfer problem, the assumption of a higher marginal propensity to spend on domestic goods of residents relative to foreigners implies that a transfer of resources from the home to the foreign country will increase world demand for foreign goods and decrease demand for domestic goods, thus implying the need for a real depreciation. To the extent that domestic output falls, this will mitigate the need for a real depreciation because of the induced fall in supply of domestic goods, relative to the supply of foreign goods. To the extent that corporate debt is denominated in foreign currency, the real depreciation could mess up the balance sheet of the firm and reduce its collateral, forcing the firm to borrow and invest at a reduced level. This mechanism can bring about the aforementioned reversal in capital flows in a self-fulfilling expectations manner; see also Aghion, Baccheta, and Banerjee (1998).

Example Three

Chang and Velasco (1998) provide a link between the literature on bank runs and the literature on international financial crises; see Chap. 7. A reduction in the availability of international liquidity can exacerbate the illiquidity of domestic banks, leading to a collapse in the banking system. This would cause an output decline and a collapse in asset prices. Under a fixed exchange rate, a run on the banks becomes a run on the currency if the central bank attempts to act as a lender of last resort.

For example, Korea's banks had sizable short-term foreign-currency liabilities and matching foreign-currency assets. At the beginning of the 1998 crisis, foreign banks refused to roll over long term their short-term foreign-currency assets vis-à-vis offshore and onshore Korean banks. The attempts by the central bank to shore up the foreign liquidity position of banks simply led to the rapid loss of foreign-currency reserves and the collapse of the currency [e.g., Dooley and Shin (1999)].

Insofar as current account reversals occur in periods of economic distress, with liquidity constraints that are due to a reversal in capital flows, we would expect a link between reversals and large currency depreciations. However, this may not be the case when reversals are induced by other factors, such as favorable terms-of-trade developments. The empirical work reported in the next sections characterizes empirical regularities associated with both current account reversals and currency crashes, attempts to shed light on what indicators provide a signal of the likelihood of these events occurring, and looks at whether reversals and currency crises are related.

THE DATA

The data set consists of 105 low- and middle-income countries (48 African countries, 26 Asian countries, 26 countries from Latin America and the Caribbean, and 5 European countries). A complete list of countries is in Appendix 12.1. In the empirical analysis, use is made of a reduced sample, comprising 39 middle-income countries with population above 1 million.[5] These countries are indicated with an asterisk in Appendix 12.1. The main source of data is the World Bank (World Development Indicators and Global Development

Finance); Appendix 12.2 describes data sources and definitions. In addition to standard macroeconomic and external variables, the data set includes a number of financial-sector variables and variables reflecting the composition of external liabilities, whose role in determining the likelihood of external crises has been emphasized in recent literature [see, for example, Calvo (1997)]. The data belong to different categories:

Macroeconomic variables such as economic growth, real consumption growth, the rate of investment, the fiscal balance, the level of GDP per capita.

External variables such as the current account balance (exclusive and inclusive of official transfers), the real effective exchange rate, the degree of real exchange-rate overvaluation,[6] the degree of openness to trade, the level of external official transfers as a fraction of GDP.

Debt variables such as the ratio of external debt to output, the interest burden of debt as a fraction of the GNP, the share of concessional debt, short-term debt, public debt and multilateral debt in total debt, and the ratio of FDI flows to debt outstanding.

Financial variables such as the ratio of M_2 to GDP, the credit growth rate, and the ratio of private credit to GDP.

Foreign variables such as the real interest rate in the U.S. (as a proxy for world interest rates), the rate of growth in OECD countries, and the terms of trade.[7]

Dummy variables such as regional dummies, a dummy for the exchange-rate regime that takes the value 1 if the country's exchange rate is pegged and zero otherwise, and a dummy that takes the value 1 if the country has an International Monetary Fund (IMF) program in place for at least six months during the year.

INDICATORS OF CURRENT ACCOUNT REVERSALS

The definition of reversal events captures large and persistent improvements in the current account balance that go beyond short-run current account fluctuations as a result of consumption smoothing. The underlying idea is that "large" events provide more information on determinants of reductions in current account deficits than short-run fluctuations. These events have to satisfy three requirements:

1. an average reduction in the current account deficit of at least three (or, in another alternative, five) percentage points of the GDP over a period of 3 years with respect to the 3 years before the event;
2. the maximum deficit after the reversal must be no larger than the minimum deficit in the three years preceding the reversal;
3. the average current account deficit must be reduced by at least one third.

The first and second requirements should ensure that only reductions of sustained current account deficits, rather than sharp but temporary reversals, are captured. The third requirement is necessary so as to avoid counting as a reversal a reduction in the current account deficit from, say, 15% to 12%.

Because events are defined on 3-year averages, the actual sample period during which reversal events can be measured is 1973–1994. According to this definition, reversals can occur in consecutive years; in this case, however, they are not independent events. The empirical analysis that follows excludes reversals occurring within 2 years of a previous one. Table 12.1 summarizes the number of events according to different definitions.

Table 12.1. Current Account Reversals

		A. Geographical Distribution			
Size of Reversal	Total	Africa (48 countries)	Asia (26 countries)	Europe (5 countries)	Latin American/ Carribbean (26 countries)
3% (no transfers)	152	67	48	4	33
3%, window (no transfers)	100	43	29	3	25
5% (no transfers)	117	55	38	2	22
5%, window (no transfers)	77	35	22	1	19
3%	167	76	48	4	39
3%, window	107	47	30	3	27

	B. Time Distribution				
Size of Reversal	Before 1978	1978–1981	1982–1985	1986–1989	1990–1994
3% (no transfers)	7	17	66	41	21
3%, window (no transfers)	7	14	41	23	15
5% (no transfers)	4	13	54	35	12
5%, window (no transfers)	4	10	34	21	8
3%	7	20	67	49	24
3%, window	7	17	39	29	15

Notes: 3(5)%: reduction in the current account deficit by at least 3(5)% over three years with respect to the preceding 3 years. No-transfers definition excludes official transfers from the current account. Window: excludes crises occurring within 3 years of another crisis.

The first notable feature is that reversal events are by no means rare. For example, for a 3% average reduction in the current account deficit (excluding official current transfers), there are 152 episodes in 69 countries; for a 5% reduction, 117 episodes in 59 countries. If reversals occurring within 2 years of a previous one are excluded, the total is 100 episodes (77 for a 5% reduction). The geographical distribution of reversals is relatively uniform across continents, once an adjustment is made for the number of countries in the sample. An analysis of the time distribution shows, not surprisingly, that a significant share of total reversals occurs in the period immediately following the debt crisis, as well as in the late 1980s. The number of reversals during the 1970s is instead fairly low.[8] The size of the reversals is also noteworthy. For 3% events (excluding transfers), the median reversal (which is smaller than the average) is 7.4 percentage points of the GDP, from a deficit of 10.3% to a deficit of 2.9%. Malaysia, for example, had an average current account deficit of over 11% in 1981–1983, but only of 2.5% in 1984–1986.

These numbers confirm that reversal episodes are associated with major changes in acountry's external position. What are their implications for the path of other macroeconomic and financial variables? In order to address this question, a methodology developed in Eichengreen, Rose, and Wyplosz (1995) is followed. The basic idea of this event-study methodology is to distinguish between periods of "turbulence" – those within 3 years of a reversal event – and the remaining, "tranquil" periods. Graphs allow a comparison of variables during turbulent periods with their (average) value during tranquil periods.

Figures 12.1 and 12.2 depict the behavior of a set of variables during periods of turbulence (around the time of reversals) for the whole sample and for the reduced sample comprising 39 middle-income countries, respectively. Each panel shows deviations of these variables from their mean during periods of tranquility, except for the first panel, which plots the median rate of depreciation in turbulent periods, as a deviation from the sample median in tranquil periods. The plotted values for the remaining panels refer to reversal events and are the means (plus or minus two standard deviations) of the variable during each year of the reversal episode (from $t-3$ to $t+3$) as a deviation from the sample mean of the variable during tranquil periods. Hence, a positive value for a variable indicates that it tends to be higher in "turbulent" than in "tranquil" periods.[9]

The figures show that the real exchange rate starts out more appreciated than average before reversal periods and then depreciates throughout the period. This comovement between the real exchange rate and the current account is clearly in line with the standard analysis of the transfer problem; see example two above. The panel depicting the behavior of the nominal exchange rate shows indeed an acceleration in the median rate of currency depreciation that occurs a couple of years before reversals. Reversals tend also to be preceded by unfavorable terms of trade, low foreign exchange reserves (e.g., example one), a high-interest burden of external debt, low consumption growth, and a high but

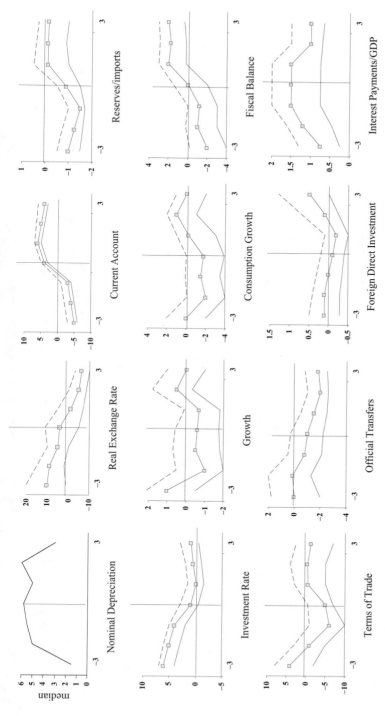

Fig. 12.1. Current account reversals (whole sample).

Notes: Data for 100 reversals from 105 countries, 1970–1996. A reversal is defined as an average improvement in the current account (net of Official transfers) of at least 3% over a period of 3 years with respect to the previous 3 years. "Turbulent" periods are those within 3 years of a current account reversal, and "tranquil" periods are those that are not within 3 years of a reversal. For each variable, the plots depict the difference between the variable mean during turbulent periods and its mean during periods of tranquility, and the two-standard-deviation band. The first panel depicts instead the difference between the median during the two periods. Scales and data vary by panel.

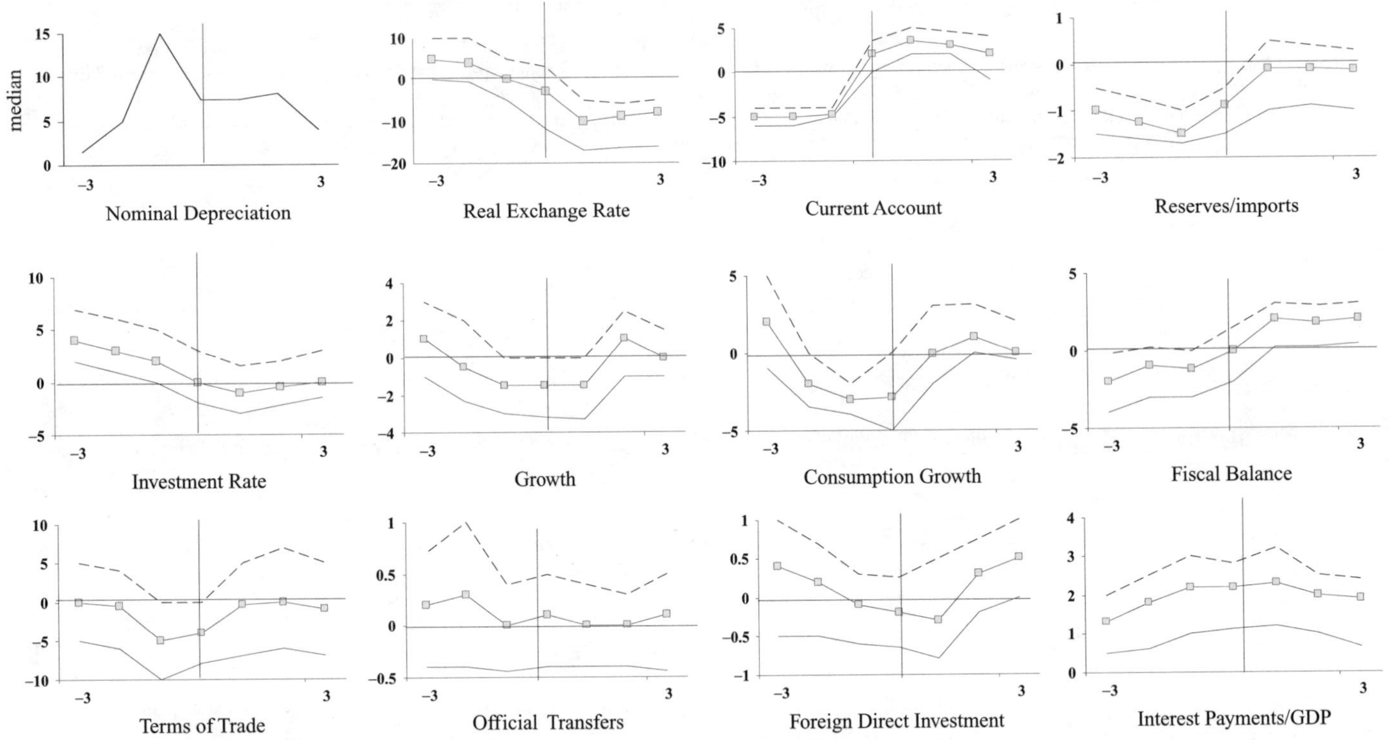

Fig. 12.2. Current account reversals (middle-income sample).

Notes: Data for 47 reversals from 39 countries, 1970–1996. A reversal is defined as an average improvement in the current account (net of Official transfers) of at least 3% over a period of 3 years with respect to the previous 3 years. "Turbulent" periods are those within 3 years of a current account reversal, and "tranquil" periods are those that are not within 3 years of a reversal. For each variable, the plots depict the difference between the variable mean during turbulent periods and its mean during periods of tranquility, and the two-standard-deviation band. The first panel depicts the difference between the median during the two periods. Scales and data vary by panel.

declining fiscal deficit. After a reversal occurs, reserves tend to rise, the fiscal balance continues to improve, and the real exchange rate to depreciate. Note also that no clear pattern for output growth characterizes the period preceding or following a reversal. This finding runs counter to the conventional wisdom that sharp reductions in current account deficits reflect an external crisis and that they are achieved by protracted domestic output compression so as to reduce import demand.

A multivariate probit analysis is then used to examine whether a set of explanatory variables helps predict whether a country is going to experience a reversal in current account imbalances. More specifically, an estimate of the probability of a reversal occurring at time t (meaning a 3% average decline of the current account deficit between t and $t + 2$ with respect to the period between $t - 1$ and $t - 3$) as a function of variables at $t - 1$ and of contemporaneous exogenous variables (terms of trade, industrial countries growth, world interest rates) is provided. The choice of the set of explanatory variables is motivated by existing research on currency and banking crises, as well as by previous work comparing episodes of persistent current account deficits, that identified a number of potential indicators of sustainability. Among them are the current account deficit (CA), economic growth (GROW), the investment rate (INV), GDP per capita (GDP), the real effective exchange rate (RER), openness to trade (OPEN), foreign exchange reserves as a fraction of imports (RES), the level of external official transfers as a fraction of GDP (OT), the ratio of external debt to GDP (DEBTY), the share of concessional debt in total debt (CONRAT), the share of public debt in total debt (PUBRAT), and the ratio of credit to GDP (CRED) (a proxy for financial development). Other variables, such as the ratio of FDI flows to GDP (FDI) and the share of short-term debt in total debt (SHORT) were excluded from the probit because they turned out to be economically and statistically insignificant. Also excluded is the fiscal deficit, because of problems with data availability – it did not enter significantly in the probit analysis, and it reduced sample size considerably. Note that the definition of the event is based on changes in the current account balance, and therefore it is important to control for the level of the current account balance prior to the reversal.

Included among the exogenous variables are the lagged and contemporaneous real interest rate in the U.S. (RINT, as a proxy for world interest rates), the lagged and contemporaneous rate of growth in OECD countries (GROECD), the lagged level of the terms of trade (TT) and the change in the terms of trade in the reversal period [$\Delta TT(t + 1)$]. Dummies for the exchange-rate regime (PEG) and the one for an IMF program (IMF) are also used.[10] For some of the lagged explanatory variables, namely the current account, the rate of growth and the investment share, a 3-year average (over the period $t - 1$ to $t - 3$), are used rather than their level at $t - 1$ to ensure consistency with the way reversals are measured.

It is clearly incorrect to interpret this probit analysis in a structural way, given that many of the explanatory variables are endogenous. Nevertheless, the analysis can provide a useful multivariate statistical characterization of reversal events as well as identify potential leading indicators. Probit results are presented in Table 12.2. Overall, the empirical analysis identifies a number of robust predictors of reversals in current account imbalances, regardless of the sample definition:

Current account deficit: Not surprisingly, reversals are more likely in countries with large current account deficits. This result is consistent with solvency and willingness to lend considerations.

Foreign exchange reserves: countries with lower reserves (expressed in months of imports) are more likely to experience a reversal. Clearly, low reserves make it difficult to sustain large external deficits and may reduce the willingness to lend of foreign investors. The ratio of reserves to M_2 also appears to signal reversals ahead of time in the sample (see example one).

GDP per capita: Countries with higher GDP per capita are more likely to experience reversals. The coefficient on this variable captures the difficulty of extremely poor countries in reversing external imbalances. The positive coefficient is also consistent with the theory of stages in the balance of payments: As a country gets richer, a reduction in deficits (or a shift to surpluses) is more likely.

Terms of trade: Reversals seem more likely in countries with worsened terms of trade. One interpretation of this finding is that countries that have suffered terms-of-trade deterioration are more likely to experience a reversal of capital flows and may therefore be forced to adjust. The evidence is also in line with what was suggested by Kraay and Ventura (1997), as the countries in the sample are almost entirely net debtors, and by Tornell and Lane (1998), who argue that the common pool problem may be exacerbated by favorable terms-of-trade shocks, thus leading to a more than proportional increase in absorption.

There is some evidence that reversals are more likely in countries with high investment: Insofar as high investment contributes to export capacity, it can lead to a narrowing of external imbalances. Reversals also appear less likely in countries that peg their exchange rates. If a peg precludes an adjustment in the nominal (and real) exchange rate, it can hamper the reduction of external imbalances.

When the full sample, which includes a large number of very poor countries, is considered, the following additional indicators are found:

Concessional debt: The higher the share of concessional debt in total debt, the less likely is a current account reversal. Concessional debt flows are less likely to be reversed, and they are likely to be higher in those countries that have more difficulties reducing their external imbalances and servicing their external obligations. The statistical significance of the share of concessional debt vanishes once the poorest countries are excluded from the sample, and therefore the variable was excluded form the last probit model (Table 12.2, column 4).

Official international transfers: A current account reversal is less likely when official transfers are high. Clearly, higher official transfers reduce the need to

Table 12.2. Indicators of Reversals

Indicator	1 With Adjacent Events, Full Sample	2 No Adjacent Events, Full Sample	3 No Adjacent Events, Average CA >10%	4 No Adjacent Events, Middle- Income Countries
Average CA	−0.60**	−0.44**	−0.63**	−0.62**
	(0.11)	(0.10)	(0.20)	(0.21)
Average GROW	−0.05	−5.7E−3	0.070	−0.10
	(0.13)	(0.10)	(0.11)	(0.15)
Average INV	0.145*	0.075	0.12**	0.19**
	(0.082)	(0.063)	(0.068)	(0.095)
GDP	1.2E−3**	7.8E−4**	6.5E−4**	1.2E−3**
	(4.6E−4)	(4.1E−4)	(3.6E−4)	(5.3E−4)
OPEN	−0.028	−0.013	−0.013	−0.017
	(0.019)	(0.014)	(0.015)	(0.020)
RES	−0.81**	−0.60**	−0.45**	−0.50**
	(0.24)	(0.21)	(0.17)	(0.22)
RER	0.007	7.4E−3	0.016**	7.0E−3
	(0.012)	(0.012)	(0.009)	(0.016)
OT	−0.64**	−0.49**	−0.44*	
	(0.20)	(0.17)	(0.29)	
DEBT	−0.019**	−0.024**	0.012	0.029*
	(0.009)	(0.009)	(0.009)	(0.017)
PUBRAT	0.050	0.036	0.045**	
	(0.035)	(0.025)	(0.022)	
CONRAT	−0.091**	−0.076**	−0.074**	
	(0.032)	(0.026)	(0.030)	
CREDIT	0.018	0.029	0.024	0.061**
	(0.029)	(0.023)	(0.021)	(0.031)
TT	−0.074**	−0.054**	−0.044**	−0.042**
	(0.026)	(0.021)	(0.020)	(0.025)
$\Delta TT(t+1)$	4.4E−3	1.8E−3		
	(2.8E=3)	(0.019)		
RINT	0.83**	2.72*	0.12	0.24
	(0.32)	(1.60)	(0.16)	(0.22)
GROECD	−0.37	−0.20	−0.18	−0.49*
	(0.33)	(0.24)	(0.22)	(0.37)
GROECD(t+1)	1.28**	0.58**		
	(0.41)	(0.28)		
PEG	−2.22*	−1.77*	−1.62**	−2.03**
	(1.32)	(1.13)	(1.02)	(1.36)
IMF	1.52	1.38*	0.37	−0.12
	(1.09)	(0.91)	(0.72)	(1.14)
Pseudo R^2	0.22	0.26	0.36	0.36
Observations	1301	1044	762	489

(continued)

Table 12.2 (*continued*)

Model (1)		Predicted		
		0	1	Total
	0	1186	7	1193
Actual	1	101	7	108
	Total	1287	14	1301

Model (2)		Predicted		
		0	1	Total
	0	972	4	976
Actual	1	60	8	68
	Total	1032	12	1044

Model (3)		Predicted		
		0	1	Total
	0	695	6	701
Actual	1	44	17	61
	Total	739	23	762

Model (4)		Predicted		
		0	1	Total
	0	444	4	448
Actual	1	28	13	41
	Total	472	17	489

Notes: A dependent variable takes the value 1 if a reversal of at least 3% takes place at time $t + 1$, and zero otherwise. Estimation by probit. The table reports probit slope derivatives (and associated z statistics in parentheses) times 100. Standard errors are corrected with the Huber–White sandwich estimator of variance. **(*) indicate statistical significance at the 95% (90%) confidence level. The variables CA, GROW, and INV are averages over the 3 years preceding the event. The variables OPEN, CONRAT, PUBRAT, OT, RER, TT, GDP, RINT, GROECD are levels. The first three probits include continent dummies (coefficients not reported). Omitted variables in models 3 and 4 were excluded based on a joint F test. Definitions of the indicators are given in the text.

adjust the current account (the current account that is measured is net of such transfers).

OECD growth: Reversals in developing countries are more likely to occur in years when the growth rate in industrial countries is high. High growth increases the demand for exports from developing countries, helping to narrow current account deficits.

U.S. Interest Rates: Reversals are more likely after a period of high real interest rates in industrial countries. High real interest rates increase the cost of borrowing for developing countries and reduce the incentive for capital to flow into developing countries.

Note that the coefficient on the level of external debt has the wrong sign in the first two probit models, reflecting the fact that several poor countries are highly indebted but have persistently high current account deficits, without reversals. Indeed, when these countries are eliminated from the sample the coefficient on external debt changes sign (see columns 3 and 4). Reversals do not appear to be systematically correlated with GDP growth before the event; no significant links between the level or rate of change of the real exchange rate (or degree of overvaluation) before the event and current account reversals are found. This finding is, of course, conditional on a given initial current account deficit (see also Figs. 12.1 and 12.2).

The second part of Table 12.2 shows the goodness of fit of the probit model, under the assumption that a crisis is correctly predicted if the estimated probability is above 0.5. Note that the fit improves considerably when very poor countries are eliminated from the sample. This is not surprising; indeed, one can think that the determinants of swings in the current account can differ substantially between countries that rely exclusively on official transfers, mostly on concessional terms, and those that have more access to international capital markets.

The results presented so far have to be interpreted with taking into account the fact that the empirical analysis aggregates reversal events that have quite different features; it includes both full-fledged balance-of-payments crises as in, say, Mexico 1982, and improvements in the current account spurred by favorable terms-of-trade developments or a timely correction in macroeconomic policy. A better understanding of the dynamics of current account reversals and of the role of economic policy will require a classification of these events based on their salient features (terms-of-trade shocks, swings in capital flows, etc.). This would provide an opportunity for a closer match between intertemporal models of current account determination and developing countries' data.

CURRENT ACCOUNT REVERSALS AND OUTPUT PERFORMANCE

In this section, we examine the behavior of output growth in countries that experienced sharp reductions in current account imbalances. The focus is on two issues: first, whether reversals are costly in terms of output, and, second, what factors determine a country's rate of growth during a reversal period. Output costs clearly arise when reversals are associated with macroeconomic crises, and more generally can be due to macroeconomic adjustment and sectoral reallocation of resources. For the purpose of this "before–after" analysis the 3% event definition is selected and adjacent events are eliminated.[11] This leaves 100 reversal episodes for the definition excluding official transfers.

The first interesting finding is that the median change in output growth between the period after and before the event is around zero, suggesting that reversals in current account deficits are not necessarily associated with domestic output compression. However, output performance is very heterogeneous. For example, Uruguay's average growth was 7% in the period 1982–1984, compared with 4% in the period 1979–1981; Malaysia instead went from a growth of 2.4% in 1984–1986 to a growth of close to 8% over the following 3 years.

The dependent variable in the regression analysis is the average rate of output growth during the 3 years of the reversal period, as deviation from OECD average during the same period. The deviation of growth from the OECD average is used because reversal events occur in different years, and an attempt is made to provide some (rough) correction of each country's performance for the overall behavior of the world economy during that period. The explanatory variables include average growth (also as a deviation from the OECD average), average investment, the average current account balance, GDP per capita (a conditional convergence term), the ratio of external debt to GDP (DEBTY), the overvaluation of the real exchange rate, official transfers, and U.S. real interest rates. They are all dated before to the reversal.[12] Results are presented in Table 12.3. The table shows that countries more open to trade and with a less appreciated level of the exchange rate before the event are likely to grow faster after the event. The size of the point estimates indicates that the effects of these variables are also economically significant: for example, a country that has an overvaluation of 10% before the reversal is likely to grow 0.7% slower for the following 3 years. We also find some evidence that countries with high external debt and those that receive high official transfers tend to grow more slowly. The latter finding could of course simply reflect the fact that poor countries that grow slowly tend to receive large transfers. Indeed, when countries with low per-capita income are excluded, the coefficient on official transfers changes sign and becomes statistically insignificant (regression not reported). Note also that the correlation of growth before and after the event is low and statistically insignificant, with the exception of the regression for the group of middle-income countries.

Overall, the empirical analysis seems to provide a reasonable characterization of short/medium-run output performance during periods of substantial reduction in external imbalances. A noteworthy finding is that reversal events seem to entail substantial changes in macroeconomic performance between the period before and the period after the crisis, but are not systematically associated with a growth slowdown.

PREDICTORS OF CURRENCY CRASHES

In this section, we extend and refine work by Frankel and Rose (1996) by considering a longer sample and alternative definitions of currency crises. Four definitions of currency crises are used. The first one (CRISIS1), used by Frankel and Rose (1996), requires an exchange rate depreciation vis-à-vis the dollar of 25%, which is at least 10% higher than the depreciation the previous year. The main problem with this definition is that it considers as a crisis an episode in which the rate of depreciation increases from, say, 50% to

Table 12.3. Consequences of Reversals

		Dependent Variable is Output Growth During Reversal Period (As Deviation from OECD average)		
Variable	Full Sample	Full Sample, Regional Dummies	Average CA> −10%, Regional Dummies	Middle-Income Countries, Regional Dummies
Lagged Dependent Variable	0.10 (0.11)	0.10 (0.11)	0.10 (0.10)	0.32** (0.12)
CA	−0.10 (0.08)	−0.14* (0.07)	−0.13 (0.08)	−0.07 (0.09)
OVERVA	−0.076** (0.017)	−0.078** (0.016)	−0.069** (0.018)	−0.070** (0.023)
OPEN	0.030** (0.011)	0.021* (0.011)	0.026** (0.013)	0.031* (0.016)
DEBTY	−0.018** (0.07)	−0.016** (0.079)	−0.018 (0.011)	−0.025** (0.009)
RINT	−0.23 (0.17)	−0.29* (0.16)	−0.20 (0.17)	−0.42 (0.18)
OT	−0.29** (0.11)	−0.31** (0.10)	−0.55 (0.35)	
GDP	−3.1E−4 (2.4E−4)	−1.4E−4 (2.6E−4)	−3.0E−4 (−2.9E−4)	−1.6E−4 (−2.8E−4)
INV	0.058 (0.044)	0.067 (0.048)	−0.067 (0.044)	−0.037 (0.067)
R^2	0.35	0.40	0.44	0.58
Observations	84	84	66	44

Notes: Estimation by Ordinary Least Squares (OLS) with White's correction for heteroskedasticity; standard errors in parentheses**(*) indicate statistical significance at the 95% (90%) confidence level. The dependent variable is a 3-year average expressed as deviation from the OECD average during the same period. The explanatory variables CA and INV are averages over the 3 years preceding the event; the variables OPEN, GDP, RER, TT, OT and DEBTY are levels the year before the event.

61%. To avoid capturing the large exchange-rate fluctuations associated with high-inflation episodes, the second definition (CRISIS2) requires, in addition to a 25% depreciation, at least a doubling in the rate of depreciation with respect to the previous year and a rate of depreciation the previous year below 40%. The third and fourth definitions (CRISIS3 and CRISIS4) focus on those episodes in which the exchange rate was relatively stable the previous year and that therefore may be closer to the concept of currency crisis implicit in theoretical models. CRISIS3 requires a 15% minimum rate of depreciation, a minimum 10% increase in the rate of depreciation with respect to the previous year, and a rate of depreciation the previous year of below 10%. Finally, CRISIS4 is analogous

Table 12.4. Currency Crashes

A. Geographical Distribution

Type of Crisis	Total	Africa (48 countries)	Asia (26 countries)	Europe (5 countries)	Latin American/ Caribbean (26 countries)
CRISIS2 (no window)	168(142*)	85(59*)	30	6	47
CRISIS1 (window)	172(146*)	81(55*)	30	7	54
CRISIS2 (window)	142(116*)	73(47*)	27	4	38
CRISIS3 (window)	162(136*)	84(58*)	33	7	38
CRISIS4 (window)	119	67(41*)	17	7	28

B. Time Distribution

Type of Crisis	Before 1978	1978–1981	1982–1985	1986–1989	1990–1994	1995–96
CRISIS2 (no window)	15	33(20*)	33	29	52(39*)	6
CRISIS1 (window)	16	32(19*)	37	26	53(40*)	8
CRISIS2 (no transfers)	14	30(17*)	28	20	45(32*)	5
CRISIS3 (window)	29	36(23*)	30	18	41(28*)	8
CRISIS4 (window)	21	30(17*)	19	14	30(17*)	5

Notes: CRISIS1: depreciation of 25%, at least 10% higher than the previous year.
CRISES2: depreciation of 25%, at least double the previous year, with the latter below 40%.
CRISIS3: depreciation of 15%, at least 10% higher than the previous year, with the latter below 10%.
CRISIS4: same as CRISIS3 plus pegged exchange rate the year before the crisis.
Window: excludes crises occurring within 3 years of another crisis.
* Counting the depreciation of the CFA franc as a single crash.

to CRISIS3 with the additional requirement that the exchange rate be pegged the year before the crisis.

Not considered as a crisis are events that occur within 3 years of another crisis; therefore a window is constructed around each crisis event that is distinguished from periods of tranquility. This reduces the total amount of crises; Table 12.4 summarizes the currency crisis episodes according to the different definitions. There is clearly a large degree of overlap among these definitions of crises. Practically all episodes in CRISIS2 (138 of them) are also episodes of CRISIS1.[13] The overlap between CRISIS3 and CRISIS1 (or CRISIS2) is smaller (109 cases) but still significant. Note also that the number of crashes depends crucially on whether one counts countries that experienced a crash or currencies that crashed. The six members of the Central African Economic and Monetary Union (Cameroon, Central African Republic, Chad, Congo, Equatorial Guinea and Gabon), the seven members of the West African Economic and Monetary Union (Benin, Burkina Faso, Côte d'Ivoire, Mali, Niger, Senegal and Togo) plus the republic of the Comoros share the same currency (the CFA franc) which was set as a fixed rate vis-à-vis the French franc until 1994, and then devalued by 50%.[14] The definition of crisis therefore captures 14 country episodes that year and also in 1981 (because of the depreciation of the French franc vis-à-vis the U.S. dollar).

The geographical distribution of currency crashes show that African and Latin American countries tend to experience more crashes than Asian countries (adjusting by the number of countries in the sample). Recall, however, that the recent 1998 Asian currency crashes are not in the sample. The time distribution of currency crashes is more uniform than the distribution of reversals, with the highest number of crashes in the early 1980s (the period of the debt crisis) and, more surprisingly, in the early 1990s. The increase in capital mobility during the latter period may be one possible explanation of this pattern.

Table 12.5 summarizes changes in the exchange-rate regime in countries that suffered currency crashes. In the whole sample, the exchange rate is pegged 69% of the time. The data show that number of countries abandon the exchange-rate peg the year of the crisis and a few more the following year.

As in the case of current account reversals, Figs. 12.3 and 12.4 present some evidence on the behavior of key variables around the time of the crisis for the whole sample and for the sample of middle-income countries, respectively (the graphs refer to CRISIS2; the graphs for the other crises are similar, and available on request). The first two panels of Figs. 12.3 and 12.4 depict the

Table 12.5. Currency Crashes and Exchange-Rate Regime

Type of Crisis	Total*	Peg Year Before Crisis	Peg Year of the Crisis	Peg Year After Crisis
CRISIS1 (window)	164	99	87	79
CRISIS2 (window)	136	97	83	76
CRISES3 (window)	146	114	98	89
CRISES4 (window)	115	115	95	87

Note: *Counting the depreciation of the CFA franc as a single crash.

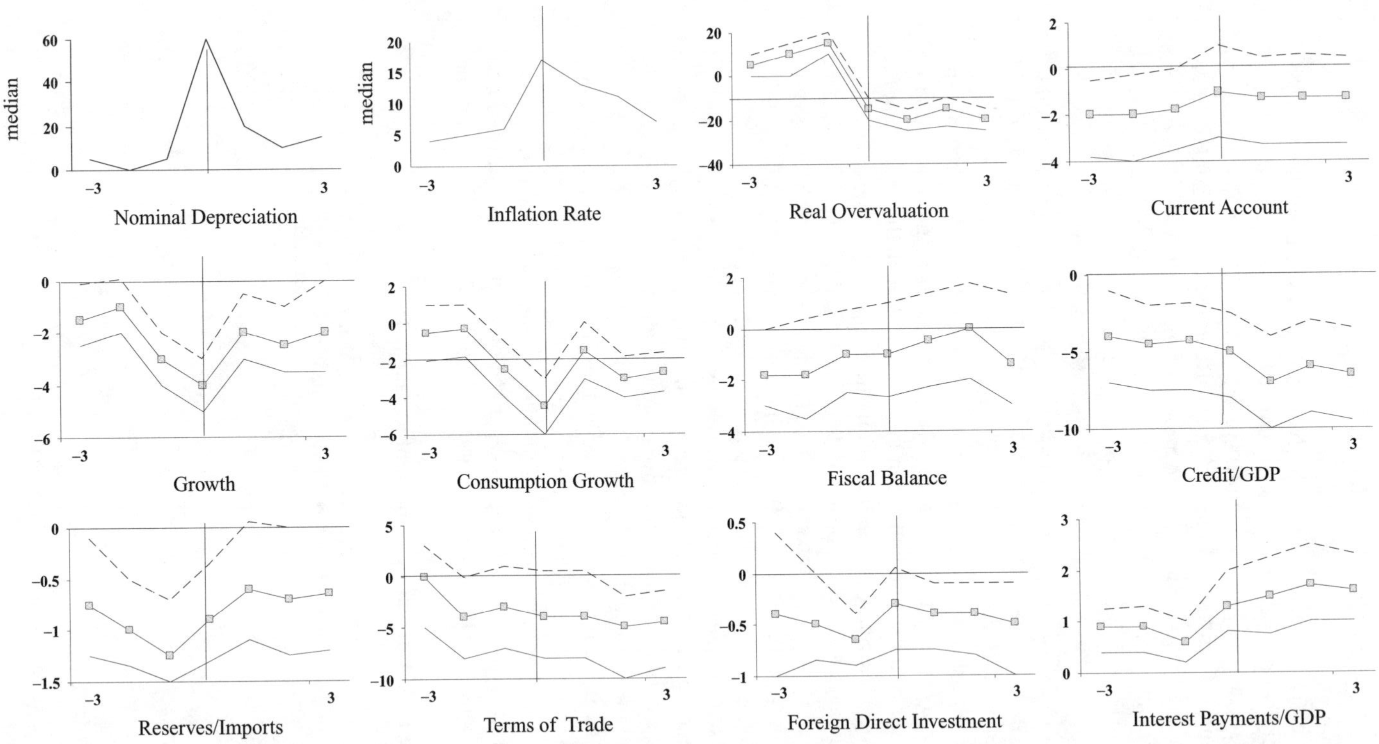

Fig. 12.3. Currency crashes (whole sample).

Notes: Data for 142 crashes from 105 countries, 1970–1996. A crash is defined as a nominal exchange-rate depreciation of at least 25%, which is at least double the previous year's depreciation rate, as long as the latter is below 40%. "Turbulent" periods are those within 3 years of a currency crash, and "tranquil" periods are those that are not within 3 years of a crash. For each variable, the plots depict the difference between the variable mean during turbulent periods and its mean during periods of tranquility, and the two-standard-deviation band. The first two panels depict the difference between the median during the two periods. Scales and data vary by panel.

148

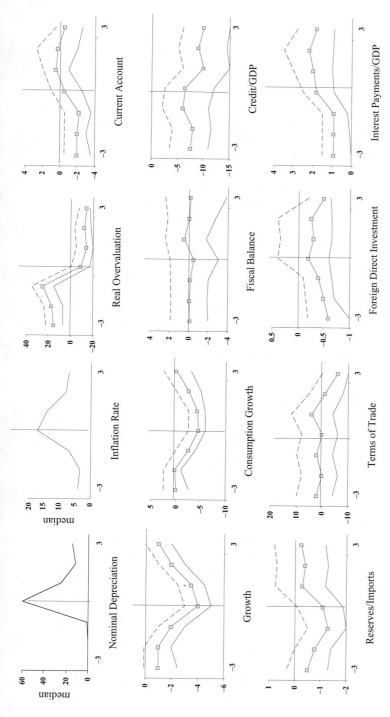

Notes: Data for 51 crashes from 39 countries, 1970–1996. A crash is defined as a nominal exchange rate depreciation of at least 25%, which is at least double the previous year's depreciation rate, as long as the latter is below 40%. "Turbulent" periods are those within 3 years of a currency crash, and "tranquil" periods are those that are not within 3 years of a crash. For each variable, the plots depict the difference between the variable mean during turbulent periods and its mean during periods of tranquility, and the two-standard-deviation band. The first two panels depict instead the difference between the median during the two periods. Scales and data vary by panel.

Fig. 12.4. Currency crashes (middle-income sample).

behavior of the median rate of depreciation and of CPI inflation around the time of a currency crash, as deviations from the sample median during periods of tranquility. The other panels depict deviations from means and standard error bands (as in Figs. 12.1 and 12.2). For the whole sample, the median rate of depreciation before crises is below 2%, close to the sample median; the median depreciation the year of the crisis is 53%, and, after the crisis, it falls to 17%. A similar pattern emerges for the rate of inflation, although the increase during the year of the crisis is much smaller than the increase in the rate of depreciation. This is reflected in the behavior of the real exchange rate (or the degree of overvaluation): these increase before the crisis and fall the year of the crisis and do not seem to recover within the 3-year window. Another notable feature of crisis years (and of the year preceding a crisis) is a decline in the rate of output and consumption growth, with a rebound taking place after the crisis. The median consumption growth rate over the 3 years preceding a crisis is 3.3%, the year of the crisis, 0.2% and the following 3 years 2.2%. For output growth, the numbers are 2.6%, 1.4%, and 3.1%, respectively. Not surprisingly, foreign exchange reserves around crisis periods tend to be lower than during tranquil periods and the terms of trade less favorable. There is some evidence that current account deficits are larger before crises than in tranquil periods; however, the figures show an improvement in the current account position after the devaluation only for middle-income countries.

Turn now to multivariate probit analysis. The probability of a currency crisis at time $t + 1$, as a function of a set of explanatory variables at time t and of "external factors" at time t and $t + 1$, is estimated. The set of explanatory variables is similar to the one used for reversals; also reported here are results obtained with the ratio of reserves to M_2 (*RESM2*) as an alternative to reserves measured in months of imports (RES). Results are presented in Table 12.6. The first four columns report probit analysis by use of the full sample and the four different definitions of crises, and the last two columns report the results for the sample of 39 middle-income countries. Overall, these results suggest some robust leading indicators of currency crashes, regardless of the precise definition of the crash:

Foreign exchange reserves: Crashes are more likely in countries with low foreign exchange reserves, measured as a fraction of imports or as a fraction of M_2.[15] This finding is clearly in line with theoretical models of currency crises; see example one.

Real exchange rate overvaluation: Crashes are more likely in countries in which the real exchange rate is appreciated relative to its historical average. This finding suggest that even the crude measure of exchange-rate misalignments adopted here provides some useful information on the likelihood of exchange-rate collapse.[16]

U.S. interest rates: Crashes are more likely when real interest rates in the U.S. are (or have been) high. Higher interest rates in industrial countries make

Table 12.6. Indicators of Currency Crashes

Indicator	1 CRISIS1, Full Sample	2 CRISIS2, Full Sample	3 CRISIS3, Full Sample	4 CRISIS4, Full Sample	5 CRISIS2, Middle Income	6 CRISIS3, Middle Income
CA	−0.25	−0.036	−0.11	−0.07	−0.36*	−0.39**
	(0.19)	(0.16)	(0.17)	(0.09)	(0.21)	(0.19)
GROW	0.11	0.18	0.53**	0.22*	0.27	−0.02
	(0.23)	(0.20)	(0.22)	(0.12)	(0.23)	(0.17)
INV	−0.15	−0.14	−0.21	−0.13	−0.12	−0.08
	(0.15)	(0.14)	(0.15)	(0.08)	(0.15)	(0.10)
GDP	−1.9E−4	−9.9E−4	−1.6E−3*	−2.5E−4	2.1E−4	2.4E−4
	(8.5E−4)	(6.3E−4)	(8.4E−4)	(4.5E−4)	(7.4E−4)	(5.7E−4)
OPEN	−0.15**	−0.054*	0.038	0.028*	0.05	0.11**
	(0.04)	(0.029)	(0.029)	(0.015)	(0.04)	(0.04)
RES	−1.37**	−1.23**			−0.75**	
	(0.35)	(0.32)			(0.30)	
RES2			−15.3**	−7.27**		−15.5**
			(−3.64)	(2.26)		(4.17)
OVERVAL	0.13**	0.15**	0.24**	0.17**	0.24**	0.17**
	(0.04)	(0.04)	(0.04)	(0.03)	(0.06)	(0.06)
DEBTY	−0.001	0.007	0.014	0.009	0.037*	0.01
	(0.01)	(0.009)	(0.011)	(0.006)	(0.024)	(0.02)
VARRAT	−0.01	−0.16**	−0.042	0.009		
	(0.07)	(0.06)				
CONRAT	−0.17**	−0.16**	−0.042	0.009		
	(0.06)	(0.05)	(0.039)	(0.02)		
FDI	−0.43	−0.31	−0.012	0.23	−0.84	−0.56
	(0.56)	(0.41)	(0.50)	(0.30)	(0.61)	(0.54)
CRED	0.07	−0.02	0.073	0.017	−0.03	−0.06*
	(0.06)	(0.05)	(0.051)	(0.03)	(0.04)	(0.035)
TT	−0.11**	−0.10**	−0.061	−0.060**	−0.064*	−0.057**
	(0.04)	(0.04)	(0.038)	(0.023)	(0.037)	(0.030)
ΔTT($t+1$)	−0.10*	−0.08	−0.099*	−0.066**		
	(0.06)	(0.05)	(0.053)	(0.031)		
RINT	0.34	−0.20	−0.014	−0.31	1.15**	0.45*
	(0.55)	(0.48)	(0.50)	(0.29)	(0.37)	(0.27)
RINT($t+1$)	1.24**	1.08**	1.36**	0.62**		
	(0.51)	(0.44)	(0.46)	(0.28)		
GROECD	−1.74**	−1.34**	−1.61**	−0.49**	−0.49	−0.84**
	(0.54)	(0.48)	(0.50)	(0.28)	(0.48)	(0.42)
GROECD($t+1$)	−0.20	−0.24	−0.53	0.13	1.32**	0.37
	(0.66)	(0.57)	(0.62)	(0.35)	(0.58)	(0.43)
PEG	−7.57**	−2.61	1.34		−0.60	2.26*
	(2.51)	(1.78)	(1.59)		(1.43)	(1.38)
IMF	−2.84**	−2.58*	0.63	0.58	−2.32	1.01
	(1.45)	(1.30)	(1.64)	(0.99)	(−1.38)	(1.44)
Pseudo R^2	0.29	0.24	0.27	0.29	0.36	0.36
Observations	838	897	878	985	474	472

(*continued*)

Table 12.6 (*continued*)

Model (1)

		0	1	Total
	0	725	9	734
Actual	1	71	33	104
	Total	796	42	838

Predicted

Model (2)

		0	1	Total
	0	808	5	813
Actual	1	70	14	84
	Total	878	19	897

Predicted

Model (3)

		0	1	Total
	0	779	7	786
Actual	1	69	23	92
	Total	848	30	878

Predicted

Model (4)

		0	1	Total
	0	913	4	917
Actual	1	56	12	68
	Total	969	16	985

Predicted

Model (5)

		0	1	Total
	0	430	3	433
Actual	1	26	15	41
	Total	456	18	474

Predicted

Model (6)

		0	1	Total
	0	442	4	426
Actual	1	30	16	46
	Total	452	20	472

Predicted

Notes: Estimation by probit. The table reports probit slope derivatives (and associated z statistics in parentheses) multiplied by 100. A dependent variable takes the value 1 if a currency crash occurs at time $t + 1$, and zero otherwise. **(*) indicates statistical significance at the 95% (90%) confidence level. The variables CA, GROW, and INV are averages over the 3 years preceding the event. Variables are dated at time t unless otherwise marked. Regressions include continent dummies (coefficients not reported). Omitted variables in models 5 and 6 were excluded based on a joint F test.

investment in developing countries less attractive and are more likely to cause reversals in capital flows.

Growth in industrial countries: Crashes are more likely if growth in industrial countries has been sluggish. A possible channel is through lower demand for developing countries exports, a decline in foreign exchange reserves and a more likely collapse of the currency.

Terms of trade: A crisis is less likely when the terms of trade are favorable. This is another intuitive finding: Better terms of trade should improve a country's creditworthiness (and its cash flow) and make it less vulnerable to speculative attacks.

When the whole sample is used, a number of other factors are good leading predictors of crises according to CRISIS1 and CRISIS2, but not CRISIS3 and CRISIS4:

Share of concessional debt: Crashes are less likely in countries with a large share of debt at concessional terms. This may be explained by the fact that these flows are less likely to be reversed.

Trade Openness: More open economies are less likely to suffer an exchange rate crash. This evidence suggests that when crises associated with high inflation episodes are included, the benefits of trade openness outweigh the higher vulnerability to external shocks. This is not the case, however, when the focus is on crashes that were preceded by more stable exchange rates (see columns 3, 4, and 6).[17]

IMF dummy: Countries with an IMF program in place are less likely to suffer a crash the following year. In addition to a possible credibility effect, this finding could reflect the fact that programs are approved, or remain in place, in countries willing to strengthen their fundamentals.

For the sample of middle-income countries, a crash is more likely when the current account deficit is large. For the full sample, which includes several low-income countries with very large current account deficits throughout the period, the current account has the expected sign, but is statistically insignificant. The finding that countries with a pegged exchange rate are less likely to suffer a crash of type 1 (CRISIS1) may simply reflect the fact that the rate of depreciation tends to be lower in countries with a pegged exchange rate than in countries with a floating exchange rate (the median rate of depreciation in the sample for countries that peg is zero, whereas it is 12% for countries with a floating exchange rate). Indeed, when the definition of crisis is limited to countries with a low initial rate of depreciation (CRISIS3, CRISIS4), the coefficient on the peg variable changes sign.

The second part of Table 12.6 reports the goodness of fit of the model. As in the case of reversals, goodness of fit improves when the sample is restricted to middle-income countries. Note also the difference in the classification accuracy for the full sample between CRISIS1 and CRISIS2: This is due to the fact that the model predicts easily accelerations in the rate of depreciation associated with episodes of high inflation. Overall, these results are broadly in line with those reported by Frankel and Rose (1996). They highlight domestic factors, such as the degree of overvaluation and the level of reserves, and external factors, such as growth and interest rates in industrial countries and the terms of trade, that tend to precede currency crashes.

CURRENCY CRISES AND OUTPUT PERFORMANCE

This section characterizes output performance after a currency crisis. The objective is twofold: first, to identify stylized facts regarding the behavior of macroeconomic variables before and after crises, and second, to investigate which factors help explain output growth after crises.

A stylized fact that emerged from the analysis of the previous section is that output and consumption growth the year of the crisis are lower than the average during the 3 preceding years and during the 3 following years. This finding suggests that the analysis is indeed picking up events that have disruptive effects on macroeconomic activity, at least in the short run. One telling example is Korea, which experienced a currency crisis (according to the first three definitions) in 1980. Its average growth in the 3 years preceding the crisis was above 10%, in 1980 output fell by close to 3%, and in the 3 successive years growth was back at 8%. The regression analysis explores the determinants of output performance in the three years following a currency crash. The dependent variable is the average growth rate in the three years following the crash as a deviation from OECD average during the same period. The independent variables include the average growth rate in the 3 years preceding the crisis, the growth rate the year of the crisis (both expressed as deviation from the OECD average during those periods), the average investment rate and current account balance the three years before the crisis, the change in the terms of trade between the two periods, as well as the debt-to-GDP ratio, the degree of real exchange-rate overvaluation, GDP per capita, the real interest rate in the U.S. and the ratio of external transfers to GDP, all measured the year before the crisis. Results are presented in Table 12.7. Overall, the most robust predictor of output performance after a crisis appears to be the average growth rate before the crisis. Evidence is also found that countries more open to trade tend to grow faster after a currency crisis. Although the latter finding is in line with that reported earlier for the before–after analysis of current account reversals, the former is different and suggests a stronger degree of continuity in output performance in the case of currency crises than in the case of reversals, especially for the sample of middle-income countries. The growth rate the year of the crisis and the current account balance before the crisis are not good predictors of subsequent performance, after controlling for other growth determinants. It is interesting to note that the real exchange rates (or the degree of overvaluation) that seem to play an important role both in explaining output performance after reversals and in triggering currency crises are not good predictors of

Table 12.7. Consequences of Currency Crashes

	Dependent Variable is Average Output Growth After a Currency Crash (As deviation from OECD growth)					
Variable	CRISIS1, Full Sample	CRISIS2, Full Sample	CRISIS3, Full Sample	CRISIS1, Middle Income	CRISIS2, Middle Income	CRISIS3, Middle Income
Lagged Dependent Variable	0.37** (0.12)	0.33** (0.14)	0.21* (0.12)	0.54** (0.17)	0.59** (0.20)	0.65** (0.21)
Growth (crisis year)	0.03 (0.07)	0.07 (0.08)	0.13 (0.08)	−0.05 (0.08)	0.07 (0.17)	0.08 (0.12)
CA	0.14 (0.12)	0.16 (0.14)	0.11 (0.09)	0.14 . (0.14)	0.32* (0.17)	0.07 (0.15)
RER	−0.01 (0.02)	0.014 (0.009)	0.006 (0.01)	−0.01 (0.01)	0.008 (0.02)	−0.03 (0.02)
ΔTT	0.063** (0.026)	0.054* (0.030)	0.026 (0.023)	0.055* (0.029)	0.056 (0.033)	−0.005 (0.03)
OPEN	0.058** (0.021)	0.074** (0.023)	0.056** (0.018)	0.03 (0.02)	0.063** (0.031)	0.03 (0.03)
DEBTY	−0.010 (0.011)	−0.012 (0.012)	−0.011 (0.009)	−0.006 (0.01)	−0.0017 (0.016)	−0.014 (0.014)
RINT	−0.06 (0.17)	−0.12 (0.21)	0.12 (0.15)	−0.04 (0.21)	−0.17 (0.26)	−0.003 (0.22)
OT	−0.13 (0.17)	−0.17 (0.18)	−0.17* (0.10)			
GDP	−4.0E−5 (5.1E−4)	−3.5E−4 (6.2E−4)	−4.1E−4 (6.5E−4)	6.4E−5 (3.2E−4)	−5.5E−5 (4.3E−4)	1.2E−4 (4.4E−4)
INV	−0.09 (0.10)	−0.07 (0.13)	0.02 (0.09)	−0.23** (0.09)	−0.25* (0.13)	−0.23** (0.11)
R^2	0.35	0.39	0.40	0.47	0.55	0.56
Observations	85	69	80	53	37	42

Notes: Estimation by OLS with White's correction for heteroscedasticity; standard errors are given in parentheses. **(*) indicate statistical significance at the 95% (90%) confidence level. The dependent variable is a 3-year average, expressed as deviations from the OECD average during the same period. The explanatory variables CA and INV are averages over the 3 years preceding the event; the variables OPEN, GDP, RER, OT and DEBTY are levels the year before the event; the variable ΔTT is the percentage of change in the average level of the terms of trade between the period after and the period before the event.

economic performance after a currency crash. A regression of the growth rate the year of the crisis on the set of lagged dependent variables (not reported) also does not find any economically and statistically significant effect of the degree of overvaluation. Finally, in the sample of middle-income countries the investment rate before the crisis is statistically significant, but has the wrong sign.

Table 12.8. Currency Crashes and Reversals

		A. Number of Reversals Preceded by Currency Crashes*						
Sample	Total	CRISES1 (no window)	CRISIS2 (no window)	CRISIS3 (no window)	CRISES1 (window)	CRISES2 (window)	CRISES3 (window)	CRISES4 (window)
3% (full sample)	152	54	43	51				
3%, window (full sample)	100				31	26	33	24
3%, window (middle income countries)	47				18	14	21	14
5% (full sample)	117	43	36	43				
5%, window (full sample)	77				25	22	27	20

		B. Growth Before and After Reversals†			
Sample	Total	Growth before reversal (average)	Growth before reversal (median)	Growth after reversal (average)	Growth after reversal (median)
3%	97	3.5	3.2	3.6	3.6
3%+CRISIS1	30	2.7	2.9	3.1	3.1
3% no CRISIS1	67	3.9	3.6	3.8	4.1
3%+CRISIS3	32	3.4	3.1	3.5	2.8
3%, no CRISIS3	65	3.6	3.3	4.0	3.6

* Number of reversals accompanied by a currency crash or preceded in at least one of the three previous years by a crash. The current account is defined net of official transfers.

† Reversals do not include adjacent events and are defined on the basis of the current account net of official transfers. They are divided into those accompanied or preceded by a currency crisis (in one of the previous 3 years) and those that are not. CRISIS1 is a depreciation of 25% or more that is at least 10% higher than the previous year's depreciation. CRISIS3 is a depreciation of 15% or more that is at least 10% higher than the previous year, with the previous year's depreciation below 10%. Growth before reversal: average (median) growth the three years before a reversal. Growth after reversal: average (median) growth rate the year of the reversal and the two succeessive years.

These findings also suggest that currency crashes and reversals in current account imbalances have indeed different characteristics and have a different impact on macroeconomic performance. In the next section, we explore this issue in more detail.

CRISES AND REVERSALS: A COMPARISON

Are reversals usually preceded by a currency crisis? The stylized facts presented in Figs. 12.1–12.4 and especially the time profile of crashes and reversals presented in Tables 12.1 and 12.4 suggest that these two events have different characteristics. Indeed, Table 12.8 shows that only around a third of reversals are accompanied by, or preceded by, a currency crisis; the median rate of depreciation in the year of a current account reversal and in the two preceding years is around 7%, well below all the thresholds used for currency crashes.[18]

A first stylized fact is that, as expected, when crises precede or accompany reversals they tend to occur 1 or 2 years before a reversal. A second stylized fact is that reversals are more likely to be preceded by currency crises in Latin America and the Caribbean than they are in Asia. For example, for the Frankel–Rose definition of CRISIS1, 12 reversals (out of 25) in Latin America were preceded by a crash, but only five (out of 29) in Asia.[19] If the definition of crisis is changed so as to exclude countries that had high rates of depreciation before a crash (that is, CRISIS3) the numbers change (nine out of 25 for Latin America, six out of 29 for Asia) but not the qualitative finding. For African countries, approximately 30% of reversals are preceded by a crisis. There are more similarities between the stylized features of reversals and crises for the sample of middle-income countries (see the exchange-rate depreciation panel in Fig. 12.2 and the current account panel in Fig 12.4). However, as shown in the third row of Table 12.8A, the fraction of reversals preceded by exchange-rate crashes is still below 50%.

The final question briefly addressed is whether countries that suffer a currency crisis before a reversal tend to perform less well after the reversal. Table 12.8B provides summary statistics for median and average growth before and after reversals, separating those preceded by crises from those that are not.[20] It shows that average and median growth performance after the reversal is worse for countries that suffered a currency crisis of type 1 (CRISIS1), but not a crisis of type 3 (CRISIS3). The explanation for this finding may lie in the worse growth performance of countries that suffered bouts of high inflation and currency depreciation (that are excluded from crises of type 3).

CONCLUSION

This chapter provides a broad-brush characterization of sharp reductions in current account deficits and of currency crises in low- and middle-income countries. Reversals in current account imbalances are more likely to occur in countries that have run persistent deficits, low reserves, and unfavorable terms of trade, and are less likely to occur in countries that receive high official transfers and whose debt is largely on concessional terms. Growth performance after reversals tends to be better in more open economies and in countries whose real exchange rate was less appreciated before the reversal. Reversals are not systematically associated with a decline in output growth; indeed, median growth after a reversal in the current account is the same as before the reversal. Currency crises are more likely to occur when reserves are low, the real exchange rate is appreciated, and when external conditions are unfavorable – high interest rates and low growth in industrial countries. Growth tends to decline the year of the crisis and to recover thereafter. Economies more open to trade seem to perform better after a crisis. A comparison of currency crashes and current account reversals shows that these are, in general, distinct events. Less than a third of all reversals are preceded by a currency crisis, however defined. This suggests that the conventional wisdom that large nominal depreciations precede a turnaround in the current account is not accurate and points to the need of looking more closely at different types of reversals.

APPENDIX 12.1. LIST OF COUNTRIES

Algeria*	Egypt*	Liberia	Sao Tomé and Princ.
Argentina*	El Salvador*	Madagascar	Senegal
Bangladesh	Equat. Guinea	Malawi	Seychelles
Barbados	Ethiopia	Malaysia*	Sierra Leone
Belize	Fiji	Maldives	Solomon Islands
Benin	Gabon	Mali	Somalia
Bhutan	Gambia	Malta	South Africa*
Bolivia*	Ghana	Mauritania	Sri Lanka*
Botswana*	Grenada	Mauritius*	St. Vincent and Gren.
Brazil*	Guatemala*	Mexico*	Sudan
Burkina Faso	Guinea	Morocco*	Swaziland
Burundi	Guinea Bissau	Myanmar	Syria*
Cameroon	Guyana	Nepal	Tanzania
Cape Verde	Honduras	Nicaragua	Thailand*
Central African Rep.	Haiti	Niger	Togo
Chad	Hungary*	Nigeria	Trinidad* and Tobago
Chile*	India	Oman*	Tunisia*
China	Indonesia*	Pakistan	Turkey*
Colombia*	Iran*	Panama*	Uganda
Comoros	Jamaica*	Papua New Guinea	Uruguay*
Congo	Jordan	Paraguay*	Vanuatu
Costa Rica*	Kenya	Peru*	Venezuela*
Cote d'Ivoire*	Korea*	Philippines*	Western Samoa
Djibouti	Laos	Portugal*	Yemen
Dominican Rep.*	Lebanon	Romania*	Zaire
Ecuador*	Lesotho	Rwanda	Zambia
			Zimbabwe

* Indicates a middle-income country.

APPENDIX 12.2. DATA SOURCES AND DEFINITIONS

CA: Current account balance (excluding official transfers) as a fraction of GDP. Source: World Bank, World Tables.

GDP: GDP per capita (chain rule). Source: Summers and Heston, Penn Table 5.6.

FISC: Fiscal balance (including grants) as a fraction of GDP. Source: World Bank, World Tables.

OT: Official transfers in US$. Source: World Bank, World Tables.

INV: Share of investment in GDP. Source: World Bank, World Tables.

GROW: Growth rate of real GDP (constant 1987 prices). Source: World Bank, World Tables.

TT: Terms of trade index (period average = 100). Source: World Bank, World Tables.

OVERVAL: Rate of real exchange-rate overvaluation vis-à-vis the U.S. dollar, based on relative GDP deflators (percentage deviation from the average level 1970–1996).

RER: CPI- based real effective exchange-rate index (period average = 100). Source: International Monetary Fund, Information Notice System.

OPEN: Average share of exports and imports to GDP. Source: authors calculations, based on World Bank, World Tables.

RES: Foreign exchange reserves in months of imports. Source: World Bank, Global Development Finance.

RESM2: Foreign exchange reserves as a fraction of $M2$. Source: Authors calculations based on World Bank, World Tables and Global Development Finance.

DEBTX: Ratio of external debt to exports. Source: World Bank, Global Development Finance.

DEBTY: Ratio of external debt to GNP. Source: World Bank, Global Development Finance.

INTGNP: Ratio of interest payments on external–INTGNP debt to GNP. Source: World Bank, Global Development Finance.

CONRAT: Share of concessional debt in total debt. Source: World Bank, Global Development Finance.

PUBRAT: Share of public debt in total debt. Source: World Bank, Global Development Finance.

SHORT: Share of short-term debt in total debt. Source: World Bank, Global Development Finance.

FDI: Net FDI flows as a fraction of GDP. Source: World Bank, Global Development Finance.

PORTF: Net portfolio flows as a fraction of GDP. Source: World Bank, Global Development Finance.

RINT: U.S. prime lending rate, deflated by the U.S. GDP deflator. Source: International Monetary Fund, International Financial Statistics.

GROECD: Real growth rate in OECD countries. Source: International Monetary Fund, International Financial Statistics.

PEG: Dummy variable taking the value of 1 if the exchange rate is fixed or fluctuates within a narrow band and 0 otherwise. Source: Cottarelli and Giannini (1997) and IMF, Exchange Arrangements and Exchange Restrictions (various issues).

IMF: Dummy variable taking the value of 1 if the country has an IMF program in place for at least 6 months during the year, and zero otherwise. Source: Cottarelli and Giannini (1997).

Notes

CHAPTER 1

1. See, for instance, the World Bank (1999).
2. We are indebted to Tamim Bayoumi for this observation.
3. GNP of the home country consists of its GDP which is $O_H MRE$, less the income accruing to foreign owners of capital, which is $AQRE$.
4. The GNP of the foreign country consists of its GDP, which is $O_F NRE$, plus foreign-source income, which is $AQRE$.
5. In fact, indirect taxes levied uniformly across commodities and over time amount to a tax on labor income; see, for instance, Frenkel, Razin, and Sadka (1991).
6. Such taxes are called source-based taxes because they are determined according to the source of the income rather than the residency of the recipient of the income; see Frenkel, Razin, and Sadka (1991) for a full-fledged (positive and normative) analysis of the source and residence principles of taxation.
7. See Eqs. (1.11a)–(1.11c).
8. Note that there is a nontraded good in this model. Its relative price is not equalized across countries by trade. Hence, neither are factor prices equalized by trade in goods. Therefore, there is a scope for factor mobility. As we shall see in the Chap. 2, if all goods are traded, then such trade may equalize factor prices, making factor mobility redundant.

CHAPTER 2

1. Strictly speaking, this graphic exposition is correct only for fixed unit-input-requirement coefficients (the a's). However, it provides a linear approximation around the equilibrium factor-price point also for variable unit-input requirements.
2. Strictly speaking, factor-price equalization can still result from free trade if the latter leads to complete specialization in at least one of the two countries. We are indebted to Lars Svensson for this point.
3. Leamer (1984, p. 11) reports that a sample of 32 countries' hourly wages in agriculture range from $0.46 in India to $2.04 in Denmark. As he puts it: "Part of these differences might be explained by skill differences, but agricultural wages seem unlikely to include a reward for skills that is sufficiently variable to account for the

data. . . . This observation encourages a search for assumptions that do not necessarily imply factor price equalization."

CHAPTER 3

1. For a survey of various reform proposals see Heller (1998).
2. See, for instance, Lalonde and Topel (1997), Borjas and Trejos (1991), and Borjas (1994).
3. This intertemporal aspect of the net contribution of low-skilled migrants to the welfare state seems to be absent from the static measures of the fiscal burden imposed by migrants provided in much of the empirical literature cited earlier. The fact that the fiscal burden is not necessarily a good welfare indicator is also a drawback of this literature.
4. This factor-price effect of migration arises either when there is an adequate inflow of capital in conjunction with the influx of labor or when the economy is large enough so as not to be a price taker in the global economy.
5. For instance, Altonji and Card (1991) find that a 1% increase in a country's labor force that due to immigration lowers wages by 1.2%.
6. We could have also introduced an income tax, in addition to the social security tax, whereby interest income would be taxed too without affecting the results.
7. Strictly speaking, a DB program links benefits to wages before retirement. However, the link is very loose and there is a clear redistributive element in most publicly funded DB plans. In order to highlight the distributive nature of the DB program, we simply assume that the benefit is in a form of a demogrant.
8. Evidently we can repeat this exercise period after period, thereby compounding the effect obtained in this chapter.
9. See also the discussion in Hemming (1998) about the role of r and n in the transition from a PAYG-DB pension system to a fully funded, defined-contribution system. Cooley and Soares (1999), Rangel (2000), and Razin, Sadka, and Swagel (2000) study political economy implications of social security in an overlapping-generations model.

CHAPTER 4

1. The idea that redistributive taxation is a form of social insurance can be traced back to Musgrave and Domar (1944), who pointed out that such taxation reduces the risk of income uncertainty. More recently, Rawls (1971) viewed income redistribution as a form of social insurance that reduces the risk of the income profile of people who are still behind "a veil of ignorance" in the "original position."
2. This version is based on (but not identical to) the model used in Razin and Sadka (1995a).
3. In the context of the Chap. 3, b was a uniform pension benefit.
4. Note that because of the constant-returns-to-scale assumption, net output $(Y - K)$ is equal to $wL + rK$.
5. To see this, note first that

$$G(e) = e,$$

and that

$$dG = de.$$

Hence,

$$L = \int_0^{e^*} (1 - e)de + q(1 - e^*) + qm$$

$$= -\frac{1}{2}(1 - e^*)^2 + \frac{1}{2} + q(1 - e^*) + qm.$$

Substituting $e^* = (1 - q)$ into the latter equation yields Eq. (4.4′).

6. To see this, observe that by substituting $Y = (1 + r)K + wL$ into the government's budget constraint (4.7) we get

$$b = \tau \frac{rK + wL}{1 + m} = \frac{\tau r K}{1 + m} + \frac{\tau w L}{1 + m} > \frac{\tau r K}{1 + m} + \frac{\tau w q(1 + m)}{1 + m},$$

because $L > (1 + m)q$ (as long as there are some skilled individuals who each supply more than q units of effective labor). Thus,

$$b > \frac{\tau r K}{1 + m} + \tau w q > \tau w q.$$

7. See also Berry and Soligo (1969).

8. Note from Eq. (A4.7) that positive b and τ are possible in this case of free migration of both low- and high-skill migrants only when the wage differential at the source country (that is, w_h^*/w_ℓ^*) is lower than the wage differential at the destination country (that is, $1/q$).

CHAPTER 5

1. Note that the fixed factor-price assumption is not compatible with free migration. When the opportunity income (w^*) of the migrants is below their net income in the destination country [$(1 - \tau)qw + b$], then m will grow without bounds.

2. The possibility that the median voter is a migrant is admittedly unrealistic, and the reason we consider it at all is just for the sake of intellectual curiosity.

CHAPTER 6

1. In some countries, such as Germany, gaining citizenship is quite difficult for migrants and very few do – less than 1% of Turkish immigrants, for example. In others, such as Denmark and the Netherlands, immigrants can vote in local elections, and immigrants from Commonwealth countries can vote in all elections in the U.K.; see the *Economist*, February 15, 1992.

2. For example, we multiply

$$\left(\frac{\text{immigrants}}{\text{population}} \right)_{1974-92} \times \left(\frac{\text{Low-Education immigrants}}{\text{immigrants}} \right)_{1995}$$

to derive a variable that gives the share of low-education immigrants in the population.

3. As a rough attempt to investigate this possible reverse causality, we used the data on the source of immigrants to create variables of the per capita GDP and growth

differentials between the 11 destination countries and the average source countries. Using these as instruments for the share of immigrants generally made the coefficients on immigrants more negative as would be expected from the discussion above. However, it would be reasonable to expect richer countries to have more elaborate social welfare systems, so that GDP differentials might not be suitable instruments for taxes and benefits.

4. These results may change when dynamic considerations are introduced; see, for instance, Razin and Sadka (1999). See also Cremer and Pestieau (1998), who examine the political economy approach to the choice of the payroll tax in the context of tax competition between tax countries in the presence of labor mobility, and Canova and Ravn (1998), who look at how the system of income distribution matters for the welfare consequences of migration on the native born.

CHAPTER 7

1. See Kaminsky and Reinhart (1999) for a recent empirical study of the relationship between banking crises and currency crises.
2. This risk-aversion assumption is not essential for establishing the risk-sharing role of the financial intermediaries in this model. It is made solely for the sake of concreteness in drawing the diagram below. This assumption will become essential later when we introduce aggregate uncertainty.
3. The grand consumption-possibility frontier is restricted also by an incentive-compatibility constraint that states that it does not pay a late consumer to behave as an early consumer, provided that she or he expects that all other late consumers will indeed behave as late consumers and will not "run" on the bank in period two. This restricts the grand consumption-possibility frontier to the region where $(1 + d_S)(1 + r_S) \leqq (1 + d_L)^2$.
4. In fact, the model used by Goldstein and Pauzner (1999) is slightly different in some inessential details from the model described here.
5. See, for instance, Chang and Velasco (1998) and Allen and Gale (2000).
6. See also Kremer and Mehta (2000).

CHAPTER 8

1. This formulation of the risk in the economy follows that of Gordon and Bovenberg (1996).
2. For later use, we also denote by $e^+(\bar{\varepsilon}^j)$ the mean value of ε realized by the high-productivity firms, that is, $e^+(\varepsilon^j) \equiv E(\varepsilon/\varepsilon \geq \bar{\varepsilon}^j)$. Note that the weighted average of $e^-(\bar{\varepsilon}^j)$ and $e^+(\bar{\varepsilon}^j)$ must yield the average value of ε, that is, $\Phi(\bar{\varepsilon}^j)e^-(\bar{\varepsilon}^j) + [1 - \Phi(\bar{\varepsilon}^j)]e^+(\bar{\varepsilon}^j) = E(\varepsilon) = 0$. This, in turn, implies that $e^-(\bar{\varepsilon}^j) < 0$, whereas $e^+(\bar{\varepsilon}^j) > 0$, that is, the expected value of ε for the "bad" ("good") firm is negative (positive).

CHAPTER 10

1. During a crisis, though, foreign direct investors may contribute to capital withdrawals by accelerating profit remittances or reducing the liabilities of affiliates toward their

mother companies. Although these are not recorded as negative FDI flows, they result from decisions made by foreign investors.

2. See, for example, Lipsey (2000) who studied empirically the inward and the outward FDIs among developed countries. He concludes, "There is little evidence that the flows of FDI are a major influence on capital formation. The lack of effects on capital formation suggests that financing capital formation is not a primary role of FDI."

3. The existence of wealthy individuals or families in the home country may possibly limit the scope of our analysis to the extent that they can compete with the foreign direct investors on control over these greenfield investment sites. Our analysis will carry over, however, if they form joint ventures with the foreign direct investors. On the other hand, the foreign direct investors need not be excessively resourceful. Even a small technological advantage they may enjoy over and above the domestic investors will enable them to bid up all these investment sites from the domestic investors and to gain control of these industries.

4. Note that Eq. (10.3') is analogous to Eq. (9.1), except that the roles of domestic savers and foreigners are reversed (because here the foreigners are better informed). Note also that ε_0 in Eq. (10.3') is not the same as ε_0 in Eq. (9.1).

5. The ε_0 condition, as given by Eq. (10.3), is determined by equilibrium in the equity market. As such, it will not be taken into account by the price-taking firms when choosing their investment levels.

6. Borensztein, De Gregorio, and Lee (1998) estimated that a dollar of FDI generates \$2.5 of domestic investment. They interpreted this higher-than-one coefficient to imply that FDI has positive externalities for all firms in the host economy, enhancing them to increase their investments. However, we may alternatively interpret this coefficient as reflecting the feature of our model rather than foreign savings financing only a portion ($1/2.5 = 0.4$) of the capital accumulation generated by FDI; see also Bosworth and Collins (1999).

CHAPTER 11

1. See also Eaton and Kortum (1999), Borensztein, Gregorio, and Lee (1998), and Helpman, Coe, and Hoffmaister (1997).

2. See also a similar setup in Borensztein, Gregorio, and Lee (1998).

CHAPTER 12

1. Note that the capital account balances are not identical to current account balances because of changes in international reserves.

2. Difference in the ratio of current account to GDP between 1998 and the average 1995–1997.

3. Real effective exchange rate depreciation between July 1997–December 1998 and January 1995–June 1997 (period averages).

4. Contagion effects, broadly defined, can (but need not) have "fundamental" origins; for example, a large depreciation in a country can imply a loss of competitiveness and a decline in external demand for a neighboring country. Eichengreen, Rose, and Wyplosz (1996) try empirically to distinguish between different types of contagion.

5. These countries had income per capita (Summers and Heston definition) above $1500, and population above 1 million in 1985, as well as an average current account deficit during the sample period below 10% of the GDP.

6. For the CPI-based real effective exchange rate (period average = 100), an increase represents a real *appreciation*. The degree of real overvaluation, calculated with a bilateral rate vis-a-vis the U.S. dollar, is for every country the percentage deviation from the country's sample average, as in Frankel and Rose (1996). Goldfajn and Valdes (1999) study the dynamics of real exchange-rate appreciations and the probability of their "unwinding."

7. For the terms-of-trade index, the average value over the sample is set equal to 100 for each country. An increase in the index represents an improvement in the terms of trade.

8. In this respect, note that several oil-producing countries in the Middle East (such as Iraq, Saudi Arabia, Kuwait, UAE, Bahrein) are excluded from the sample.

9. One potential problem with this methodology is that the time distribution of reversal episodes is concentrated in the 1980s, and therefore the characteristics of reversal events identified are in part influenced by the characteristics of the 1980s with respect to the 1970s and the 1990s. However, the graphs restricted to the 1980s show the same overall pattern as that of Fig. 12.1.

10. Santaella (1996) and Knight and Santaella (1997) study the determinants of IMF programs and characterize the stylized facts that precede them.

11. In Milesi-Ferretti and Razin (1998) events occurring in adjacent years for the same country are grouped, counting them as a single, longer-lasting reversal.

12. All averages are calculated over the 3-year period preceding the reversal. The percentage of change in the terms of trade between the two periods was statistically insignificant and was excluded from the regression so as to increase sample size.

13. Effects of windowing account for the CRISIS2 episodes that are not also CRISIS1.

14. Technically, the Islamic Federal Republic of Comoros uses a different currency, the CV, which is tied to the French franc in an analogous fashion to the CFA.

15. The regressions by use of RESM2 instead of RES are not reported. Klein and Marion (1997) report similar results using the ratio of reserves to M_1 for a sample of Latin American countries.

16. A potential problem with this finding is that the definition of the benchmark as the sample average implies a tendency for mean reversion.

17. Klein and Marion (1997) find that openness significantly reduces the likelihood of a devaluation in a sample of Latin American countries pegging their exchange rate.

18. The crisis definition does not affect significantly the selection of reversal episodes preceded by a crisis.

19. This partly reflects the higher incidence of crashes in Latin America than in Asia (Table 12.4).

20. The table excludes CRISIS2; growth would be intermediate between CRISIS1 and CRISIS3.

References

Aghion, Philippe, Philippe Baccheta, and Abhijit Banerjee, 1998, "Financial Liberalization and Volatility in Emerging Market Economies," *Studienzentrum Gerzensee, Shiftung der Scheizerischen Nationalbank*, Working Paper 98.02.

Aizenman, Joshua and Nancy Marion, 2000, "Uncertainty and the Disappearance of International Credit," in *Financial Crises in Emerging Markets*, Reuven Glick, Mark Spiegel, and Ramon Moreno (editors), Cambridge University Press, New York.

Akerlof, George, 1970, "The Market for 'Lemons': Qualitative Uncertainty and the Market Mechanism," *Quarterly Journal of Economics*, **89**: 488–560.

Alesina, Alberto and Romain Wacziarg, 1998, "Openness, Country Size, and the Government," *Journal of Public Economics*, **69** (September): 305–321.

Allen, Franklin and Douglas Gale, 2000, "Optimal Currency Crises," Carnegie-Rochester Conference Series on Public Policy. Elsevier Science Ltd., New York.

Altonji, Joseph G. and David Card, 1991, "The Effects of Immigration on the Labor Market Outcomes of Less-Skilled Natives," in *Immigration, Trade and the Labor Market*, John Abowd and Richard Frreeman (editors), University of Chicago Press, Chicago, pp. 201–234.

Baxter, Marianne, 1995, "International Trade and Business Cycles," in *Handbook of International Economics*, Gene Grossman and Kenneth Rogoff (editors), Elsevier Science, New York, vol. 3.

Bernanke, Benjamin and Marc Gertler, 1989, "Agency Costs, Net Worth, and Business Fluctuations," *American Economic Review*, **79**: 14–31.

Berry, Albert R. and Ronald Soligo, 1969, "Some Welfare Aspects of International Migration," *Journal of Political Economy*, **77**: 778–794.

Bhagwati, Jagdish and Robert C. Feenstra (editors), 1987, *International Factor Mobility: Essays in International Economic Theory (International Factor Mobility)*, MIT Press, Cambridge, MA.

Bordo, Michael D., Barry Eichengreen, and Douglas A. Irwin, 1999, "Is Globalization Today Really Different than Globalization a Hundred Years Ago?" NBER Working Paper 7195, *National Bureau of Economic Research*. June.

Borjas, George, 1994, "Immigration and Welfare, 1970–1990," NBER Working Paper 4872, *National Bureau of Economic Research*. Cambridge, MA.

Borjas, George and S. Trejos, 1991, "Immigrant Participation in the Welfare System," *Industrial and Labor Relations Review*, **44**: 195–211.

Borensztein, Eduardo, Jose De Gregorio, and Jong-Wa Lee, 1998, "How Does Foreign Direct Investment Affect Economic Growth?" *Journal of International Economics*, **45**: 115–135.

Bosworth, Barry and Susan Collins, 1999, "Capital Flows to Developing Economies: Implications for Saving and Investment," *Brookings Papers on Economic Activity*, 1999(I): 143–80.

Brugiavini, Agar, 1999, "Social Security and Retirement in Italy," in *Social Security and Retirement Around the World*, Jonathan Gruber and David A. Wise (editors), University of Chicago Press, Chicago.

Calvo, Guillermo A., 1997, "Varieties of Capital Market Crises," in *The Debt Burden and Its Consequences for Monetary Policy*, G. A. Calvo and Mervyn King (editors), St. Martins, New York.

Calvo, Guillermo A., Leonardo Leiderman, and Carmen M. Reinhart, 1993, "Capital Inflows and Real Exchange Rate Appreciation in Latin America: The Role of External Factors," IMF Staff Papers, **40** (March): 108–151.

Calvo, Guillermo A. and Enrique Mendoza, 1996, "Rational Contagion and the Globalization of Securities Markets," mimeo, University of Maryland, College Park, Maryland.

Canova, Fabio and Morten O. Ravn, 1998, "Crossing the Rio Grande: Migrations, Business Cycles, and the Welfare State," CEPR Discussion Paper 2040, December, London, U.K.

Card, David, John DiNardo, and Eugena Estes, 1998, "The More Things Change: Immigrants and the Children of Immigrants in the 1940s, the 1970s, and the 1990s," NBER Working Paper W6519.

Caves, Richard E., Jeffrey A. Frankel, and Ronald W. Jones, 1996, *World Trade and Payments: An Introduction*, 7th ed., Harper Collins, New York.

Chang, Roberto and Andrés Velasco, 1998, "Financial Crises in Emerging Markets: A Canonical Model," NBER Working Paper 6606, June.

Cooley, Thomas F. and Jorge Soares, 1999, "A Positive Theory of Social Security Based on Reputation," *Journal of Political Economy*, **107** (No. 1, February): 135–160.

Corbo, Vittorio and Leonardo Hernández, 1996, "Macroeconomic Adjustment to Capital Inflows: Lessons from Recent East Asian and Latin American Experience," *World Bank Research Observer*, **11** (February): 61–85.

Cottarelli, Carlo and Curzio Giannini, 1997, "Credibility Without Rules? Monetary Frameworks in the Post-Bretton Woods Era," *IMF Occasional Paper*, 154 (December).

Cremer, Helmuth and Pierre Pestieau, 1998, "Social Insurance, Majority Voting, and Labor Mobility," *Journal of Public Economics*, **68**(3): 397–420.

Daveri, Francesco and Guido Tabellini, 2000, "Unemployment and Taxes: Do Taxes Affect the Rate of Unemployment?" *Economic Policy*, **15**: 48–104.

Davis, Steven J., 1992, "Cross Country Patterns of Change in Relative Wages," in *NBER Macroeconomics Annual*, Oliver J. Blanchard and Stanley Fischer (editors), MIT Press, Cambridge, MA.

Debelle, Guy and Hamid Faruqee, 1996, "What Determines the Current Account? A Cross-Sectional and Panel Approach," IMF Working Paper 96/58, June.

Deininger, Klaus and Lyn Squire, 1996, "A New Dataset Measuring Income Inequality," *World Bank Economic Review*, **10** (September): 565–591. Updated data set available on http://www.worldbank.org.

Demirgüç-Kunt, Ash and Enrica Detragiache, 1998, "The Determinants of Banking Crises in Developed and Developing Countries," IMF Staff Papers **45** (March): 81–109.

Diamond, Douglas W. and Philip H. Dybvig, 1983, "Bank Runs, Deposit Insurance, and Liquidity," *Journal of Political Economy*, **91**: 401–419.

Dooley, Michael and Insook Shin, 1999, "Private Inflows When Crises are Anticipated: A Case Study of Korea," mimeo, University of California at Santa Cruz.

Dornbusch, Rudiger, Ilan Goldfajn, and Rodrigo Valdés, 1995, "Currency Crises and Collapses," *Brookings Papers on Economic Activity*, **2**: 219–293.

Dornbusch, Rudiger, Stanley Fisher, and Paul A. Samuelson, 1977, "Comparative Advantage, Trade, and Payments in Ricardian Model with a Continuum of Goods," *American Economic Review*, **67** (December): 823–839.

Eaton, Jonathan and Samuel Kortum, 1999, "International Technology Diffusion: Theory and Management," *International Economic Review*, **40**: 537–570.

Edwards, Sebastian, 1989, *Real Exchange Rates, Devaluation and Adjustment*, MIT Press, Cambridge, MA.

Eichengreen, Barry, Andrew K. Rose, and Charles Wyplosz, 1995, "Exchange Market Mayhem: The Antecedents and Aftermath of Speculative Attacks," *Economic Policy*, **21** (October): 249–312.

Eichengreen, Barry, Andrew K. Rose, and Charles Wyplosz, 1996, "Contagious Currency Crises," CEPR Discussion Paper 1453, August.

Feldstein, Martin, S. and C. Horioka, 1980, "Domestic Savings and International Capital Flows," *Economic Journal*, **90** (June): 314–329.

Fernández-Arias, Eduardo, 1996, "The New Wave of Private Capital Inflows: Push or Pull?" *Journal of Development Economics*, **48**: 389–418.

Fernández-Arias, Eduardo and Peter Montiel, 1996, "The Surge in Capital Inflows to Developing Countries: An Analytical Overview," *World Bank Economic Review*, **10** (January): 51–77.

Flood, Robert and Peter Garber, 1984, "Collapsing Exchange Rate Regimes: Some Linear Examples," *Journal of International Economics*, **17**: 1–13.

Frankel, Jeffrey A. and Andrew K. Rose, 1996, "Currency Crashes in Emerging Markets: An Empirical Treatment," *Journal of International Economics*, **41** (November): 351–366.

French, K. and James Poterba, 1991, "Investor Diversification and International Equity Markets," *American Economic Review*, **81** (May): 222–226.

Frenkel, Jacob A., Assaf Razin, and Efraim Sadka, 1991, *International Taxation in an Integrated World*, MIT Press, Cambridge, MA.

Goldfajn, Ilan and Rodrigo Valdés, 1997, "Capital Flows and The Twin Crises: The Role of Liquidity," IMF Working Paper 97–87, July.

Goldfajn, Ilan and Rodrigo Valdés, 1999, "The Aftermath of Appreciations," *Quarterly Journal of Economics*, **104** (February): 229–262.

Goldstein, Itay, 2000, "Independent Banking and Currency Crises in a Model of Self-Fulfilling Beliefs," mimeo, Tel-Aviv University.

Goldstein, Itay and Ady Pauzner, 1999, "Endogenous Probability of Bank Runs in a Rational Expectations Model," mimeo, Tel-Aviv University.

Gordon, Roger, and Lars A. Bovenberg, 1996, "Why is Capital So Immobile Internationally?: Possible Explanations and Implications for Capital Income Taxation," *American Economic Review*, **86**: 1057–1075.

Gruber, Jonathan and David A. Wise (editors), 1999, *Social Security and Retirement Around the World*, The University of Chicago Press, Chicago.

Hall, Robert E., 1986, "The Relation Between Price and Marginal Cost in U.S. Industry," *Journal of Political Economy*, **96** (October): 921–947.

Hatton, Timothy I. and Jeffrey G. Williamson, 1992, "International Migration and World Development: A Historical Perspective," NBER Historical Paper 4, Cambridge, MA.

Hatton, Timothy I. and Jeffrey G. Williamson, 1998, *The Age of Mass Migration: An Economic Analysis*, Oxford University Press, New York.

Heller, Peter S., 1998, "Rethinking Public Pension Reform Initiatives," IMF Working Paper 98/61, Washington, D.C.

Helpman, Elhanan, 1999, "R&D and Productivity: The International Connection," in *The Economics of Globalization: Policy Perspectives from Public Economics*, Assaf Razin and Efraim Sadka (editors), Cambridge University Press, New York, pp. 17–30.

Helpman, Elhanan and Assaf Razin, 1983, "Increasing Returns, Monopolistic Competition, and Factor Movements: A Welfare Analysis," *Journal of International Economics*, **14**: 263–276.

Helpman, Elhanan, David T. Coe, and Alexander W. Hoffmaister, 1997, "North–South R&D Spillovers," *Economic Journal*, **107** (January).

Hemming, Richard, 1998, "Should Public Pensions be Funded?" IMF Working Paper 98/35, Washington, DC.

Huberman, Gur, 1997, "Familiarity Breeds Investment," mimeo, Columbia University Business School.

Jeanne, Olivier, 1997, "Are Currency Crises Self-Fulfilling? A Test," *Journal of International Economics*, **43**(3/4): 163–186.

Jones, Ronald W., 1965, "The Structure of Simple General Equilibrium Models," *The Journal of Political Economy*, **73**: 557–572.

Jones, Ronald W., 1967, "International Capital Movements and the Theory of Tariffs and Trade," *Quarterly Journal of Economics*, **81**: 1–38.

Kaminsky, Graciela and Carmen M. Reinhart, 1999, "The Twin Crises: The Causes of Banking and Balance of Payments Problems," *American Economic Review*, **89** (June): 473–500.

Kaminsky, Graciela, Saul Lizondo, and Carmen M. Reinhart, 1998, "Leading Indicators of Currency Crises," *IMF Staff Papers*, **45** (March): 1–48.

Klein, Michael W. and Nancy P. Marion, 1997, "Explaining the Duration of Exchange-Rate Pegs," *Journal of Development Economics*, **54** (December): 387–404.

Knight, Malcolm A. and Julio A. Santaella, 1997, "Economic Determinants of IMF Financial Arrangements" *Journal of Development Economics*, **54**(2): 405–436.

Kraay, Aart and Jaume Ventura, 1997, "Current Accounts in Debtor and Creditor Countries," mimeo. World Bank, Washington D.C.

Kremer, Michael and Paras Mehta, 2000, "Globalization and International Public Finance," NBER Working Paper 7575.

Krugman, Paul, 1979, "A Model of Balance-of-Payments Crises," *Journal of Money, Credit and Banking*, **11** (August): 309–325.

Krugman, Paul, 1996, "Are Currency Crises Self-Fulfilling?" *NBER Macroeconomics Annual*, pp. 345–377.

Krugman, Paul, 1999, "Balance Sheets, the Transfer Problem, and Financial Crises," *International Tax and Public Finance*, **6** (No. 4, November): 152–176.

Lalonde, Robert J. and Robert H. Topel, 1997, "Economic Impact of International Migration and the Economic Performance of Migrants," in *Handbook of Population and Family Economics*, Mark R. Rosenweig and Oded Stark (editors), Elsevier, New York, Vol. 1B.

Lane, Philip and Roberto Perotti, 1998, "The Trade Balance and Fiscal Policy in the OECD," *European Economic Review*, **42** (May): 887–895.

Layard, Richard, Oliver Blanchard, Rudiger Dornbusch, and Paul Krugman, 1992, *East–West Migration*, MIT Press, Cambridge, MA.

Leamer, Edward E., 1984, *Sources of International Comparative Advantage*, MIT Press, Cambridge MA.

Lipsey, Robert E., 2000, "FDI Flows among Developed Countries and the Location of Production," NBER, mimeo, New York.

Lewis, Karen, 1999, "Trying to Explain the Home Bias in Equities and Consumption," *Journal of Economic Literature*, **37** (June): 571–608.

Lovell, Michael C., 1975, "The Collective Allocation of Commodities in a Democratic Society," *Public Choice*, **24**(1): 71–92.

MacDougall, G. D. A., 1960, "The Benefits and Costs of Private Investment from Abroad: A Theoretical Appoach," *Economic Record*, **36**: 13–35.

Markusen, James R., 1983, "Factor Movements and Commodity Trade as Complements," *Journal of International Economics*, **22** (May): 341–356.

Masson, Paul, 1998, "Contagion: Monsoonal Effects, Spillovers, and Jumps Between Multiple Equilibria," IMF Working Paper 98/142 (September).

Mendoza, Enrique, Assaf Razin, and Linda Tesar, 1994, "Effective Tax Rates in Macroeconomics: Cross-Country Estimates of Tax Rates on Factor Income and Consumption, *Journal of Monetary Economics*, **34**: 297–323.

Milesi-Ferretti, Gian Maria and Assaf Razin, 1996a, "Current Account Sustainability," *Princeton Studies in International Finance*, No. 81 (October).

Milesi-Ferretti, Gian Maria and Assaf Razin, 1996b, "Current Account Sustainability: Selected East Asian and Latin American Experiences," NBER Working Paper 5791 (October).

Milesi-Ferretti, Gian Maria, Enrique Mendoza, and Patrick Asea, 1997, "On the Ineffectiveness of Tax Policy in Altering Long-Run Growth: Harberger's Superneutrality Conjecture," *Journal of Public Economics*, **66** (October): 99–126.

Milesi-Ferretti, Gian Maria and Assaf Razin, 1998, "Sharp Reductions in Current Account Deficits: An Empirical Analysis," *European Economic Review*, **42** (May): 897–908.

Milesi-Ferretti, Gian Maria and Assaf Razin, 2000, "Current Account Reversals and Currency Crises: Empirical Regularities," in *Currency Crises*, Paul Krugman (editor), University of Chicago Press, Chicago.

Mirrlees, James A., 1971, "An Exploration in the Theory of Optimum Income Taxation," *Review of Economic Studies* **38** (114, April): 175–208.

Morris, Stephen and Hyun Song Shin, 2000, "Rethinking Multiple Equilibria in Macro-economic Modelling," *NBER Macroeconomic Annual 2000*, MIT Press, Cambridge, MA.

Morris, Stephen and Hyun Song Shin, 1998, "Unique Equilibrium in a Model of Self-Fulfilling Currency Attacks," *American Economic Review*, **88**: 587–597.

Mundell, Robert A., 1957, "International Trade and Factor Mobility," *American Economic Review*, 47: 321–335.

Musgrave, Richard A. and Evsey D. Domar, 1944, "Proportional Income Taxation and Risk-Taking," *Quarterly Journal of Economics*, **58**: 387–422.

Obstfeld, Maurice, 1982, "Aggregate Spending and the Terms-of-Trade: Is there a Laursen–Metzler Effect?" *Quarterly Journal of Economics*, **97** (May): 251–270.

Obstfeld, Maurice, 1994, "The Logic of Currency Crises," *Cahiers Economiques et Monétaires* (Banque de France), **43**: 189–213.

Obstfeld, Maurice, 1995, "International Capital Mobility in the 1990s," in *Understanding Interdependence: The Macroeconomics of the Open Economy*, Peter B. Kenen (editor), Princeton University Press, Princeton, NJ.

Obstfeld, Maurice and Kenneth Rogoff, 1996, *Foundations of International Macroeconomics*, MIT Press, Cambridge, MA.

Persson, Torsten and Guido Tabellini, 1999, "Political Economics and Public Finance," NBER Working Paper 7097 (April).

Portes, Richard and Hélène Rey, 1999, "The Determinants of Cross-Border Equity Flows: The Geography of Information," NBER Working Paper 7336.

Rangel, Antonio, 2000, "Forward and Backward Intergenerational Goods: A Theory of Intergenerational Exchange," NBER Working Paper 7518 (February).

Ratelet, Steven and Jeffrey Sachs, 1999, "The Onset of the East Asian Financial Crisis," in *Currency Crises*, Paul Krugman (editor), University of Chicago Press, Chicago.

Rawls, John, 1971, *The Theory of Justice*, Harvard University Press, Cambridge, MA.

Razin, Assaf, Efraim Sadka, and Phillip Swagel, 2001, "Tax Burden and Migration: A Political Economy Theory and Evidence," *Journal of Public Economics*.

Razin, Assaf, Efraim Sadka, and Phillip Swagel, 2000, "The Aging Population and the Size of the Welfare State," mimeo, Tel-Aviv University.

Razin, Assaf, Efraim Sadka, and Chi-Wa Yuen, 2001, "Excessive FDI Flows under Asymmetric Information," in *Financial Crises in Emerging Markets*, Glick Reuven, Ramon Moreno, and Mark Spiegel (editors), Cambridge University Press, Cambridge, U.K.

Razin, Assaf and Efraim Sadka, 2001, "Country Risk and Capital Flow Reversals," *Economics Letters*, **70**(4): 502–510.

Razin, Assaf, Efraim Sadka, and Chi-Wa Yuen, 2000, "Social Benefits and Losses from FDI: Two Non-Traditional Views," in *Regional and Global Capital Flows: Macroeconomic Causes and Consequences*, Takatoshi Ito and Anne O. Krueger (editors), University of Chicago Press, Chicago.

Razin, Assaf and Efraim Sadka, 2000, "Unskilled Migration: A Burden or a Boon for the Welfare State?" *Scandinavian Journal of Economics*, **102**: 463–479.

Razin, Assaf and Efraim Sadka, 1999a, "Migration and Pension with International Capital Mobility," *Journal of Public Economics*, **74**: 141–150.

Razin, Assaf and Efraim Sadka (editors), 1999b, *The Economics of Globalization: Policy Perspective from Public Economics*, Cambridge University Press, Cambridge, U.K.

Razin, Assaf and Efraim Sadka, 1997, "International Migration and International Trade," in *Handbook of Population and Family Economics*, Mark R. Rosenzweig and Oded Stark (editors), Elsevier Science B.V., Amsterdam, pp. 851–887.

Razin, Assaf, Efraim Sadka, and Chi-Wa Yuen, 1998, "A Pecking Order of Capital Inflows and International Tax Principles," *Journal of International Economics*, **44**: 45–68.

Razin, Assaf and Efraim Sadka, 1995a, "Resisting Migration: Wage Rigidity and Income Distribution," *American Economic Review, Papers and Proceedings*, **85** (May): 312–316.

Razin, Assaf and Efraim Sadka, 1995b, *Population Economics*, MIT Press, Cambridge, MA.

Rodrik, Dani, 1998, "Why Do More Open Economies Have Bigger Governments?" *Journal of Political Economy*, **106** (October): 997–1032.

Rotemberg, Julio J. and Michael Woodford, 1995, "Dynamic General Equilibrium Models with Imperfectly Competitive Product Markets," in *Frontiers of Business Cycle Research*, Thomas F. Cooley (editor), Princeton University Press, Princeton, NJ.

Rybczynski, T. M., 1955, "Factor Endowment and Relative Commodity Prices," *Economica*, **22**: 336–341.

Sachs, Jeffrey, 1981, "The Current Account and Macroeconomic Adjustment in the 1970s," *Brookings Papers on Economic Activity*, 201–268.

Sachs, Jeffrey, 1982, "The Current Account in the Macroeconomic Adjustment Process," *Scandinavian Journal of Economics*, **84** (2): 147–159.

Sachs, Jeffrey, Aaron Tornell, and Andrés Velasco, 1996, "Financial Crises in Emerging Markets: Lessons from 1995," *Brookings Papers on Economic Activity*, **1**: 147–198.

Samuelson, Paul A., 1958, "An Exact Consumption Loan Model with or without the Social Contrivance of Money," *Journal of Political Economy*, **66**: 467–482.

Santaella, Julio A., 1996, "Stylized Facts Before IMF-Supported Macroeconomic Adjustment," *IMF Staff Papers*, **43** (September): 502–544.

Smith, James, P. and Barry Edmonston (editors), 1997, *The New American: Economic, Demographic, and Fiscal Effects of Immigration*, National Academy Press, Washington, D.C.

Stark, Oded, 1991, *The Migration of Labor*, Blackwell, Oxford, U.K.

Stopler, W. and Paul A. Samuelson, 1941, "Protection and Real Wages," *Review of Economic Studies*, **9**: 58–73.

Svensson, Lars E. O. and Assaf Razin, 1983, "The Terms-of-Trade and the Current Account: The Harberger–Laursen–Metzler Effect," *Journal of Political Economy*, **91** (February): 91–125.

Tesar, Linda L. and Ingrid M. Werner, 1995, "U.S. Equity Investment in Emerging Stock Markets," *World Bank Economic Review*, **9**: 109–30.

Tornell, Aaron and Philip Lane, 1998, "Are Windfalls a Curse? A Non-Representative Agent Model of the Current Account and Fiscal Policy," *Journal of International Economics*, **44** (February): 83–112.

Townsend, Robert M., 1979, "Optimal Contracts and Competitive Markets with Costly State Verification, *Journal of Economic Theory*, **21**: 265–293.

Vanek, Jaroslav, 1968, "The Factor Proportion Theory: The N-Factor Case," *Kyklos*, **21**(4): 749–756.

Wildasin, David E., 1994, "Income Redistribution and Migration," *Canadian Journal of Economics*, **27** (3, August): 637–656.

Wong, Kar-Yiu, 1995, *International Trade in Goods and Factor Mobility*, MIT Press, Cambridge, MA.

The World Bank, 1999, *World Development Report, 1999–2000*, Washington, D.C.

Wyplosz, Charles, 1986, "Capital Controls and Balance-of-Payments Crises," *Journal of International Money and Finance*, **5** (June): 167–179.

Index